AN ANTHOLOGY OF
MODERN FRENCH POETRY

AN ANTHOLOGY OF MODERN FRENCH POETRY (1850–1950)

SELECTED AND EDITED BY
PETER BROOME
Senior Lecturer in French, Queen's University, Belfast

AND
GRAHAM CHESTERS
Lecturer in French at the University of Hull

CAMBRIDGE UNIVERSITY PRESS
CAMBRIDGE
LONDON . NEW YORK . MELBOURNE

Published by the Syndics of the Cambridge University Press
The Pitt Building, Trumpington Street, Cambridge CB2 1RP
Bentley House, 200 Euston Road, London NW1 2DB
32 East 57th Street, New York, NY 10022, USA
296 Beaconsfield Parade, Middle Park, Melbourne 3206, Australia

First published 1976

Printed in Great Britain
at the University Printing House, Cambridge
(Euan Phillips, University Printer)

Library of Congress Cataloguing in Publication Data
Main entry under title:

An Anthology of modern French poetry (1850–1950)

A companion volume to The appreciation of modern French
poetry, 1850–1950, by P. Broome and G. Chesters.
  Includes bibliographies and index.
  1. French poetry–19th century. 2. French poetry–20th
century. I. Broome, Peter, 1937– II. Chesters, Graham.
III. Broome, Peter, 1937– The appreciation of modern French
poetry, 1850–1950.
PQ1183.A5 841'.8'08 75–40769
ISBN 0 521 20793 2 hard covers
ISBN 0 521 20929 3 limp

CONTENTS

Contents

PREFACE

This *Anthology of Modern French Poetry* is the companion volume of *The Appreciation of Modern French Poetry*. It follows on from the general introduction to poetry and the select commentaries by providing a well-balanced, fully annotated anthology. It is hoped that the two works will be used in close conjunction, the comments of the one (on rhythm, verse-form, imagery, structure, etc.) helping towards a live and appreciative reading of the texts of the other, the details of the individual commentaries reflecting on and enriching the suggestions contained within the notes, and vice versa. Together, they offer the student the means of gaining a close, inquiring and genuine relationship with the work of the poets concerned, as well as with the major developments of over a hundred years of French poetry.

Our selection covers fourteen of the most influential or symptomatic poets of the period 1850 – 1950: Hugo, Nerval, Baudelaire, Mallarmé, Cros, Verlaine, Rimbaud, Laforgue, Valéry, Apollinaire, Supervielle, Eluard, Michaux and Desnos. The choice from each is intended to show something of the variety as well as the underlying unity of his work, different tones as well as the uniqueness of the poet's voice. We have sought a balance: of long and short poems (*Le Bateau ivre* and *O saisons, ô châteaux...*), poems with distinctively different verse-forms (*Possession* and *Hiéroglyphe*), strictly governed metres and free verse (*La Tzigane* and *1909*), parisyllabic and imparisyllabic lines (*Recueillement* and *L'Invitation au voyage*), brief 'weightless' lines and more extensive cumbersome ones (*Chanson d'automne* and *Sonnet boiteux*), epic and lyrical tones (*Booz endormi* and *Demain, dès l'aube...*) and so on: the contrasts and comparisons that one could make are almost unlimited. Similarly, though many consecrated anthology pieces command a prominent place here, these are joined by lesser known texts whose artistic richness has gone largely unexhibited. So, one will find not only Hugo's *Pasteurs et troupeaux* but *Je suis fait d'ombre et de marbre...* and *Jour de fête*; not only Baudelaire's *Harmonie du soir* but *Avec ses vêtements ondoyants et nacrés...* and *Un Fantôme*; not only Verlaine's *Le ciel est, par-dessus le toit...* but *C'est l'extase langoureuse...* and *Sonnet boiteux*; not only Apollinaire's *Le Pont Mirabeau* but *1909* and *Liens*. We have regretfully left aside Hugo's, Mallarmé's and Valéry's longer poems

(*Le Satyre, L'Après-midi d'un faune, La Jeune Parque*). In this, our criterion has been to provide poems which can be conveniently studied in a relatively short space of time and, almost without exception, we have preferred to restrict ourselves to works conceived and fashioned as complete artistic unities rather than include extracts, however magnificent or illustrative. The anthologist runs more than a normal risk of offending, and we have certainly omitted major poets (one thinks, in the twentieth century, of Claudel or Saint-John Perse). This is not to underestimate their importance. It is simply that the selection does not pretend to give a complete survey of the history of modern French poetry, but only a soundly based initiation to some of its most significant figures which will then lead the reader elsewhere; and in our blending (which includes the lesser known poets Cros and Desnos) we have wanted at this stage to avoid tilting the balance excessively towards the weightier and reputedly more 'difficult' poets.

The notes on the poems are aids to individual study. Whereas the practical commentaries in *The Appreciation of Modern French Poetry*, with their fuller treatment, sketch out a critical approach and act as preliminary exercises in close appreciation, the notes here leave the initiative far more to the reader: they are condensed 'blocks' of comments and suggestions pointing to the artistic essentials of each text and opening up a number of paths of reading to be explored and drawn together.

In this same volume, we have also included a brief introduction to each poet, summarizing his distinctive place in the changing patterns of modern French poetry, and a set of essay questions for group discussion or written work: these will help, finally, to set the individual poems of the anthology in a wider perspective and encourage comparative assessments.

P. B.
G. C.

ACKNOWLEDGEMENTS

The editors and publisher would like to thank Editions Gallimard for permission to quote material which is their copyright, as follows: *J'ai tant rêvé de toi, Non, l'amour n'est pas mort, Comme une main à l'instant de la mort, A la faveur de la nuit, La Voix de Robert Desnos* and *Ombres des arbres dans l'eau*... by Robert Desnos from *Domaine public* (1953); *L'Amoureuse, La courbe de tes yeux..., Tu te lèves l'eau se déplie..., Sans âge, Je ne suis pas seul, Critique de la poésie, Bonne justice* and *Semaine* by Paul Eluard from *Choix de poèmes* (1951); *Emportez-moi, La jeune fille de Budapest, Dans la nuit, Icebergs, Clown, Ainsi, ce jour-là fut*... by Henri Michaux from *L'Espace du dedans* (1966) and 66 lines from *Portrait des Meidosems* by Henri Michaux from *La Vie dans les plis* (1949) and *Dans le cercle brisant de la jeune magicienne* by Henri Michaux from *Face aux verrous* (1954); *Prophétie, Montévidéo, Haute mer, Sous le large, Le Sillage, Le Nuage, Visite de la nuit* and *Tristesse de Dieu* by Jules Supervielle from *Choix de poèmes* (1947); *L'Abeille, Les Pas, La Ceinture, Le Sylphe, L'Insinuant, Les Grenades, Le Cimetière marin* and *La Caresse* by Paul Valéry from *Œuvres* Bibliothèque de la Pléiade (1957).

For Di and Anne

TEXTS

Victor Hugo

(1802–1885)

'Le Maître', 'le géant', 'invincible', 'incomparable artisan', 'parfait artiste' are all terms which French poets have used to acknowledge Hugo's greatness. By any standards, he is the colossus of nineteenth-century French literature: his poetic career, in a massively sustained surge of creative energy, spanned over sixty-five years; endlessly versatile, he wrote plays, novels, as well as poems; in his poetry, he tapped every lyrical source, plunged fearlessly into the cauldron of satirical verse (*Les Châtiments*, 1853), produced epic frescoes of human history (*La Légende des Siècles*, 1859, 1877, 1883), wrote frivolous, exotic, erotic and impressionistic pictorial poems, and explored a vast range of verse-forms.

Partly because of the sheer volume of his work, much of it lax and with a tendency towards facile self-repetition, many modern critics have been grudging about Hugo's achievement: the novelist Gide, asked who was France's greatest poet, replied 'Hugo, hélas!'. But his influence on modern French poetry is indubitable. For the Hugo who emerges from *Les Contemplations* (1856) is the major propagator of that spirit of inquiry which is subsequently to suffuse the work of a Rimbaud, a Mallarmé, a Supervielle or even a Michaux, and in which poetic vision becomes a vital instrument in man's relations with his own beyond, not merely an aesthetic colouring. Many of Hugo's poems are a cosmic confrontation: on the bare dunes or beetling cliffs of the Channel Isles, he apprehends the vulnerability of man and probes the mystery and threat of the bottomless reaches of space. In others, the décor of life collapses to reveal the heaving forces, the endless spirals or the beckoning apparitions which underlie human destiny. Indeed, these poems are not merely a lyrical outlet for personal obsessions, but a splendid and frightening assumption of the human predicament in its entirety: 'Quand je vous parle de moi, je vous parle de vous', he writes in his Preface to *Les Contemplations*. He was always conscious of the poet's social function as a 'rêveur sacré', the chosen intermediary between humanity and God, between the workaday world and the obscurities of the universe, or between the superficial pretentions of society and the ultimate seriousness of divine retribution. Here, too, Hugo's passage has been inestimable: in giving new depth and compass to the rôle of the poet.

Whatever the subject, a chief characteristic of Hugo's poetry is its dramatic directness and visual appeal, whether to the pictorial eye or an imaginative inner eye. As a critic once said, in a comparison of different Romantic poets, 'Victor Hugo est un œil, Lamartine est une âme'; and even the rebelliously dismissive Rimbaud had to confess that 'Hugo (...) a bien du *vu* dans les derniers volumes'. Even when pursuing the most abstract of ideas, he avoids ambiguity and abstruseness. Ideas, moods and intuitions are seized in stark concrete terms. His imagery, especially in his post-1850 poetry, is rarely banal or ornamental, but seems physically wedded to his experience, often uncomfortably so: 'la Dame blanche' and the images associated with her are a sensed *reality* and not a piece of literary symbolism. Similarly, his startling personifications spring, not from rhetorical caprice, but from his deep-rooted and disturbing belief in an animating spirit in every recess of the universe. Equally forceful is his use of antithesis. In innumerable poems he opposes God and Satan, Being and Void, the firmament and 'fange', light and dark, faith and despair, the sublime and the coarse, the innocuous and the threatening, the minute and the immeasurable. Such a reliance on antithesis in both structure and detail, often abetted by a wave-like enumerative technique, has laid Hugo open to the criticism of facile construction. One can only suggest that his faults are also his qualities: the simplicity of his 'black and white' vision is a prime source of dramatic tension, giving one the feeling that great scales are being tipped through the strained pivot of the individual; while his excess is at the same time a passionate energy, an exalted verbal genesis, the sign of an infinitely creative mind.

Perhaps Hugo's greatest legacy has been in his versification and use of language: his supple handling of the Alexandrine, his audacity with stress, his use of the expressive *enjambement*, his unashamed choice of plebeian words which the petrified traditions of Classicism had rejected, the absence of contorted syntax and the infusion of new blood into the old figures of rhetoric. Aware of his own achievements, he saw himself as the literary equivalent of Danton and Robespierre:

> Je fis souffler un vent révolutionnaire.
> Je mis un bonnet rouge au vieux dictionnaire.

Without some knowledge of the style of literature preceding Hugo (largely characterized in its poetry by an insipid reliance on traditional metaphors, a taste for sedate expression and a mistrust of the passionate and boldly imaginative), it is not easy to assess this historical impact. But a glance at the immense variety of styles which developed during his life-time gives proof enough of that spirit of innovation to which he provided the gigantic breath.

For the modern reader Hugo's appeal is unlikely to be based on an intellectual acceptance of his spiritual convictions. What one will recognize as evergreen in his poetry is the artistic ambition to capture fugitive impressions within a stoutly mastered framework; the strength, verve and resonance of his emotions; the tremor of disquiet or fear caused by his intuitions of an awesome other-world; and the feeling that one is in touch with the fertile and vivid imagination of a genius.

SELECT BIBLIOGRAPHY

P. Albouy, *La Création mythologique chez Victor Hugo*, Corti, 1963.
J. Barrère, *Hugo: l'homme et l'œuvre*, (Connaissance des lettres), Hatier, 1952.
J. Barrère, *La Fantaisie de Victor Hugo*, 3 vols., Corti, 1949–60; repr. Klincksieck, 1972–3.
C. Baudelaire, 'Réflexions sur quelques-uns de mes contemporains: Victor Hugo' in *Œuvres complètes*, eds. Y.–G. Le Dantec, C. Pichois, (Bibliothèque de la Pléiade), Gallimard, 1961.
J. Gaudon, *Le Temps de la contemplation*, Flammarion, 1969.
C. Gely, *Victor Hugo, poète de l'intimité*, Nizet, 1969.
C. Renouvier, *Victor Hugo, le poète*, Armand Colin, 1926.

Souvenir de la nuit du 4

L'enfant avait reçu deux balles dans la tête.
Le logis était propre, humble, paisible, honnête;
On voyait un rameau bénit sur un portrait.
Une vieille grand-mère était là qui pleurait.   4
Nous le déshabillions en silence. Sa bouche,
Pâle, s'ouvrait; la mort noyait son œil farouche;
Ses bras pendants semblaient demander des appuis.
Il avait dans sa poche une toupie en buis.   8
On pouvait mettre un doigt dans les trous de ses plaies.
Avez-vous vu saigner la mûre dans les haies?
Son crâne était ouvert comme un bois qui se fend.
L'aïeule regarda déshabiller l'enfant,   12
Disant: – Comme il est blanc! approchez donc la lampe.
Dieu! ses pauvres cheveux sont collés sur sa tempe! –
Et quand ce fut fini, le prit sur ses genoux.
La nuit était lugubre; on entendait des coups   16
De fusil dans la rue où l'on en tuait d'autres.
– Il faut ensevelir l'enfant, dirent les nôtres.
Et l'on prit un drap blanc dans l'armoire en noyer.
L'aïeule cependant l'approchait du foyer   20
Comme pour réchauffer ses membres déjà roides.
Hélas! ce que la mort touche de ses mains froides
Ne se réchauffe plus aux foyers d'ici-bas!
Elle pencha la tête et lui tira ses bas,   24
Et dans ses vieilles mains prit les pieds du cadavre.

– Est-ce que ce n'est pas une chose qui navre !
Cria-t-elle ! monsieur, il n'avait pas huit ans !
Ses maîtres, il allait en classe, étaient contents.   28
Monsieur, quand il fallait que je fisse une lettre,
C'est lui qui l'écrivait. Est-ce qu'on va se mettre
A tuer les enfants maintenant ? Ah ! mon Dieu !
On est donc des brigands ! Je vous demande un peu,   32
Il jouait ce matin, là, devant la fenêtre !
Dire qu'ils m'ont tué ce pauvre petit être !
Il passait dans la rue, ils ont tiré dessus.
Monsieur, il était bon et doux comme un Jésus.   36
Moi je suis vieille, il est tout simple que je parte ;
Cela n'aurait rien fait à monsieur Bonaparte
De me tuer au lieu de tuer mon enfant ! –
Elle s'interrompit, les sanglots l'étouffant,   40
Puis elle dit, et tous pleuraient près de l'aïeule :
– Que vais-je devenir à présent toute seule ?
Expliquez-moi cela, vous autres, aujourd'hui.
Hélas ! je n'avais plus de sa mère que lui.   44
Pourquoi l'a-t-on tué ? je veux qu'on me l'explique.
L'enfant n'a pas crié vive la République. –
Nous nous taisons, debout et graves, chapeau bas,
Tremblant devant ce deuil qu'on ne console pas.   48

Vous ne compreniez point, mère, la politique.
Monsieur Napoléon, c'est son nom authentique,
Est pauvre et même prince ; il aime les palais ;
Il lui convient d'avoir des chevaux, des valets,   52
De l'argent pour son jeu, sa table, son alcôve,
Ses chasses ; par la même occasion, il sauve
La famille, l'église et la société ;
Il veut avoir Saint-Cloud, plein de roses l'été,   56
Où viendront l'adorer les préfets at les maires ;
C'est pour cela qu'il faut que les vieilles grand-mères,
De leurs pauvres doigts gris que fait trembler le temps,
Cousent dans le linceul des enfants de sept ans.   60

L'Homme a ri

M. Victor Hugo vient de publier à Bruxelles un livre qui a pour
titre : *Napoléon le Petit*, et qui renferme les calomnies les plus
odieuses contre le prince-président.

On raconte, qu'un des jours de la semaine dernière un fonction-
naire apporta ce libelle à Saint-Cloud. Lorsque Louis Napoléon le
vit, il le prit, l'examina un instant avec le sourire du mépris sur les
lèvres; puis s'adressant aux personnes qui l'entouraient, il dit, en
leur montrant le pamphlet: 'Voyez, messieurs, voici Napoléon-le-
petit, par Victor Hugo-le-grand'.

Journaux élyséens, août 1852.

Ah! tu finiras bien par hurler, misérable!
Encor tout haletant de ton crime exécrable,
Dans ton triomphe abject, si lugubre et si prompt,
Je t'ai saisi. J'ai mis l'écriteau sur ton front;   4
Et maintenant la foule accourt et te bafoue.
Toi, tandis qu'au poteau le châtiment te cloue,
Que le carcan te force à lever le menton,
Tandis que, de ta veste arrachant le bouton,   8
L'histoire à mes côtés met à nu ton épaule,
Tu dis: je ne sens rien! et tu nous railles, drôle!
Ton rire sur mon nom gaîment vient écumer;
Mais je tiens le fer rouge et vois ta chair fumer.   12

Demain, dès l'aube...

Demain, dès l'aube, à l'heure où blanchit la campagne,
Je partirai. Vois-tu, je sais que tu m'attends.
J'irai par la forêt, j'irai par la montagne.
Je ne puis demeurer loin de toi plus longtemps.   4

Je marcherai les yeux fixés sur mes pensées,
Sans rien voir au-dehors, sans entendre aucun bruit,
Seul, inconnu, le dos courbé, les mains croisées,
Triste, et le jour pour moi sera comme la nuit.   8

Je ne regarderai ni l'or du soir qui tombe,
Ni les voiles au loin descendant vers Harfleur,
Et quand j'arriverai, je mettrai sur ta tombe
Un bouquet de houx vert et de bruyère en fleur.   12

Paroles sur la dune

Maintenant que mon temps décroît comme un flambeau,
    Que mes tâches sont terminées;
Maintenant que voici que je touche au tombeau
    Par les deuils et par les années,   4

Et qu'au fond de ce ciel que mon essor rêva,
    Je vois fuir, vers l'ombre entraînées,
Comme le tourbillon du passé qui s'en va,
    Tant de belles heures sonnées;   8

Maintenant que je dis: – Un jour, nous triomphons;
    Le lendemain, tout est mensonge! –
Je suis triste, et je marche au bord des flots profonds,
    Courbé comme celui qui songe.   12

Je regarde, au-dessus du mont et du vallon,
    Et des mers sans fin remuées,
S'envoler, sous le bec du vautour aquilon,
    Toute la toison des nuées;   16

J'entends le vent dans l'air, la mer sur le récif,
    L'homme liant la gerbe mûre;
J'écoute et je confronte en mon esprit pensif
    Ce qui parle à ce qui murmure;   20

Et je reste parfois couché sans me lever
    Sur l'herbe rare de la dune,
Jusqu'à l'heure où l'on voit apparaître et rêver
    Les yeux sinistres de la lune.   24

Elle monte, elle jette un long rayon dormant
    A l'espace, au mystère, au gouffre;
Et nous nous regardons tous les deux fixement,
    Elle qui brille et moi qui souffre.   28

Où donc s'en sont allés mes jours évanouis?
    Est-il quelqu'un qui me connaisse?
Ai-je encor quelque chose en mes yeux éblouis,
    De la clarté de ma jeunesse?   32

Tout s'est-il envolé? Je suis seul, je suis las;
    J'appelle sans qu'on me réponde;
O vents! ô flots! ne suis-je aussi qu'un souffle, hélas!
    Hélas! ne suis-je aussi qu'une onde?   36

Ne verrai-je plus rien de tout ce que j'aimais?
    Au-dedans de moi le soir tombe.
O terre, dont la brume efface les sommets,
    Suis-je le spectre, et toi la tombe?   40

Ai-je donc vidé tout, vie, amour, joie, espoir?
    J'attends, je demande, j'implore;
Je penche tour à tour mes urnes pour avoir
    De chacune une goutte encore!   44

Comme le souvenir est voisin du remord!
    Comme à pleurer tout nous ramène!
Et que je te sens froide en te touchant, ô mort,
    Noir verrou de la porte humaine!   48

Et je pense, écoutant gémir le vent amer,
    Et l'onde aux plis infranchissables;
L'été rit, et l'on voit sur le bord de la mer
    Fleurir le chardon bleu des sables.   52

Pasteurs et troupeaux

Le vallon où je vais tous les jours est charmant,
Serein, abandonné, seul sous le firmament,
Plein de ronces en fleurs; c'est un sourire triste.
Il vous fait oublier que quelque chose existe,   4
Et sans le bruit des champs remplis de travailleurs,
On ne saurait plus là si quelqu'un vit ailleurs.
Là, l'ombre fait l'amour; l'idylle naturelle
Rit; le bouvreuil avec le verdier s'y querelle,   8
Et la fauvette y met de travers son bonnet;
C'est tantôt l'aubépine et tantôt le genêt;
De noirs granits bourrus, puis des mousses riantes;
Car Dieu fait un poëme avec des variantes;   12
Comme le vieil Homère, il rabâche parfois,
Mais c'est avec les fleurs, les monts, l'onde et les bois!
Une petite mare est là, ridant sa face,
Prenant des airs de flot pour la fourmi qui passe,   16
Ironie étalée au milieu du gazon,
Qu'ignore l'océan grondant à l'horizon.
J'y rencontre parfois sur la roche hideuse
Un doux être; quinze ans, yeux bleus, pieds nus, gardeuse   20
De chèvres, habitant, au fond d'un ravin noir,
Un vieux chaume croulant qui s'étoile le soir;
Ses sœurs sont au logis et filent leur quenouille;
Elle essuie aux roseaux ses pieds que l'étang mouille;   24
Chèvres, brebis, béliers, paissent; quand, sombre esprit,
J'apparais, le pauvre ange a peur, et me sourit;
Et moi, je la salue, elle étant l'innocence.
Ses agneaux, dans le pré plein de fleurs qui l'encense,   28
Bondissent, et chacun, au soleil s'empourprant,
Laisse aux buissons, à qui la bise le reprend,
Un peu de sa toison, comme un flocon d'écume.
Je passe, enfant, troupeau, s'effacent dans la brume;   32

Le crépuscule étend sur les longs sillons gris
Ses ailes de fantôme et de chauve-souris;
J'entends encore au loin dans la plaine ouvrière
Chanter derrière moi la douce chevrière,   36
Et, là-bas, devant moi, le vieux gardien pensif
De l'écume, du flot, de l'algue, du récif,
Et des vagues sans trêve et sans fin remuées,
Le pâtre promontoire au chapeau de nuées,   40
S'accoude et rêve au bruit de tous les infinis,
Et, dans l'ascension des nuages bénis,
Regarde se lever la lune triomphale,
Pendant que l'ombre tremble, et que l'âpre rafale   44
Disperse à tous les vents avec son souffle amer
La laine des moutons sinistres de la mer.

J'ai cueilli cette fleur . . .

J'ai cueilli cette fleur pour toi sur la colline.
Dans l'âpre escarpement qui sur le flot s'incline,
Que l'aigle connaît seul et peut seul approcher,
Paisible, elle croissait aux fentes du rocher.   4
L'ombre baignait les flancs du morne promontoire;
Je voyais, comme on dresse au lieu d'une victoire
Un grand arc de triomphe éclatant et vermeil,
A l'endroit où s'était englouti le soleil,   8
La sombre nuit bâtir un porche de nuées.
Des voiles s'enfuyaient, au loin diminuées;
Quelques toits, s'éclairant au fond d'un entonnoir,
Semblaient craindre de luire et de se laisser voir.   12
J'ai cueilli cette fleur pour toi, ma bien-aimée.
Elle est pâle, et n'a pas de corolle embaumée.
Sa racine n'a pris sur la crête des monts
Que l'amère senteur des glauques goëmons;   16
Moi, j'ai dit: 'Pauvre fleur, du haut de cette cime,
Tu devais t'en aller dans cet immense abîme
Où l'algue et le nuage et les voiles s'en vont.
Va mourir sur un cœur, abîme plus profond.   20
Fane-toi sur ce sein en qui palpite un monde.
Le ciel, qui te créa pour t'effeuiller dans l'onde,
Te fit pour l'océan, je te donne à l'amour.'
Le vent mêlait les flots; il ne restait du jour   24

Qu'une vague lueur, lentement effacée.
Oh! comme j'étais triste au fond de ma pensée
Tandis que je songeais, et que le gouffre noir
M'entrait dans l'âme avec tous les frissons du soir!   28

A celle qui est voilée

Tu me parles du fond d'un rêve
Comme une âme parle aux vivants.
Comme l'écume de la grève,
Ta robe flotte dans les vents.   4

Je suis l'algue des flots sans nombre,
Le captif du destin vainqueur;
Je suis celui que toute l'ombre
Couvre sans éteindre son cœur.   8

Mon esprit ressemble à cette île,
Et mon sort à cet océan;
Et je suis l'habitant tranquille
De la foudre et de l'ouragan.   12

Je suis le proscrit qui se voile,
Qui songe, et chante, loin du bruit,
Avec la chouette et l'étoile,
La sombre chanson de la nuit.   16

Toi, n'es-tu pas, comme moi-même,
Flambeau dans ce monde âpre et vil,
Ame, c'est-à-dire problème,
Et femme, c'est-à-dire exil?   20

Sors du nuage, ombre charmante.
O fantôme, laisse-toi voir!
Sois un phare dans ma tourmente,
Sois un regard dans mon ciel noir!   24

Cherche-moi parmi les mouettes!
Dresse un rayon sur mon récif,
Et, dans mes profondeurs muettes,
La blancheur de l'ange pensif!   28

Sois l'aile qui passe et se mêle
Aux grandes vagues en courroux.
Oh, viens! tu dois être bien belle,
Car ton chant lointain est bien doux;   32

Car la nuit engendre l'aurore;
C'est peut-être une loi des cieux
Que mon noir destin fasse éclore
Ton sourire mystérieux!   36

Dans ce ténébreux monde où j'erre,
Nous devons nous apercevoir,
Toi, toute faite de lumière,
Moi, tout composé de devoir!   40

Tu me dis de loin que tu m'aimes,
Et que, la nuit, à l'horizon,
Tu viens voir sur les grèves blêmes
Le spectre blanc de ma maison.   44

Là, méditant sous le grand dôme,
Près du flot sans trêve agité,
Surprise de trouver l'atome
Ressemblant à l'immensité,   48

Tu compares, sans me connaître,
L'onde à l'homme, l'ombre au banni,
Ma lampe étoilant ma fenêtre
A l'astre étoilant l'infini!   52

Parfois, comme au fond d'une tombe,
Je te sens sur mon front fatal,
Bouche de l'Inconnu d'où tombe
Le pur baiser de l'Idéal.   56

A ton souffle, vers Dieu poussées,
Je sens en moi, douce frayeur,
Frissonner toutes mes pensées,
Feuilles de l'arbre intérieur.   60

Mais tu ne veux pas qu'on te voie;
Tu viens et tu fuis tour à tour;
Tu ne veux pas te nommer joie,
Ayant dit: Je m'appelle amour.   64

Oh! fais un pas de plus! viens, entre,
Si nul devoir ne le défend;
Viens voir mon âme dans son antre,
L'esprit lion, le cœur enfant;   68

Viens voir le désert où j'habite
Seul sous mon plafond effrayant;
Sois l'ange chez le cénobite,
Sois la clarté chez le voyant.   72

Change en perles dans mes décombres
Toutes mes gouttes de sueur!
Viens poser sur mes œuvres sombres
Ton doigt d'où sort une lueur!   76

Du bord des sinistres ravines
Du rêve et de la vision,
J'entrevois les choses divines... –
Complète l'apparition!   80

Viens voir le songeur qui s'enflamme
A mesure qu'il se détruit,
Et, de jour en jour, dans son âme
A plus de mort et moins de nuit!   84

Viens! viens dans ma brume hagarde,
Où naît la foi, d'où l'esprit sort,
Où confusément je regarde
Les formes obscures du sort.   88

Tout s'éclaire aux lueurs funèbres;
Dieu, pour le penseur attristé,
Ouvre toujours dans les ténèbres
De brusques gouffres de clarté.   92

Avant d'être sur cette terre,
Je sens que jadis j'ai plané;
J'étais l'archange solitaire,
Et mon malheur, c'est d'être né.   96

Sur mon âme, qui fut colombe,
Viens, toi qui des cieux as le sceau.
Quelquefois une plume tombe
Sur le cadavre d'un oiseau.   100

Oui, mon malheur irréparable,
C'est de pendre aux deux éléments,
C'est d'avoir en moi, misérable,
De la fange et des firmaments!   104

Hélas! hélas! c'est d'être un homme;
C'est de songer que j'étais beau,
D'ignorer comment je me nomme,
D'être un ciel et d'être un tombeau!   108

C'est d'être un forçat qui promène
Son vil labeur sous le ciel bleu;
C'est de porter la hotte humaine
Où j'avais vos ailes, mon Dieu!   112

C'est de traîner de la matière;
C'est d'être plein, moi, fils du jour,
De la terre du cimetière,
Même quand je m'écrie: Amour!　　　116

Booz endormi

Booz s'était couché de fatigue accablé;
Il avait tout le jour travaillé dans son aire;
Puis avait fait son lit à sa place ordinaire;
Booz dormait auprès des boisseaux pleins de blé.　　　4

Ce vieillard possédait des champs de blés et d'orge;
Il était, quoique riche, à la justice enclin;
Il n'avait pas de fange en l'eau de son moulin;
Il n'avait pas d'enfer dans le feu de sa forge.　　　8

Sa barbe était d'argent comme un ruisseau d'avril.
Sa gerbe n'était point avare ni haineuse;
Quand il voyait passer quelque pauvre glaneuse:
'Laissez tomber exprès des épis', disait-il.　　　12

Cet homme marchait pur loin des sentiers obliques,
Vêtu de probité candide et de lin blanc;
Et, toujours du côté des pauvres ruisselant,
Ses sacs de grains semblaient des fontaines publiques.　　　16

Booz était bon maître et fidèle parent;
Il était généreux, quoiqu'il fût économe;
Les femmes regardaient Booz plus qu'un jeune homme,
Car le jeune homme est beau, mais le vieillard est grand.　　　20

Le vieillard, qui revient vers la source première,
Entre aux jours éternels et sort des jours changeants;
Et l'on voit de la flamme aux yeux des jeunes gens,
Mais dans l'œil du vieillard on voit de la lumière.　　　24

*

Donc, Booz dans la nuit dormait parmi les siens.
Près des meules, qu'on eût prises pour des décombres,
Les moissonneurs couchés faisaient des groupes sombres;
Et ceci se passait dans des temps très anciens.　　　28

Les tribus d'Israël avaient pour chef un juge;
La terre, où l'homme errait sous la tente, inquiet
Des empreintes de pieds de géants qu'il voyait,
Etait mouillée encor et molle du déluge.   32

*

Comme dormait Jacob, comme dormait Judith,
Booz, les yeux fermés, gisait sous la feuillée;
Or, la porte du ciel s'étant entre-bâillée
Au-dessus de sa tête, un songe en descendit.   36

Et ce songe était tel, que Booz vit un chêne
Qui, sorti de son ventre, allait jusqu'au ciel bleu;
Une race y montait comme une longue chaîne;
Un roi chantait en bas, en haut mourait un Dieu.   40

Et Booz murmurait avec la voix de l'âme:
'Comment se pourrait-il que de moi ceci vînt?
Le chiffre de mes ans a passé quatre-vingt,
Et je n'ai pas de fils, et je n'ai plus de femme.   44

'Voilà longtemps que celle avec qui j'ai dormi,
O Seigneur! a quitté ma couche pour la vôtre;
Et nous sommes encor tout mêlés l'un à l'autre,
Elle à demi vivante et moi mort à demi.   48

'Une race naîtrait de moi! Comment le croire?
Comment se pourrait-il que j'eusse des enfants?
Quand on est jeune, on a des matins triomphants;
Le jour sort de la nuit comme d'une victoire;   52

'Mais, vieux, on tremble ainsi qu'à l'hiver le bouleau;
Je suis veuf, je suis seul, et sur moi le soir tombe,
Et je courbe, ô mon Dieu! mon âme vers la tombe,
Comme un bœuf ayant soif penche son front vers l'eau.'   56

Ainsi parlait Booz dans le rêve et l'extase,
Tournant vers Dieu ses yeux par le sommeil noyés;
Le cèdre ne sent pas une rose à sa base,
Et lui ne sentait pas une femme à ses pieds.   60

*

Pendant qu'il sommeillait, Ruth, une moabite,
S'était couchée aux pieds de Booz, le sein nu,
Espérant on ne sait quel rayon inconnu,
Quand viendrait du réveil la lumière subite.   64

Booz ne savait point qu'une femme était là,
Et Ruth ne savait point ce que Dieu voulait d'elle.
Un frais parfum sortait des touffes d'asphodèle ;
Les souffles de la nuit flottaient sur Galgala.   68

L'ombre était nuptiale, auguste et solennelle ;
Les anges y volaient sans doute obscurément,
Car on voyait passer dans la nuit, par moment,
Quelque chose de bleu qui paraissait une aile.   72

La respiration de Booz qui dormait,
Se mêlait au bruit sourd des ruisseaux sur la mousse.
On était dans le mois où la nature est douce,
Les collines ayant des lys sur leur sommet.   76

Ruth songeait et Booz dormait ; l'herbe était noire ;
Les grelots des troupeaux palpitaient vaguement ;
Une immense bonté tombait du firmament ;
C'était l'heure tranquille où les lions vont boire.   80

Tout reposait dans Ur et dans Jérimadeth ;
Les astres émaillaient le ciel profond et sombre ;
Le croissant fin et clair parmi ces fleurs de l'ombre
Brillait à l'occident, et Ruth se demandait,   84

Immobile, ouvrant l'œil à moitié sous ses voiles,
Quel dieu, quel moissonneur de l'éternel été,
Avait, en s'en allant, négligemment jeté
Cette faucille d'or dans le champ des étoiles.   88

Jour de fête aux environs de Paris

Midi chauffe et sèche la mousse ;
Les champs sont pleins de tambourins ;
On voit dans une lueur douce
Des groupes vagues et sereins.   4

Là-bas, à l'horizon, poudroie
Le vieux donjon de saint Louis ;
Le soleil dans toute sa joie
Accable les champs éblouis.   8

L'air brûlant fait, sous ses haleines
Sans murmures et sans échos,
Luire en la fournaise des plaines
La braise des coquelicots.   12

Les brebis paissent inégales;
Le jour est splendide et dormant;
Presque pas d'ombre; les cigales
Chantent sous le bleu flamboiement. 16

Voilà les avoines rentrées.
Trêve au travail. Amis, du vin!
Des larges tonnes éventrées
Sort l'éclat de rire divin. 20

Le buveur chancelle à la table
Qui boite fraternellement.
L'ivrogne se sent véritable;
Il oublie, ô clair firmament, 24

Tout, la ligne droite, la gêne,
La loi, le gendarme, l'effroi,
L'ordre; et l'échalas de Surène
Raille le poteau de l'octroi. 28

L'âne broute, vieux philosophe;
L'oreille est longue, l'âne en rit,
Peu troublé d'un excès d'étoffe,
Et content si le pré fleurit. 32

Les enfants courent par volée.
Clichy montre, honneur aux anciens!
Sa grande muraille étoilée
Par la mitraille des prussiens. 36

La charrette roule et cahote;
Paris élève au loin sa voix,
Noir chiffonnier qui dans sa hotte
Porte le sombre tas des rois. 40

On voit au loin les cheminées
Et les dômes d'azur voilés;
Des filles passent, couronnées
De joie et de fleurs, dans les blés. 44

– *Va-t'en, me dit la bise*..

– Va-t'en, me dit la bise,
C'est mon tour de chanter. –
Et, tremblante, surprise,
N'osant pas résister, 4

Fort décontenancée
Devant un *Quos ego*,
Ma chanson est chassée
Par cette virago.   8

Pluie. On me congédie
Partout, sur tous les tons.
Fin de la comédie,
Hirondelles, partons.   12

Grêle et vent. La ramée
Tord ses bras rabougris ;
Là-bas fuit la fumée,
Blanche sur le ciel gris.   16

Une pâle dorure
Jaunit les coteaux froids.
Le trou de ma serrure
Me souffle sur les doigts.   20

Je suis fait d'ombre et de marbre...

Je suis fait d'ombre et de marbre.
Comme les pieds noirs de l'arbre,
Je m'enfonce dans la nuit.
J'écoute ; je suis sous terre ;
D'en bas je dis au tonnerre :
Attends ! ne fais pas de bruit.   6

Moi qu'on nomme le poète,
Je suis dans la nuit muette
L'escalier mystérieux ;
Je suis l'escalier Ténèbres ;
Dans mes spirales funèbres
L'ombre ouvre ses vagues yeux.   12

Les flambeaux deviendront cierges.
Respectez mes degrés vierges,
Passez, les joyeux du jour !
Mes marches ne sont pas faites
Pour les pieds ailés des fêtes,
Pour les pieds nus de l'amour.   18

Devant ma profondeur blême
Tout tremble, les spectres même
Ont des gouttes de sueur.
Je viens de la tombe morte ;

J'aboutis à cette porte
Par où passe une lueur. 24

Le banquet rit et flamboie.
Les maîtres sont dans la joie
Sur leur trône ensanglanté;
Tout les sert, tout les encense;
Et la femme à leur puissance
Mesure sa nudité. 30

Laissez la clef et le pène.
Je suis l'escalier; la peine
Médite; l'heure viendra;
Quelqu'un qu'entourent les ombres
Montera mes marches sombres,
Et quelqu'un les descendra. 36

Qui sait si tout n'est pas . . .

Qui sait si tout n'est pas un pourrissoir immense?
Qui sait si ce qu'on croit gloire, vie et semence,
  N'est pas horreur et deuil?
Contemplateur sur qui le rayon des nuits tombe,
Qui sait si ce n'est pas de néant et de tombe
  Que tu remplis ton œil? 6

Qui sait, espaces noirs, éthers, vagues lumières,
Si le fourmillement mystérieux des sphères
  Ne ronge pas le ciel?
Et si l'aube n'est pas la rougeur d'une torche
Qui passe, et que quelqu'un promène sous le porche
  Du sépulcre éternel? 12

Peut-être que l'abîme est un vaste ossuaire,
Que la comète rampe aux plis d'un noir suaire,
  O vivants pleins de bruit,
Peut-être que la Mort, colossale et hagarde,
Est sous le firmament penchée, et vous regarde
  Ayant pour front la nuit! 18

Peut-être que le monde est une chose morte;
Peut-être que le ciel où la saison apporte
  Tant de rayons divers,
O mortels, est soumis à la loi qui vous navre,
Et que de cet énorme et splendide cadavre
  Les astres sont les vers! 24

Gérard de Nerval

(1808–1855)

There are few poets who have written as little poetry as Nerval and yet been accorded a major place in the development of French verse. Nerval himself would have certainly been surprised at the lasting admiration which *Les Chimères* (1854), a slender collection of eight poems of which five are printed here, has provoked. (It might have been some consolation for a life marred by an unhappy childhood, an unreciprocated love and a series of mental crises, and finally brought mysteriously to an end one January morning in 1855: he was found hanged not far from Les Halles.) His dense, allusive poetry which intimates the existence of a buried, gestating 'Idéal' waiting to flower again and redeem life, made him a natural precursor of the Symbolists (although their 'Idéal' was more distilled and celestial than Nerval's); while his composition of poems 'dans cet état de rêverie *super-naturaliste*' and his interest in dreams gained for him the adulation of the Surrealists. In direct opposition to the effusiveness of some Romantic poets, he introduced a new concept of poetic concentration into French verse, making his sonnets a kind of ritual theatre, and dispersing his expression of emotions among a play of ciphers — a formula so disturbingly new that Alexandre Dumas seems to have looked upon *El Desdichado* as a sign of the poet's madness.

The title, *Les Chimères*, announces two of Nerval's major preoccupations: his obsession with the universe of myth ('les chimères' are legendary creatures, half-lion, half-goat) and his awareness that the 'Idéal' he pursues is a dream and an illusion ('une chimère' also means a vain imagining). A central dilemma in Nerval's work is what Baudelaire was later to call '...un monde où l'action n'est pas la sœur du rêve'. A nostalgic poet, haunted by the persons and places of a *vie antérieure*, he looks to dreams, love and mystical experience as the key to a magical return; and over all his restless efforts there reigns the vision of a luminous realm associated with the Golden Age, the pagan gods, and Man's primitive harmony with the earth. It is the sense of exclusion or severed contact from this realm which inspires images of the *déshérité* (Nerval is at the same time El Desdichado, Cain and an Amalekite; in *Myrtho*, the act of revitalization is sensed to be taking place 'là-bas'; in *Delfica*, the aspirations of the poet and Dafné are barred by 'le sévère portique'); images of the persecutor ('le duc normand', 'Constantin', 'Jéhovah' are all Christian conquerors of paganism); and images of lost or uncertain identity. But on the other hand there are images of resurgence, reconciliation and victory, so that the poems, individually and taken together, are the richly symbolic expression of a battle of tensions within the poet's mind. One notices equally that the weapons with which Nerval fights towards his 'Idéal' have an ambiguity of their own. The fantastic dreams of the poet come uncomfortably close to the dreams of the madman; the image of the woman is intoxicating *and* dangerous; the fire of intense mystical experience fascinates *and* destroys.

El Desdichado suggests that the very act of transmuting experience into poetry is the only reliable resolution of his ambiguities. The forces of the irrational which capture the man do not capture the poet unawares; they are themselves captured by a mysterious poetic reason and tamed in the tightly-knit system of the sonnet. In *Les Chimères*, Nerval has answered his own questions: 'Pourquoi ne point enfin forcer les portes mystiques, armé de toute ma volonté, et dominer mes sensations au lieu de les subir? N'est-il pas possible de dompter cette chimère attrayante et redoutable, d'imposer une règle à des esprits de nuits qui se jouent de notre raison?' His poetry is an act of will imposed on dream-like vision. It is not difficult to understand how important such an act might be to a person of Nerval's instability; nor to imagine that the terse, mysterious titles had the effect of a talisman on the poet.

The sonnets of *Les Chimères* are obscure to varying degrees. But their aura of poetry is beautifully transparent, impressing the reader with the magical sound of proper names, evocations of strangely familiar myths, the balanced cadences of the Alexandrine, the sonnet's phonetic web, and the stimulating contrast between the logic of the form and the apparent unreason of the content. The initial savouring of what has been called Nerval's 'pure poetry' does not have to disappear once the effort to interpret begins, if one always remembers that *Les Chimères* are poems, not hieroglyphics. There is a valid form of aesthetic satisfaction in tracing the patterns of suggestion which lie behind the allusions. Indeed, to understand the subtleties and the wilful order of Nerval's poetry, one must learn to uncover the associations he attaches to mythical, Biblical and historical figures and to certain elemental images. It is a confirmation of his poetry's power that such a process brings just reward: a feeling of having penetrated into a richly imaginative, timeless universe in which the irrational has been brought under some control and ancient forces have been brought back to life.

SELECT BIBLIOGRAPHY

J. Dhaenens, *Le destin d'Orphée: étude sur 'El Desdichado' de Nerval*, Minard, 1972.
R. Jean, *Nerval par lui-même*, Seuil, 1964.

J. Richer, *Gérard de Nerval*, (Poètes d'aujourd'hui, 21), Seghers, 1950.
N. Rinsler, *Gérard de Nerval*, (Athlone French Poets), Athlone Press, 1973.
N. Rinsler, *Les Chimères*, (Athlone French Poets), Athlone Press, 1973.
K. Schärer, *Thématique de Nerval*, Minard, 1968.

El Desdichado

Je suis le ténébreux, – le veuf, – l'inconsolé,
Le prince d'Aquitaine à la tour abolie:
Ma seule *étoile* est morte, – et mon luth constellé
Porte le *Soleil noir* de la *Mélancolie*.   4

Dans la nuit du tombeau, toi qui m'as consolé,
Rends-moi le Pausilippe et la mer d'Italie,
La *fleur* qui plaisait tant à mon cœur désolé,
Et la treille où le pampre à la rose s'allie.   8

Suis-je Amour ou Phébus?...Lusignan ou Biron?
Mon front est rouge encor du baiser de la reine;
J'ai rêvé dans la grotte où nage la syrène...   11

Et j'ai deux fois vainqueur traversé l'Achéron:
Modulant tour à tour sur la lyre d'Orphée
Les soupirs de la sainte et les cris de la fée.   14

Myrtho

Je pense à toi, Myrtho, divine enchanteresse,
Au Pausilippe altier, de mille feux brillant,
A ton front inondé des clartés d'Orient,
Aux raisins noirs mêlés avec l'or de ta tresse.   4

C'est dans ta coupe aussi que j'avais bu l'ivresse,
Et dans l'éclair furtif de ton œil souriant,
Quand aux pieds d'Iacchus on me voyait priant,
Car la Muse m'a fait l'un des fils de la Grèce.   8

Je sais pourquoi là-bas le volcan s'est rouvert...
C'est qu'hier tu l'avais touché d'un pied agile,
Et de cendres soudain l'horizon s'est couvert.   11

Depuis qu'un duc normand brisa tes dieux d'argile,
Toujours, sous les rameaux du laurier de Virgile,
Le pâle Hortensia s'unit au Myrthe vert!   14

Antéros

Tu demandes pourquoi j'ai tant de rage au cœur
Et sur un col flexible une tête indomptée;
C'est que je suis issu de la race d'Antée,
Je retourne les dards contre le dieu vainqueur.　　　　4

Oui, je suis de ceux-là qu'inspire le Vengeur,
Il m'a marqué le front de sa lèvre irritée,
Sous la pâleur d'Abel, hélas! ensanglantée,
J'ai parfois de Caïn l'implacable rougeur!　　　　8

Jéhovah! le dernier, vaincu par ton génie,
Qui, du fond des enfers, criait: 'O tyrannie!'
C'est mon aïeul Bélus ou mon père Dagon...　　　　11

Ils m'ont plongé trois fois dans les eaux du Cocyte,
Et protégeant tout seul ma mère Amalécyte,
Je ressème à ses pieds les dents du vieux dragon.　　　　14

Delfica

La connais-tu, DAFNÉ, cette ancienne romance,
Au pied du sycomore, ou sous les lauriers blancs,
Sous l'olivier, le myrthe ou les saules tremblants,
Cette chanson d'amour...qui toujours recommence!　　　　4

Reconnais-tu le TEMPLE, au péristyle immense,
Et les citrons amers où s'imprimaient tes dents?
Et la grotte, fatale aux hôtes imprudents,
Où du dragon vaincu dort l'antique semence.　　　　8

Ils reviendront ces dieux que tu pleures toujours!
Le temps va ramener l'ordre des anciens jours;
La terre a tressailli d'un souffle prophétique...　　　　11

Cependant la sibylle au visage latin
Est endormie encor sous l'arc de Constantin:
– Et rien n'a dérangé le sévère portique.　　　　14

Gérard de Nerval

Vers dores

Eh quoi! tout est sensible!
PYTHAGORE

Homme, libre penseur! te crois-tu seul pensant
Dans ce monde où la vie éclate en toute chose?
Des forces que tu tiens ta liberté dispose,
Mais de tous tes conseils l'univers est absent.   4

Respecte dans la bête un esprit agissant:
Chaque fleur est une âme a la Nature éclose;
Un mystère d'amour dans le métal repose;
'Tout est sensible!' Et tout sur ton être est puissant.   8

Crains, dans le mur aveugle, un regard qui t'épie:
A la matière même un verbe est attaché...
Ne la fais pas servir à quelque usage impie!   11

Souvent dans l'être obscur habite un Dieu cache;
Et comme un œil naissant couvert par ses paupières,
Un pur esprit s'accroît sous l'écorce des pierres!   14

Charles Baudelaire

(1821–1867)

Baudelaire, more than any French poet before him, is the poet of consciousness of sin: man is a fallen creature, trapped in a material world far inferior
to the spiritual paradise which has perennially haunted human dreams.
Much of the tension of Baudelaire's work stems from opposite polarities,
the endless conflict between degraded human nature and aspiration, between
wilful self-possession and the pleasures of self-abandonment, between
journeys to exotic dreamlands and plunges into the *gouffre*. But instead of
falling passive victim to the contradictions of the human fate, the poet
tries to transcend them through beauty, his aim being to 'extraire l'or du
fumier du réel', to cultivate radiant flowers from the morass of evil – hence
the title of his major volume of poetry, *Les Fleurs du mal* (1857), from which
the poems in the present anthology – except *Recueillement* – are taken.
Woman has a particular place in this region of Baudelaire's inspiration,
being the symbolic focus of the essential duality: on the one hand, the
figure which tantalizes and is never wholly possessed, which man trans-
figures and even deifies in his imagination; on the other hand, the fatal
force which draws man to degrade himself and sell his soul in the sophisticated hell of carnality.

Baudelaire defines the function of his poetry as 'une aspiration humaine
vers une beauté supérieure', his belief in a world of superior beauty being
based as much on his own sensitive contact with the outside world as on
any specifically religious awareness. Everyone, he says, has known privileged
moments when the world seems intensely alive, full of meaning and exciting
to the senses; the disaster is that these moments of heightened perception
cannot be prolonged. Instead, one is plunged back into the 'lourdes ténèbres
de l'existence', into the drabness of a routine life of which every moment is a
relentless step towards death and of which the most crushing evil is a helpless
feeling of boredom and spiritual sterility. From his earliest years, Baudelaire
was acutely aware of the agonizing gap between these two forms of experience; he oscillates between an aspiration towards the glimpsed world of
beauty (the 'Idéal' which, being an aesthetic rather than a moral ideal,
does not necessarily have anything in common with the conventional notion
of good) and the negative pull of lethargy and stagnation ('Spleen').

Through his art, Baudelaire seeks to create and preserve a feeling of intensity akin to that experienced at 'supernatural' moments. His poetry sharpens the senses, draws them into a relationship with each other which seems to take one beyond mere sense-perception, and provokes the imagination into seeing things in a richly harmonic way. His intention is not to describe objects in accurate, picturesque detail, but to reveal what complexity of sensation they release and the patterns of meaning they evoke for him (e.g. the woman's hair in *La Chevelure* is not described for itself, but is only a starting-point for an exploration of the entrancing effect it has on the poet himself; and even in the *Spleen* poem 'Pluviôse...', the disturbing atmosphere in the garret, symbolic of the poet's mood, sends the mind floating far beyond the mere visual details from which it emanates). Art's aim is not slavishly to copy the outside world, but, according to Baudelaire, to 'créer une magie suggestive contenant à la fois l'objet et le sujet, le monde extérieur à l'artiste et l'artiste lui-même'. Such a 'magie suggestive' was to become the centre of the aesthetic of poets in the last quarter of the century (Mallarmé, Verlaine, Rimbaud) who, abandoning the explicit and transparent, perfected an art of the implicit and half-obscure. For Baudelaire, nature is a kind of dictionary. As a magician of language, the poet goes beyond isolated banal objects to suggest the coherent design which binds them. As a magician of the imagination, he feels out mysterious links and seals them in the image which holds the key to a fresh vision of the world.

Baudelaire's contribution to the development of modern French verse is inestimable (while his influence on such poets as T. S. Eliot and Robert Lowell shows his importance in a wider perspective). After the occasionally self-indulgent emotionalism of the Romantics, he brings to poetry a more actual religious dimension and an intensely felt spiritual torment; instead of feeding the sentiments, he gives new liberty to the senses, provocative, insinuating, uplifting or degenerate; instead of offering a reassuring complicity, he throws man into an uncomfortable confrontation with his own duality, his unconfessed dreams and inadmissible baser instincts; in his work the poetic imagination, no longer a mere purveyor of the appropriate metaphor, takes flight in its own right as *vision* and interplay of image; his studied sonnets, with their highly polished and reflective density, break with the notion of poetic inspiration as a 'fine frenzy' or a spontaneous cry of the heart and represent the conquest of will over facility, spirit over matter, and permanence over the ephemeral; and his subtle 'tides' of rhythm and headily sensuous music envelop the reader in a way unknown in previous poetry, inviting him to join the poet in a richer world where 'les parfums, les couleurs et les sons se répondent'.

SELECT BIBLIOGRAPHY

L. J. Austin, *L'Univers poétique de Baudelaire*, Mercure de France, 1956.
A. Fairlie, *Baudelaire: Les Fleurs du mal*, (Studies in French Literature, 6), Arnold, 1960.
R. Galand, *Baudelaire: poétiques et poésie*, Nizet, 1969.
F. W. Leakey, *Baudelaire and nature*, Manchester University Press, 1969.
P. Pia, *Baudelaire par lui-même*, Seuil, 1952.
G. Poulet, *Qui était Baudelaire?*, Skira, 1969.
J. Prévost, *Baudelaire: essai sur l'inspiration et la création poétiques*, Mercure de France, 1953.
J.-P. Richard, 'Profondeur de Baudelaire' in *Poésie et profondeur*, Seuil, 1955.
M.-A. Ruff, *Baudelaire*, (Connaissance des lettres), Hatier, 1955.
P. Valéry, 'Situation de Baudelaire' in *Œuvres*, ed. J. Hytier, (Bibliothèque de la Pléiade), Gallimard, 1957.

Correspondances

La Nature est un temple où de vivants piliers
Laissent parfois sortir de confuses paroles;
L'homme y passe à travers des forêts de symboles
Qui l'observent avec des regards familiers. 4

Comme de longs échos qui de loin se confondent
Dans une ténébreuse et profonde unité,
Vaste comme la nuit et comme la clarté,
Les parfums, les couleurs et les sons se répondent. 8

Il est des parfums frais comme des chairs d'enfants,
Doux comme les hautbois, verts comme les prairies,
– Et d'autres, corrompus, riches et triomphants, 11

Ayant l'expansion des choses infinies,
Comme l'ambre, le musc, le benjoin et l'encens
Qui chantent les transports de l'esprit et des sens. 14

La Chevelure

O toison, moutonnant jusque sur l'encolure!
O boucles! O parfum chargé de nonchaloir!
Extase! Pour peupler ce soir l'alcôve obscure
Des souvenirs dormant dans cette chevelure,
Je la veux agiter dans l'air comme un mouchoir! 5

La langoureuse Asie et la brûlante Afrique,
Tout un monde lointain, absent, presque défunt,
Vit dans tes profondeurs, forêt aromatique!
Comme d'autres esprits voguent sur la musique,
Le mien, ô mon amour! nage sur ton parfum. 10

J'irai là-bas où l'arbre et l'homme, pleins de sève,
Se pâment longuement sous l'ardeur des climats;
Fortes tresses, soyez la houle qui m'enlève!
Tu contiens, mer d'ébène, un éblouissant rêve
De voiles, de rameurs, de flammes et de mâts: 15

Un port retentissant où mon âme peut boire
A grands flots le parfum, le son et la couleur;
Où les vaisseaux, glissant dans l'or et dans la moire,
Ouvrent leurs vastes bras pour embrasser la gloire
D'un ciel pur où frémit l'éternelle chaleur.   20

Je plongerai ma tête amoureuse d'ivresse
Dans ce noir océan où l'autre est enfermé;
Et mon esprit subtil que le roulis caresse
Saura vous retrouver, ô féconde paresse!
Infinis bercements du loisir embaumé!   25

Cheveux bleus, pavillon de ténèbres tendues,
Vous me rendez l'azur du ciel immense et rond;
Sur les bords duvetés de vos mèches tordues
Je m'enivre ardemment des senteurs confondues
De l'huile de coco, du musc et du goudron.   30

Longtemps! toujours! ma main dans ta crinière lourde
Sèmera le rubis, la perle et le saphir,
Afin qu'à mon désir tu ne sois jamais sourde!
N'es-tu pas l'oasis où je rêve, et la gourde
Où je hume à longs traits le vin du souvenir?   35

Avec ses vêtements...

Avec ses vêtements ondoyants et nacrés,
Même quand elle marche on croirait qu'elle danse,
Comme ces longs serpents que les jongleurs sacrés
Au bout de leurs bâtons agitent en cadence.   4

Comme le sable morne et l'azur des déserts,
Insensibles tous deux à l'humaine souffrance,
Comme les longs réseaux de la houle des mers,
Elle se développe avec indifférence.   8

Ses yeux polis sont faits de minéraux charmants,
Et dans cette nature étrange et symbolique
Où l'ange inviolé se mêle au sphinx antique,   11

Où tout n'est qu'or, acier, lumière et diamants,
Resplendit à jamais, comme un astre inutile,
La froide majesté de la femme stérile.   14

Un Fantôme

I

Les Ténèbres

Dans les caveaux d'insondable tristesse
Où le Destin m'a déjà relégué;
Où jamais n'entre un rayon rose et gai;
Où, seul avec la Nuit, maussade hôtesse,   4

Je suis comme un peintre qu'un Dieu moqueur
Condamne à peindre, hélas! sur les ténèbres;
Où, cuisinier aux appétits funèbres,
Je fais bouillir et je mange mon cœur,   8

Par instants brille, et s'allonge, et s'étale
Un spectre fait de grâce et de splendeur.
A sa rêveuse allure orientale,   11

Quand il atteint sa totale grandeur,
Je reconnais ma belle visiteuse:
C'est Elle! noire et pourtant lumineuse.   14

II

Le Parfum

Lecteur, as-tu quelquefois respiré
Avec ivresse et lente gourmandise
Ce grain d'encens qui remplit une église,
Ou d'un sachet le musc invétéré?   18

Charme profond, magique, dont nous grise
Dans le présent le passé restauré!
Ainsi l'amant sur un corps adoré
Du souvenir cueille la fleur exquise.   22

De ses cheveux élastiques et lourds,
Vivant sachet, encensoir de l'alcôve,
Une senteur montait, sauvage et fauve,   25

Et des habits, mousseline ou velours,
Tout imprégnés de sa jeunesse pure,
Se dégageait un parfum de fourrure.   28

III

Le Cadre

Comme un beau cadre ajoute à la peinture,
Bien qu'elle soit d'un pinceau très-vanté,
Je ne sais quoi d'étrange et d'enchanté
En l'isolant de l'immense nature,   32

Ainsi bijoux, meubles, métaux, dorure,
S'adaptaient juste à sa rare beauté;
Rien n'offusquait sa parfaite clarté,
Et tout semblait lui servir de bordure.   36

Même on eût dit parfois qu'elle croyait
Que tout voulait l'aimer; elle noyait
Sa nudité voluptueusement   39

Dans les baisers du satin et du linge,
Et, lente ou brusque, à chaque mouvement
Montrait la grâce enfantine du singe.   42

IV

Le Portrait

La Maladie et la Mort font des cendres
De tout le feu qui pour nous flamboya.
De ces grands yeux si fervents et si tendres,
De cette bouche où mon cœur se noya,   46

De ces baisers puissants comme un dictame,
De ces transports plus vifs que des rayons,
Que reste-t-il? C'est affreux, ô mon âme!
Rien qu'un dessin fort pâle, aux trois crayons,   50

Qui, comme moi, meurt dans la solitude,
Et que le Temps, injurieux vieillard,
Chaque jour frotte avec son aile rude...   53

Noir assassin de la Vie et de l'Art,
Tu ne tueras jamais dans ma mémoire
Celle qui fut mon plaisir et ma gloire!   56

Harmonie du soir

Voici venir les temps où vibrant sur sa tige
Chaque fleur s'évapore ainsi qu'un encensoir;
Les sons et les parfums tournent dans l'air du soir;
Valse mélancolique et langoureux vertige!   4

Chaque fleur s'évapore ainsi qu'un encensoir;
Le violon frémit comme un cœur qu'on afflige;
Valse mélancolique et langoureux vertige!
Le ciel est triste et beau comme un grand reposoir.   8

Le violon frémit comme un cœur qu'on afflige,
Un cœur tendre, qui hait le néant vaste et noir!
Le ciel est triste et beau comme un grand reposoir;
Le soleil s'est noyé dans son sang qui se fige.   12

Un cœur tendre, qui hait le néant vaste et noir,
Du passé lumineux recueille tout vestige!
Le soleil s'est noyé dans son sang qui se fige...
Ton souvenir en moi luit comme un ostensoir!   16

L'Invitation au voyage

     Mon enfant, ma sœur,
     Songe à la douceur
D'aller là-bas vivre ensemble!   3
     Aimer à loisir,
     Aimer et mourir
Au pays qui te ressemble!   6
     Les soleils mouillés
     De ces ciels brouillés
Pour mon esprit ont les charmes   9
     Si mystérieux
     De tes traîtres yeux,
Brillant à travers leurs larmes.   12

Là, tout n'est qu'ordre et beauté,
Luxe, calme et volupté.   14

     Des meubles luisants,
     Polis par les ans,
Décoreraient notre chambre;   17
     Les plus rares fleurs
     Mêlant leurs odeurs
Aux vagues senteurs de l'ambre,   20

Les riches plafonds,
Les miroirs profonds,
La splendeur orientale,   23
Tout y parlerait
A l'âme en secret
Sa douce langue natale.   26

Là, tout n'est qu'ordre et beauté,
Luxe, calme et volupté.   28

Vois sur ces canaux
Dormir ces vaisseaux
Dont l'humeur est vagabonde;   31
C'est pour assouvir
Ton moindre désir
Qu'ils viennent du bout du monde.   34
– Les soleils couchants
Revêtent les champs,
Les canaux, la ville entière,   37
D'hyacinthe et d'or;
Le monde s'endort
Dans une chaude lumière.   40

Là, tout n'est qu'ordre et beauté.
Luxe, calme et volupté.   42

Chant d'automne

I

Bientôt nous plongerons dans les froides ténèbres;
Adieu, vive clarté de nos étés trop courts!
J'entends déjà tomber avec des chocs funèbres
Le bois retentissant sur le pavé des cours.   4

Tout l'hiver va rentrer dans mon être: colère,
Haine, frissons, horreur, labeur dur et forcé,
Et, comme le soleil dans son enfer polaire,
Mon cœur ne sera plus qu'un bloc rouge et glacé.   8

J'écoute en frémissant chaque bûche qui tombe;
L'échafaud qu'on bâtit n'a pas d'écho plus sourd.
Mon esprit est pareil à la tour qui succombe
Sous les coups du bélier infatigable et lourd.   12

Il me semble, bercé par ce choc monotone,
Qu'on cloue en grande hâte un cercueil quelque part.

Pour qui? – C'était hier l'été; voici l'automne!
Ce bruit mystérieux sonne comme un départ. 16

II

J'aime de vos longs yeux la lumière verdâtre,
Douce beauté, mais tout aujourd'hui m'est amer,
Et rien, ni votre amour, ni le boudoir, ni l'âtre,
Ne me vaut le soleil rayonnant sur la mer. 20

Et pourtant aimez-moi, tendre cœur! soyez mère,
Même pour un ingrat, même pour un méchant;
Amante ou sœur, soyez la douceur éphémère
D'un glorieux automne ou d'un soleil couchant. 24

Courte tâche! La tombe attend; elle est avide!
Ah! laissez-moi, mon front posé sur vos genoux,
Goûter, en regrettant l'été blanc et torride,
De l'arrière-saison le rayon jaune et doux! 28

La Musique

La musique souvent me prend comme une mer!
    Vers ma pâle étoile,
Sous un plafond de brume ou dans un vaste éther,
    Je mets à la voile; 4

La poitrine en avant et les poumons gonflés
    Comme de la toile,
J'escalade le dos des flots amoncelés
    Que la nuit me voile; 8

Je sens vibrer en moi toutes les passions
    D'un vaisseau qui souffre;
Le bon vent, la tempête et ses convulsions 11

    Sur l'immense gouffre
Me bercent. D'autres fois, calme plat, grand miroir
    De mon désespoir! 14

Spleen

Pluviôse, irrité contre la ville entière,
De son urne à grands flots verse un froid ténébreux
Aux pâles habitants du voisin cimetière
Et la mortalité sur les faubourgs brumeux. 4

Mon chat sur le carreau cherchant une litière
Agite sans repos son corps maigre et galeux ;
L'âme d'un vieux poëte erre dans la gouttière
Avec la triste voix d'un fantôme frileux.   8

Le bourdon se lamente, et la bûche enfumée
Accompagne en fausset la pendule enrhumée,
Cependant qu'en un jeu plein de sales parfums,   11

Héritage fatal d'une vieille hydropique,
Le beau valet de cœur et la dame de pique
Causent sinistrement de leurs amours défunts.   14

Spleen

Quand le ciel bas et lourd pèse comme un couvercle
Sur l'esprit gémissant en proie aux longs ennuis,
Et que de l'horizon embrassant tout le cercle
Il nous verse un jour noir plus triste que les nuits ;   4

Quand la terre est changée en un cachot humide,
Où l'Espérance, comme une chauve-souris,
S'en va battant les murs de son aile timide
Et se cognant la tête à des plafonds pourris ;   8

Quand la pluie étalant ses immenses traînées
D'une vaste prison imite les barreaux,
Et qu'un peuple muet d'infâmes araignées
Vient tendre ses filets au fond de nos cerveaux,   12

Des cloches tout à coup sautent avec furie
Et lancent vers le ciel un affreux hurlement,
Ainsi que des esprits errants et sans patrie
Qui se mettent à geindre opiniâtrement.   16

– Et de longs corbillards, sans tambours ni musique,
Défilent lentement dans mon âme ; l'Espoir,
Vaincu, pleure, et l'Angoisse atroce, despotique,
Sur mon crâne incliné plante son drapeau noir.   20

Rêve parisien

I

De ce terrible paysage,
Tel que jamais mortel n'en vit,
Ce matin encore l'image,
Vague et lointaine, me ravit.   4

Le sommeil est plein de miracles !
Par un caprice singulier
J'avais banni de ces spectacles
Le végétal irrégulier, 8

Et, peintre fier de mon génie,
Je savourais dans mon tableau
L'enivrante monotonie
Du métal, du marbre et de l'eau. 12

Babel d'escaliers et d'arcades,
C'était un palais infini,
Plein de bassins et de cascades
Tombant dans l'or mat ou bruni ; 16

Et des cataractes pesantes,
Comme des rideaux de cristal,
Se suspendaient, éblouissantes,
A des murailles de métal. 20

Non d'arbres, mais de colonnades
Les étangs dormants s'entouraient,
Où de gigantesques naïades,
Comme des femmes, se miraient. 24

Des nappes d'eau s'épanchaient, bleues,
Entre des quais roses et verts,
Pendant des millions de lieues,
Vers les confins de l'univers ; 28

C'étaient des pierres inouïes
Et des flots magiques ; c'étaient
D'immenses glaces éblouies
Par tout ce qu'elles reflétaient ! 32

Insouciants et taciturnes,
Des Ganges, dans le firmament,
Versaient le trésor de leurs urnes
Dans des gouffres de diamant. 36

Architecte de mes féeries,
Je faisais, à ma volonté,
Sous un tunnel de pierreries
Passer un océan dompté ; 40

Et tout, même la couleur noire,
Semblait fourbi, clair, irisé ;
Le liquide enchâssait sa gloire
Dans le rayon cristallisé. 44

Nul astre d'ailleurs, nuls vestiges
De soleil, même au bas du ciel,
Pour illuminer ces prodiges,
Qui brillaient d'un feu personnel!   48

Et sur ces mouvantes merveilles
Planait (terrible nouveauté!
Tout pour l'œil, rien pour les oreilles!)
Un silence d'éternité.   52

II

En rouvrant mes yeux pleins de flamme
J'ai vu l'horreur de mon taudis,
Et senti, rentrant dans mon âme,
La pointe des soucis maudits;   56

La pendule aux accents funèbres
Sonnait brutalement midi,
Et le ciel versait des ténèbres
Sur le triste monde engourdi.   60

Recueillement

Sois sage, ô ma Douleur, et tiens-toi plus tranquille.
Tu réclamais le Soir; il descend; le voici:
Une atmosphère obscure enveloppe la ville,
Aux uns portant la paix, aux autres le souci.   4

Pendant que des mortels la multitude vile,
Sous le fouet du Plaisir, ce bourreau sans merci,
Va cueillir des remords dans la fête servile,
Ma Douleur, donne-moi la main; viens par ici,   8

Loin d'eux. Vois se pencher les défuntes Années,
Sur les balcons du ciel, en robes surannées;
Surgir du fond des eaux le Regret souriant;   11

Le Soleil moribond s'endormir sous une arche,
Et, comme un long linceul traînant à l'Orient,
Entends, ma chère, entends la douce Nuit qui marche.   14

Stéphane Mallarmé

(1842–1898)

One could say that Mallarmé is the most 'spiritualized' French poet of the nineteenth century, the one with the most sacred view of the poetic art. His work takes to their most absolute and purified conclusion the implications of Baudelaire's idea of *correspondances*: the belief that behind the phenomena of the material world lies an anterior, immutable Reality; that material forms, imprisoned in the plane of the contingent and the accidental, testify nevertheless to a pattern of meaning and a mysterious order beyond themselves; and that an essential link exists between the artistic intuition, with its deep captures in the realm of aesthetic analogy, and the underlying unity of Creation. Poetry thus becomes, for Mallarmé, a religious act. From the insignificant body of things and from the base matter of human experience (mere sense-perceptions and personal emotions), he tries to disengage or resurrect the spirituality, the suggestive aura.

This means that Mallarmé's is a nebulous and obscure poetry. It makes no concessions to the idea of *l'art pour tous* and appeals unashamedly to those rarer spirits who are willing to turn themselves into initiates and whose imaginations find sustenance in an ethereal zone. As he says, 'Toute chose sacrée et qui veut demeurer sacrée s'enveloppe de mystère'. But whereas the quotation might suggest an artificial cultivation of mystery for mystery's sake, his poetry is, in fact, only inaccessible in that it is trying to evoke what may well be a 'sublime illusion' and to release from the page what cannot be grasped in words. Hence the dilemma, the explanation of so much of the theme of anguish, impotence and literary sterility in Mallarmé, that he must use words, bent as they are on the explicit and encrusted with the dross of meaning, to express the ineffable. How, indeed, can poetry be refined to become that paradoxical 'Musicienne du silence'? This is the same dilemma, never more acute than in the Symbolist period when poetry and spiritual aspiration became virtually synonymous, as that implied in Rimbaud's statement, 'J'écrivais des silences (...) je notais l'inexprimable' and in Verlaine's request that the poem should be 'la chose envolée (...) Et tout le reste est littérature'.

But Mallarmé differentiates himself from Rimbaud in one important respect. In his work there is no wild and fitful breath of inspiration, no self-abandonment to the dictates of the subconscious, no surprise-images thrown up as if by accident. He shows himself once more an inheritor from Baudelaire, just as later he is to be a model for Valéry, in saying that what he seeks is 'un livre qui soit un livre, architectural et prémédité, et non un recueil des inspirations de hasard, fussent-elles merveilleuses'. There is no more extreme example of the alchemist's studious dedication than Mallarmé, patiently and methodically conquering 'le hasard', transmuting the unkempt, disordered and indiscriminate matter of life into a fine spiritual distillation. He differentiates himself also from both Verlaine and Rimbaud by his complete break with the personal lyrical tradition and his cultivation of an anonymous poetry from which the self and its emotions are abolished. It is only when the poem has purified itself of its points of reference in the real world, the sacrilegious explicitness of words and the personality of the poet that it has a chance to become 'teinté d'absolu'.

Mallarmé's 'immaculate language', the highest expression of the Symbolist mood, uses symbols instead of statement (the window, the mirror, the lake's surface; the bird, the wing, the fan; the sea, the foam, the sunset and so on): symbols of infinite nuance, radiating within poems and between poems, which cannot be reduced to a single meaning and stay poised in the realm of the virtual. It is a language totally divorced from the function of prose. The syntax is reorganized in a baffling way, so that each word lives with an independent reverberative life and is no longer subordinate to a clearly communicative grammatical purpose: instead of a signifying agent, it becomes a musical note, a colour on a palette, a vibrancy of suggestion. It is a language, finally, which does not exclude by its obscurity, but invites the reader to become the creator himself, sharing Mallarmé's own ambitious and arduous experience of gradually conquering 'le hasard' word by word and touching something airy and beyond reality which may not exist.

SELECT BIBLIOGRAPHY

A. R. Chisholm, *Mallarmé's Grand Œuvre*, Manchester University Press, 1962.
C. Mauron, *Mallarmé par lui-même*, Seuil, 1964.
G. Michaud, *Mallarmé*, (Connaissance des lettres), Hatier, 1953.
E. Noulet, *Vingt poèmes de Mallarmé: exégèses*, Droz, 1967.
J.-P. Richard, *L'Univers imaginaire de Mallarmé*, Seuil, 1961.
J. Scherer, *L'Expression littéraire dans l'œuvre de Mallarmé*, Nizet, 1947.
A. Thibaudet, *La Poésie de Stéphane Mallarmé*, Gallimard, 1926.
P.-O. Walzer, *Stéphane Mallarmé*, (Poètes d'aujourd'hui, 94), 1963.

Brise marine

La chair est triste, hélas! et j'ai lu tous les livres.
Fuir! là-bas fuir! Je sens que des oiseaux sont ivres

D'être parmi l'écume inconnue et les cieux!
Rien, ni les vieux jardins reflétés par les yeux   4
Ne retiendra ce cœur qui dans la mer se trempe
O nuits! ni la clarté déserte de ma lampe
Sur le vide papier que la blancheur défend
Et ni la jeune femme allaitant son enfant.   8
Je partirai! Steamer balançant ta mâture,
Lève l'ancre pour une exotique nature!

Un Ennui, désolé par les cruels espoirs,
Croit encore à l'adieu suprême des mouchoirs!   12
Et, peut-être, les mâts, invitant les orages
Sont-ils de ceux qu'un vent penche sur les naufrages
Perdus, sans mâts, sans mâts, ni fertiles îlots...
Mais, ô mon cœur, entends le chant des matelots!   16

Sainte

A la fenêtre recélant
Le santal vieux qui se dédore
De sa viole étincelant
Jadis avec flûte ou mandore,   4

Est la Sainte pâle, étalant
Le livre vieux qui se déplie
Du Magnificat ruisselant
Jadis selon vêpre et complie: 8

A ce vitrage d'ostensoir
Que frôle une harpe par l'Ange
Formée avec son vol du soir
Pour la délicate phalange   12

Du doigt que, sans le vieux santal
Ni le vieux livre, elle balance
Sur le plumage instrumental,
Musicienne du silence.   16

Autre éventail

O rêveuse, pour que je plonge
Au pur délice sans chemin,
Sache, par un subtil mensonge,
Garder mon aile dans ta main.   4

Une fraîcheur de crépuscule
Te vient à chaque battement
Dont le coup prisonnier recule
L'horizon délicatement.   8

Vertige! voici que frissonne
L'espace comme un grand baiser
Qui, fou de naître pour personne,
Ne peut jaillir ni s'apaiser.   12

Sens-tu le paradis farouche
Ainsi qu'un rire enseveli
Se couler du coin de ta bouche
Au fond de l'unanime pli!   16

Le sceptre des rivages roses
Stagnants sur les soirs d'or, ce l'est,
Ce blanc vol fermé que tu poses
Contre le feu d'un bracelet.   20

Petit air

II

Indomptablement a dû
Comme mon espoir s'y lance
Éclater là-haut perdu
Avec furie et silence,   4

Voix étrangère au bosquet
Ou par nul écho suivie,
L'oiseau qu'on n'ouït jamais
Une autre fois en la vie.   8

Le hagard musicien,
Cela dans le doute expire
Si de mon sein pas du sien
A jailli le sanglot pire   12

Déchiré va-t-il entier
Rester sur quelque sentier!   14

Quand l'ombre menaça...

Quand l'ombre menaca de la fatale loi
Tel vieux Rêve, désir et mal de mes vertèbres,
Affligé de périr sous les plafonds funèbres
Il a ployé son aile indubitable en moi.   4

Luxe, ô salle d'ébène où, pour séduire un roi
Se tordent dans leur mort des guirlandes célèbres,
Vous n'êtes qu'un orgueil menti par les ténèbres
Aux yeux du solitaire ébloui de sa foi.   8

Oui, je sais qu'au lointain de cette nuit, la Terre
Jette d'un grand éclat l'insolite mystère,
Sous les siècles hideux qui l'obscurcissent moins.   11

L'espace à soi pareil qu'il s'accroisse ou se nie
Roule dans cet ennui des feux vils pour témoins
Que s'est d'un astre en fête allumé le génie.   14

Le vierge, le vivace...

Le vierge, le vivace et le bel aujourd'hui
Va-t-il nous déchirer avec un coup d'aile ivre
Ce lac dur oublié que hante sous le givre
Le transparent glacier des vols qui n'ont pas fui!   4

Un cygne d'autrefois se souvient que c'est lui
Magnifique mais qui sans espoir se délivre
Pour n'avoir pas chanté la région où vivre
Quand du stérile hiver a resplendi l'ennui.   8

Tout son col secouera cette blanche agonie
Par l'espace infligée à l'oiseau qui le nie,
Mais non l'horreur du sol où le plumage est pris.   11

Fantôme qu'à ce lieu son pur éclat assigne,
Il s'immobilise au songe froid de mépris
Que vêt parmi l'exil inutile le Cygne.   14

Au seul souci de voyager . . .

Au seul souci de voyager
Outre une Inde splendide et trouble
– Ce salut soit le messager
Du temps, cap que ta poupe double   4

Comme sur quelque vergue bas
Plongeante avec la caravelle
Écumait toujours en ébats
Un oiseau d'annonce nouvelle   8

Qui criait monotonement
Sans que la barre ne varie
Un inutile gisement
Nuit, désespoir et pierrerie   12

Par son chant reflété jusqu'au
Sourire du pâle Vasco.   14

Toute l'âme résumée . . .

Toute l'âme résumée
Quand lente nous l'expirons
Dans plusieurs ronds de fumée
Abolis en autres ronds   4

Atteste quelque cigare
Brûlant savamment pour peu
Que la cendre se sépare
De son clair baiser de feu   8

Ainsi le chœur des romances
A la lèvre vole-t-il
Exclus-en si tu commences
Le réel parce que vil   12

Le sens trop précis rature
Ta vague littérature.   14

Charles Cros

(1842–1888)

Charles Cros is not just a poet and typical figure of late nineteenth-century Bohemian Paris; he is also one of the inventors of colour photography and the gramophone. This remarkable and bizarre combination of rôles gives proof of a mind concerned with the exploration of the physical, spiritual and emotional possibilities of existence (Rimbaud, too, in this period, saw himself as 'un multiplicateur de progrès', hoping to bring a new spirit of semi-scientific discovery into poetry). For a long time Cros's work went largely unrecognized in either field, his poetic talent being overshadowed by that of greater spirits (Baudelaire, Rimbaud or Verlaine) and his theoretical research in the sciences being overtaken by the practical discoveries of others. But in the twentieth century, partly through the enthusiasm of the Surrealists for his original bent of mind, his work has aroused considerable interest. The bulk of his poetry is contained in two collections: *Le Coffret de santal* (1873) and *Le Collier de griffes* (published posthumously in 1908).

One can distinguish in Cros's verse an absorbing mixture of sensuality and detachment, of sentiment and irony. On the one hand there is the love-poet and the fascination which woman exerts over him, promising heady moments of intense feeling, excited senses and the swaying tight-rope of danger and death; she is the enchantress offering her varied potions of joy and frustration. On the other hand, there is a lucidity in Cros which makes him mistrust the pretentiousness of the emotions. Seen from the critics' box the search for love is no more than a banal drama of pleading, possession and disillusion; and, likewise, the whole range of sensual enjoyments appear as frivolous theatrical gestures disguising the void or the face of despair:

> Avec les fleurs, avec les femmes,
> Avec l'absinthe, avec le feu,
> On peut se divertir un peu,
> Jouer son rôle en quelque drame
> *(Lendemain)*.

The impression is of a poet administering his own carefully controlled and sophisticated doses of the amorous stimulant, savouring for a moment a

new and ingenious combination, then disengaging as it becomes 'fade'.
The cynicism and self-mockery implicit in such an attitude (which Laforgue
shares) add poignancy to those poems in which the poet appears as a self-
dramatized figure *(Supplication, Possession, Conquérant)*; one senses a
melancholic spirit behind the mask.

Afraid of pompous declamation, Cros has a taste for unpretentious short
lines and the controlled precision of the sonnet. Richly developed passages
such as in Baudelaire's *La Chevelure*, extended movements of graceful
music as in Verlaine are both rare in Cros (although he shares with the
powerfully influential Baudelaire an ambiguous blend of sensuality and
spirituality, a touch of perversity and sadism, an indulgence in *ivresse* and
a love of exotic imaginary landscapes; and with his contemporary, Verlaine,
a note of dreamy melancholia, and a taste for blurred or shifting outlines).
In fact, his lines have been called 'secs' (and Verlaine refers to 'la sobriété
de son verbe et de son discours'). It is as if the mistrust of his own passion
leads him to a metre whose discretion will itself stem effusiveness. The octosyllables of *J'ai bâti dans ma fantaisie...* and *Testament* are a perfect match
for the poet's mood of calm, lucid introspection and suppressed despair.
Cros has a sure touch in his choice of verse-form and in his immaculate
arrangement of effects within those forms. *Hiéroglyphe* is a quite exceptional
example of expert versification: the six syllables of the repeated formula
set up a faceted interplay with the contrasting octosyllables, the totally
unified system of rhymes gives an inexorable pull to the poet's half-willing,
half-unwilling spiral towards death, and every isolated fourth line momentarily halts the movement of hieroglyphics and modifies the mood before
reactivating them in a new combination. The work shows a masterly reciprocity between form and content.

Rather than search for deep ideas in Cros's 'théâtre aux décors divers',
one does better to listen to his 'persuasive parole' and its fluctuating moods;
to appreciate the comic and the tragic of his lyricism; to applaud the actor
and pity the man. His poetry does not break through new frontiers of spiritual
knowledge; that was never its ambition. Instead it is, in the selection given
here, a curiously varied expression of one man's awareness of himself.

SELECT BIBLIOGRAPHY

L. Forestier, P.-O. Walzer (eds.), *Œuvres complètes de Charles Cros et Tristan Corbière*,
    (Bibliothèque de la Pléiade), Gallimard, 1970.
L. Forestier, *Charles Cros: l'homme et l'œuvre*, Minard, 1969.
L. Forestier, *Charles Cros*, (Poètes d'aujourd'hui, 47), Seghers, 1972.
P. Verlaine, 'Charles Cros' in *Œuvres en prose complètes*, ed. J. Borel, (Bibliothèque
    de la Pléiade), Gallimard, 1972.

Supplication

Sonnet

Tes yeux, impassibles sondeurs
D'une mer polaire idéale,
S'éclairent parfois des splendeurs
Du rire, aurore boréale.   4

Ta chevelure, en ces odeurs
Fines et chaudes qu'elle exhale,
Fait rêver aux tigres rôdeurs
D'une clairière tropicale.   8

Ton âme a ces aspects divers :
Froideur sereine des hivers,
Douceur trompeuse de la fauve.   11

Glacé de froid, ou déchiré
A belles dents, moi, je mourrai
A moins que ton cœur ne me sauve.   14

Possession

Puisque ma bouche a rencontré
Sa bouche, il faut me taire. Trêve
Aux mots creux. Je ne montrerai
Rien qui puisse trahir mon rêve.   4

*

Il faut que je ne dise rien
De l'odeur de sa chevelure,
De son sourire aérien,
Des bravoures de son allure,   8

Rien des yeux aux regards troublants,
Persuasifs, cabalistiques,
Rien des épaules, des bras blancs
Aux effluves aromatiques.   12

*

Je ne sais plus faire d'ailleurs
Une si savante analyse,
Possédé de rêves meilleurs
Où ma raison se paralyse.   16

Et je me sens comme emporté,
Epave en proie au jeu des vagues,

Par le vertige où m'ont jeté
Ses lèvres tièdes, ses yeux vagues.   20

*

On se demandera d'où vient
L'influx tout-puissant qui m'oppresse,
Mais personne n'en saura rien
Que moi seul...et l'Enchanteresse.   24

Sonnet

J'ai bâti dans ma fantaisie
Un théâtre aux décors divers:
– Magiques palais, grands bois verts –
Pour y jouer ma poésie.   4

Un peu trop au hasard choisie,
La jeune-première à l'envers
Récite quelquefois mes vers.
Faute de mieux je m'extasie.   8

Et je déclame avec tant d'art
Qu'on me croirait pris à son fard,
Au fard que je lui mets moi-même.

Non. Sous le faux air virginal
Je vois l'être inepte et vénal,
Mais c'est le rôle seul que j'aime.   14

Conquérant

J'ai balayé tout le pays
En une fière cavalcade;
Partout les gens se sont soumis,
Ils viennent me chanter l'aubade.   4

Ce cérémonial est fade;
Aux murs mes ordres sont écrits.
Amenez-moi (mais pas de cris)
Des filles pour la rigolade.   8

L'une sanglote, l'autre a peur,
La troisième a le sein trompeur
Et l'autre s'habille en insecte.   11

Mais la plus belle ne dit rien;
Elle a le rire aérien
Et ne craint pas qu'on la respecte.   14

Hiéroglyphe

J'ai trois fenêtres à ma chambre:
    L'amour, la mer, la mort,
Sang vif, vert calme, violet.

O femme, doux et lourd trésor!   4

Froids vitraux, cloches, odeurs d'ambre.
    La mer, la mort, l'amour,
Ne sentir que ce qui me plaît...

Femme, plus claire que le jour!   8

Par ce soir doré de septembre,
    La mort, l'amour, la mer,
Me noyer dans l'oubli complet.

Femme! femme! cercueil de chair!   12

Testament

Si mon âme claire s'éteint
Comme une lampe sans pétrole,
Si mon esprit, en haut, déteint
Comme une guenille folle,   4

Si je moisis, diamantin,
Entier, sans tache, sans vérole,
Si le bégaiement bête atteint
Ma persuasive parole,   8

Et si je meurs, soûl, dans un coin
C'est que ma patrie est bien loin
Loin de la France et de la terre.   11

Ne craignez rien, je ne maudis
Personne. Car un paradis
Matinal, s'ouvre et me fait taire.   14

Paul Verlaine

(1844–1896)

Verlaine has left his mark as a supremely musical poet. Titles like *La bonne chanson*, *Romances sans paroles* and *Ariettes oubliées*, the presence of instruments such as 'violons', 'luth' and 'mandoline', and phrases such as 'en sourdine' and 'sur le mode mineur' are a token of the affinity between his poetry and the resources of music. 'De la musique avant toute chose', he writes in his *Art poétique*, at a time when Mallarmé is also shaping the spirit of Symbolism by seeking to perfect an allusive language of notes rather than meanings. But Verlaine's music is of a unique kind. It does not have the vast swelling and abating rhythms of Baudelaire, who says 'La musique souvent me prend comme une mer', nor does it have the same luxurious harmonic richness. It is very often a diminutive melodic poetry (as in the lines 'O triste, triste était mon âme/A cause, à cause d'une femme'), with single notes recurring at intervals to create the impression of a simple, ingenuous air. At other times it applies a delicate penetrating monotony, with sound-echoes spread so extensively throughout the poem that the borders of structure dissolve and the clarity of theme is submerged. It is almost invariably a suave, unobtrusive music with no grand effects: not lending dramatic accompaniment to the peaks and valleys of intense emotion, as in earlier Romantic poetry, but swathing them in a misty mood so that one can no longer be sure of their outline or feel the acuteness of their contrast. And yet lyricism is not lost: in the background is always the nagging presence of a simple and universal human emotion, melancholy, nostalgia, distress, remorse. No other French poet has enlisted such resources of rhyme, assonance and alliteration, coupled with the flexibilities of rhythm and verse-form, to drown the intellect, steep it in sound and leave it powerless to resist an elementary poignancy of feeling.

But Verlaine is not simply a poet-musician. He is also a poet-painter, whose pictorial interests are captured in such titles as *Eaux-fortes*, *Paysages tristes*, *Paysages belges* and *Aquarelles*. From the shimmering moonlight, soft blue shadows, quivering air and half-glimpsed snatches of coloured costumes filtered through the trees of the *Fêtes galantes* (1869), to the tremulous vision, plays of light on water, mist-soaked floating oak-trees, whirling roundabout and rapid brush dabs chasing the sunny zest of an outdoor beer-garden of *Romances sans paroles* (1874), one can see Verlaine contributing to the same revolution in the use of words as that accomplished by the Impressionists in the use of colours and brush-strokes. It is significant that the period of composition of the latter collection was also the period of his condemned liaison with Rimbaud *le voyant*, and nowhere else in his work is a *dérèglement* of vision more apparent: the face of reality loses its contours, becomes mobile, phantasmal and at times hallucinatory.

But Verlaine's achievement extends far beyond these two rôles. There is the religious poet of *Sagesse* (1880), expressing the crisis of his new-found faith in a variety of forms: firmly hewn allegorical vision, self-reinforcing intellectual argument, graceful dream images, peaceful descriptions of a natural scene, cryptic little songs, restless and tormented juxtapositions of metaphors and symbols. It is here that we see him putting his qualities as a musician and a landscape painter at the service of a deeper spiritual dimension; and the conflict of lucidity and inner obscurity, self-denial and escapist self-abandonment, takes on a new richness. There is also the humorous Verlaine, the poet of *caprices*: the satirical portraits, spiced with colourful vocabulary, of the early *Poèmes saturniens* (1866); the mock-gaiety, urbane ironies and ambiguous game of masks in the *Fêtes galantes*; the chameleon-like self-parody and the scabrous humour of his later works. Nor, in spite of a profusion of titles like *Melancholia* or *Paysages tristes*, can his poetic mood be limited to that of melancholy, bittersweet nostalgia or vague reverie: one finds moods of innocence, joyful simplicity, religious devotion, torment, self-castigation, plebeian bonhomie, animated banter and casual playfulness. Nor, even though it is central to all his poems inspired successively by his wife Mathilde, Arthur Rimbaud and the Christian God, is the theme of lost love and its variants his only theme: this is given subtle accompaniment by the complementary motifs of reality and appearances, the precariousness of personal identity, man's relationship with nature, oblivion and ecstasy, and so on.

Through all these manifestations, however, Verlaine's hall-marks are unmistakeable: a matchless handling of all the pliabilities of rhythm (its almost imperceptible variations, the telling irregularity, the slight palpitation, the lingering mute 'e', the tenuous tug-of-war of two alternative rhythms) and a supreme ear for the musical values of words.

SELECT BIBLIOGRAPHY

A. Adam, *Verlaine*, (Connaissance des lettres), Hatier, 1965.
J. Borel, Introductions to the various *recueils* in *Verlaine: Œuvres poétiques complètes*, (Bibliothèque de la Pléiade), Gallimard, 1962.
J.-H. Bornecque, *Verlaine par lui-même*, Seuil, 1966.
C. Chadwick, *Verlaine*, (Athlone French Poets), Athlone Press, 1973.
O. Nadal, *Paul Verlaine*, Mercure de France, 1961.

J.-P. Richard, 'Fadeur de Verlaine' in *Poésie et profondeur*, Seuil, 1955.
J. Richer. *Paul Verlaine*, (Poètes d'aujourd'hui, 38), Seghers, 1960.
E. Zimmermann, *Magies de Verlaine*, Corti, 1967.

Soleils couchants

Une aube affaiblie
Verse par les champs
La mélancolie
Des soleils couchants.   4
La mélancolie
Berce de doux chants
Mon cœur qui s'oublie
Aux soleils couchants.   8
Et d'étranges rêves,
Comme des soleils
Couchants sur les grèves,
Fantômes vermeils,   12
Défilent sans trêves,
Défilent, pareils
A des grands soleils
Couchants sur les grèves.   16

Chanson d'automne

Les sanglots longs
Des violons
   De l'automne
Blessent mon cœur
D'une langueur
   Monotone.   6

Tout suffocant
Et blême, quand
   Sonne l'heure,
Je me souviens
Des jours anciens
   Et je pleure ;   12

Et je m'en vais
Au vent mauvais
   Qui m'emporte
Deçà, delà,
Pareil à la
   Feuille morte.   18

Clair de lune

Votre âme est un paysage choisi
Que vont charmant masques et bergamasques
Jouant du luth et dansant et quasi
Tristes sous leurs déguisements fantasques. 4

Tout en chantant sur le mode mineur
L'amour vainqueur et la vie opportune,
Ils n'ont pas l'air de croire à leur bonheur
Et leur chanson se mêle au clair de lune, 8

Au calme clair de lune triste et beau,
Qui fait rêver les oiseaux dans les arbres
Et sangloter d'extase les jets d'eau,
Les grands jets d'eau sveltes parmi les marbres. 12

En sourdine

Calmes dans le demi-jour
Que les branches hautes font,
Pénétrons bien notre amour
De ce silence profond. 4

Fondons nos âmes, nos cœurs
Et nos sens extasiés,
Parmi les vagues langueurs
Des pins et des arbousiers. 8

Ferme tes yeux à demi,
Croise tes bras sur ton sein,
Et de ton cœur endormi
Chasse à jamais tout dessein. 12

Laissons-nous persuader
Au souffle berceur et doux
Qui vient à tes pieds rider
Les ondes de gazon roux. 16

Et quand, solennel, le soir
Des chênes noirs tombera,
Voix de notre désespoir,
Le rossignol chantera. 20

Colloque sentimental

Dans le vieux parc solitaire et glacé,
Deux formes ont tout à l'heure passé.

Leurs yeux sont morts et leurs lèvres sont molles,
Et l'on entend à peine leurs paroles. 4

Dans le vieux parc solitaire et glacé,
Deux spectres ont évoqué le passé.

– Te souvient-il de notre extase ancienne?
– Pourquoi voulez-vous donc qu'il m'en souvienne? 8

– Ton cœur bat-il toujours à mon seul nom?
Toujours vois-tu mon âme en rêve? – Non.

– Ah! les beaux jours de bonheur indicible
Où nous joignions nos bouches! – C'est possible. 12

– Qu'il était bleu, le ciel, et grand, l'espoir!
– L'espoir a fui, vaincu, vers le ciel noir.

Tels ils marchaient dans les avoines folles,
Et la nuit seule entendit leurs paroles. 16

C'est l'extase langoureuse...

> Le vent dans la plaine
> Suspend son haleine.
> (FAVART)

C'est l'extase langoureuse,
C'est la fatigue amoureuse,
C'est tous les frissons des bois
Parmi l'étreinte des brises,
C'est, vers les ramures grises,
Le chœur des petites voix. 6

O le frêle et frais murmure!
Cela gazouille et susurre,
Cela ressemble au cri doux
Que l'herbe agitée expire ...
Tu dirais, sous l'eau qui vire,
Le roulis sourd des cailloux. 12

Cette âme qui se lamente
En cette plainte dormante
C'est la nôtre, n'est-ce pas?

La mienne, dis, et la tienne,
Dont s'exhale l'humble antienne
Par ce tiède soir, tout bas?   18

Il pleure dans mon cœur...

> Il pleut doucement sur la ville.
> (ARTHUR RIMBAUD)

Il pleure dans mon cœur
Comme il pleut sur la ville;
Quelle est cette langueur
Qui pénètre mon cœur?
                                                4

O bruit doux de la pluie
Par terre et sur les toits!
Pour un cœur qui s'ennuie
O le chant de la pluie!
                                                8

Il pleure sans raison
Dans ce cœur qui s'écœure.
Quoi! nulle trahison?...
Ce deuil est sans raison.
                                                12

C'est bien la pire peine
De ne savoir pourquoi
Sans amour et sans haine
Mon cœur a tant de peine!
                                                16

Les chères mains qui furent miennes...

Les chères mains qui furent miennes,
Toutes petites, toutes belles,
Après ces méprises mortelles
Et toutes ces choses païennes,
                                                4

Après les rades et les grèves,
Et les pays et les provinces,
Royales mieux qu'au temps des princes,
Les chères mains m'ouvrent les rêves.
                                                8

Mains en songe, mains sur mon âme,
Sais-je, moi, ce que vous daignâtes,
Parmi ces rumeurs scélérates,
Dire à cette âme qui se pâme?
                                                12

Ment-elle, ma vision chaste
D'affinité spirituelle,
De complicité maternelle,
D'affection étroite et vaste?   16

Remords si cher, peine très bonne,
Rêves bénis, mains consacrées,
O ces mains, ces mains vénérées,
Faites le geste qui pardonne!   20

Le ciel est, par-dessus le toit...

Le ciel est, par-dessus le toit,
    Si bleu, si calme!
Un arbre, par-dessus le toit,
    Berce sa palme.   4

La cloche, dans le ciel qu'on voit,
    Doucement tinte.
Un oiseau sur l'arbre qu'on voit
    Chante sa plainte.   8

Mon Dieu, mon Dieu, la vie est là,
    Simple et tranquille.
Cette paisible rumeur-là
    Vient de la ville.   12

– Qu'as-tu fait, ô toi que voilà
    Pleurant sans cesse,
Dis, qu'as-tu fait, toi que voilà,
    De ta jeunesse?   16

Je ne sais pourquoi...

Je ne sais pourquoi
    Mon esprit amer
D'une aile inquiète et folle vole sur la mer.
    Tout ce qui m'est cher,
    D'une aile d'effroi
Mon amour le couve au ras des flots. Pourquoi, pourquoi?   6

Mouette à l'essor mélancolique,
Elle suit la vague, ma pensée,
A tous les vents du ciel balancée,
Et biaisant quand la marée oblique,
Mouette à l'essor mélancolique.   11

Ivre de soleil
Et de liberté,
Un instinct la guide à travers cette immensité.
La brise d'été
Sur le flot vermeil
Doucement la porte en un tiède demi-sommeil.   17

Parfois si tristement elle crie
Qu'elle alarme au lointain le pilote,
Puis au gré du vent se livre et flotte
Et plonge, et l'aile toute meurtrie
Revole, et puis si tristement crie!   22

Je ne sais pourquoi
Mon esprit amer
D'une aile inquiète et folle vole sur la mer.
Tout ce qui m'est cher,
D'une aile d'effroi
Mon amour le couve au ras des flots. Pourquoi, pourquoi?   28

L'échelonnement des haies...

L'échelonnement des haies
Moutonne à l'infini, mer
Claire dans le brouillard clair
Qui sent bon les jeunes baies.   4

Des arbres et des moulins
Sont légers sur le vert tendre
Où vient s'ébattre et s'étendre
L'agilité des poulains.   8

Dans ce vague d'un Dimanche
Voici se jouer aussi
De grandes brebis aussi
Douces que leur laine blanche.   12

Tout à l'heure déferlait
L'onde, roulée en volutes,
De cloches comme des flûtes
Dans le ciel comme du lait.   16

Paul Verlaine

Sonnet boiteux

Ah! vraiment c'est triste, ah! vraiment ca finit trop mal.
Il n'est pas permis d'être à ce point infortuné.
Ah! vraiment c'est trop la mort du naïf animal
Qui voit tout son sang couler sous son regard fané.   4

Londres fume et crie. O quelle ville de la Bible!
Le gaz flambe et nage et les enseignes sont vermeilles.
Et les maisons dans leur ratatinement terrible
Epouvantent comme un sénat de petites vieilles.   8

Tout l'affreux passé saute, piaule, miaule et glapit
Dans le brouillard rose et jaune et sale des Sohos
Avec des *indeeds* et des *all rights* et des *haôs*.   11

Non vraiment c'est trop un martyre sans espérance,
Non vraiment cela finit trop mal, vraiment c'est triste:
O le feu du ciel sur cette ville de la Bible!   14

Arthur Rimbaud

(1854–1891)

Rimbaud's poetry, written between the ages of sixteen and twenty-one, is marked above all by the theme of youth and an irrepressible spirit of revolt. Isolated juvenile figures wander across his colourful stage, the homeless ragamuffins of *Les Effarés* or the happy-go-lucky vagabond of *Ma Bohème*, alienated from the world at large and finding their solace in communion with nature and in a private feast of the imagination. In a poem entitled *Les Poètes de sept ans*, Rimbaud gives the most dramatic image of the nascent child-poet: gritting his teeth against authority and respectable conduct, mixing with forbidden company and finding a kind of contemplative serenity in impurity and social disgrace, turning his frustration into a pleasurable inner *vertige*, crushing his fists against his eyes to see the turning shapes and colours of his mental kaleidoscope, and feeling the effervescence and inexhaustible richness of the imagination inviting him far more persuasively than the drab surface of so-called reality.

It is only one step from such a portrait to the all-important letter written by Rimbaud in 1871 and known as the *Lettre du voyant*, in which he expresses his determination to turn himself forcibly into a poetic visionary. His intention, echoing that of Baudelaire to plunge 'Au fond de l'Inconnu pour trouver du *nouveau*' and inspired by a similar *ennui* or soul-destroying disenchantment with the material world, is nevertheless far more revolutionary and systematic. Basing his programme on the view that, set apart from the sterile and pallid workings of the rational mind, there is a deeper second self, the agent of poetry, responsive to essential intuitions from a mysterious 'âme universelle', Rimbaud resolves to explore and exploit every corner of his imaginative potential. To this end he is willing to mutilate normal perception, even destroy his own health and, by an 'immense et raisonné dérèglement de tous les sens', provoke a surreal awareness of things. A poem like *Voyelles* is a challenging illustration of all the latent imagery, depth of association and complexity of sensual impression that can lie behind a mere linguistic convention like the alphabet; while *Le Bateau ivre* represents a journey of liberation, beyond all restrictions, into fabulous oceans of vision, synaesthesia, colour and sound which seem to convey some supernatural meaning and cannot be reduced to the language of reason.

But Rimbaud's achievement cannot be summed up in any one style. Few poets have run the gamut of poetic forms more rapidly than he, contemptuously conquering then relegating one mode of expression after another. Already in *Le Bateau ivre* one can feel the stiff formality of the Alexandrine bursting at the seams, almost incapable of holding the wealth and intensity of imagery which is seeking an outlet. Shortly afterwards, influenced by a turbulent poetic and sensual relationship with the older poet Verlaine in the summer of 1872, Rimbaud is experimenting with more pliable verse-forms characterized by imparisyllabic lines, unpredictable rhythms and loose rhymes: slender and melodic pieces like *Chanson de la plus haute tour*, *L'Eternité* and *O saisons, ô châteaux...*, in which an apparently naïve lyrical vein, unpretentious as a folk song and heavy with musicality, mingles with obscurity of reference and mystical mood, to create an immediately appealing but dense and allusive poetry. But having convinced himself for a moment that he has found a formula for capturing the most evasive spiritual states and suggesting the ineffable, Rimbaud is soon to reject such false artistic subtleties, with their calculated illusion of mysticism, and turns to the form of the prose-poem. His *Illuminations*, from which *Après le déluge* and *Aube* are taken, dispense completely with the art of statement and versified rhetoric: here image is juxtaposed brutally with image, logic is left stranded, and one moves in a magical creative world where mysterious figures, legendary landscapes and colourful pictures surge spontaneously from no known source.

Whether Rimbaud is composing a sarcastic and vulgar caricature to add to the portrait-gallery of bloated and self-satisfied bourgeois that one finds in his early verse or describing the exhilarating adventures of an intoxicated imagination, certain features never fail to affect one: the sheer energy and vitality of the writing (with its inventive vocabulary and violently whipped rhythms); the total emotional commitment of the poet himself (whether in hatred, savagery, ironic amusement, excitement, wonderment or awe); the freshness and spontaneity of the childlike visions (which give one the impression of a face of the world washed clean); and above all the unending inventiveness of his imagination, which has set a new style, even a new definition, for modern French poetry.

SELECT BIBLIOGRAHY

S. Bernard, Introductions and notes to *Rimbaud: Œuvres*, Garnier, 1960.

Y. Bonnefoy, *Rimbaud par lui-même*, Seuil, 1961.

E. Etiemble and Y. Gauclère, *Rimbaud*, Gallimard, 1950.

C. A. Hackett, *Rimbaud*, Bowes and Bowes, 1957.

C.-E. Magny, *Arthur Rimbaud*, (Poètes d'aujourd'hui, 12), Seghers, 1956.

J. Plessen, *Promenade et poésie: l'expérience de la marche et du mouvement dans l'œuvre de Rimbaud*, Mouton, 1967.

J.-P. Richard, 'Rimbaud ou la poésie du devenir' in *Poésie et profondeur*, Seuil, 1955.
M.-A. Ruff, *Rimbaud*, (Connaissance des lettres), Hatier, 1968.

Les Effarés

Noirs dans la neige et dans la brume,
Au grand soupirail qui s'allume,
    Leurs culs en rond,   3

A genoux, cinq petits, – misère! –
Regardent le Boulanger faire
    Le lourd pain blond.   6

Ils voient le fort bras blanc qui tourne
La pâte grise et qui l'enfourne
    Dans un trou clair.   9

Ils écoutent le bon pain cuire.
Le Boulanger au gras sourire
    Grogne un vieil air.   12

Ils sont blottis, pas un ne bouge,
Au souffle du soupirail rouge
    Chaud comme un sein.   15

Quand pour quelque médianoche,
Façonné comme une brioche
    On sort le pain,   18

Quand, sous les poutres enfumées,
Chantent les croûtes parfumées
    Et les grillons,   21

Que ce trou chaud souffle la vie,
Ils ont leur âme si ravie
    Sous leurs haillons,   24

Ils se ressentent si bien vivre,
Les pauvres Jésus pleins de givre,
    Qu'ils sont là tous,   27

Collant leurs petits museaux roses
Au treillage, grognant des choses
    Entre les trous,   30

Tout bêtes, faisant leurs prières
Et repliés vers ces lumières
    Du ciel rouvert,   33

Si fort, qu'ils crèvent leur culotte
Et que leur chemise tremblote
Au vent d'hiver.   36

Roman

I

On n'est pas sérieux, quand on a dix-sept ans.
– Un beau soir, foin des bocks et de la limonade,
Des cafés tapageurs aux lustres éclatants!
– On va sous les tilleuls verts de la promenade.   4

Les tilleuls sentent bon dans les bons soirs de juin!
L'air est parfois si doux, qu'on ferme la paupière;
Le vent chargé de bruits, – la ville n'est pas loin, –
A des parfums de vigne et des parfums de bière...   8

II

– Voilà qu'on aperçoit un tout petit chiffon
D'azur sombre, encadré d'une petite branche,
Piqué d'une mauvaise étoile, qui se fond
Avec de doux frissons, petite et toute blanche...   12

Nuit de juin! Dix-sept ans! – On se laisse griser.
La sève est du champagne et vous monte à la tête...
On divague; on se sent aux lèvres un baiser
Qui palpite là, comme une petite bête...   16

III

Le cœur fou Robinsonne à travers les romans,
– Lorsque, dans la clarté d'un pâle réverbère,
Passe une demoiselle aux petits airs charmants,
Sous l'ombre du faux-col effrayant de son père...   20

Et, comme elle vous trouve immensément naïf,
Tout en faisant trotter ses petites bottines,
Elle se tourne, alerte et d'un mouvement vif...
– Sur vos lèvres alors meurent les cavatines...   24

IV

Vous êtes amoureux. Loué jusqu'au mois d'août.
Vous êtes amoureux. – Vos sonnets La font rire.

Tous vos amis s'en vont, vous êtes mauvais goût.
– Puis l'adorée, un soir, a daigné vous écrire!...   28

– Ce soir-là, ... – vous rentrez aux cafés éclatants,
Vous demandez des bocks ou de la limonade...
– On n'est pas sérieux, quand on a dix-sept ans
Et qu'on a des tilleuls verts sur la promenade.   32

Le Dormeur du val

C'est un trou de verdure où chante une rivière
Accrochant follement aux herbes des haillons
D'argent; où le soleil, de la montagne fière,
Luit: c'est un petit val qui mousse de rayons.   4

Un soldat jeune, bouche ouverte, tête nue,
Et la nuque baignant dans le frais cresson bleu,
Dort; il est étendu dans l'herbe, sous la nue,
Pâle dans son lit vert où la lumière pleut.   8

Les pieds dans les glaïeuls, il dort. Souriant comme
Sourirait un enfant malade, il fait un somme:
Nature, berce-le chaudement: il a froid.   11

Les parfums ne font pas frissonner sa narine;
Il dort dans le soleil, la main sur sa poitrine
Tranquille. Il a deux trous rouges au côté droit.   14

Ma Bohème

(Fantaisie)

Je m'en allais, les poings dans mes poches crevées;
Mon paletot aussi devenait idéal;
J'allais sous le ciel, Muse! et j'étais ton féal;
Oh! là là! que d'amours splendides j'ai rêvées!   4

Mon unique culotte avait un large trou.
– Petit-Poucet rêveur, j'égrenais dans ma course
Des rimes. Mon auberge était à la Grande-Ourse.
– Mes étoiles au ciel avaient un doux frou-frou   8

Et je les écoutais, assis au bord des routes,
Ces bons soirs de septembre où je sentais des gouttes
De rosée à mon front, comme un vin de vigueur;   11

Où, rimant au milieu des ombres fantastiques,
Comme des lyres, je tirais les élastiques
De mes souliers blessés, un pied près de mon cœur!   14

Les Corbeaux

Seigneur, quand froide est la prairie,
Quand dans les hameaux abattus,
Les longs angélus se sont tus...
Sur la nature défleurie
Faites s'abattre des grands cieux
Les chers corbeaux délicieux.   6

Armée étrange aux cris sévères,
Les vents froids attaquent vos nids!
Vous, le long des fleuves jaunis,
Sur les routes aux vieux calvaires,
Sur les fossés et sur les trous
Dispersez-vous, ralliez-vous!   12

Par milliers, sur les champs de France,
Où dorment des morts d'avant-hier,
Tournoyez, n'est-ce pas, l'hiver,
Pour que chaque passant repense!
Sois donc le crieur du devoir,
O notre funèbre oiseau noir!   18

Mais, saints du ciel, en haut du chêne,
Mât perdu dans le soir charmé,
Laissez les fauvettes de mai
Pour ceux qu'au fond du bois enchaîne,
Dans l'herbe d'où l'on ne peut fuir,
La défaite sans avenir.   24

Voyelles

A noir, E blanc, I rouge, U vert, O bleu: voyelles,
Je dirai quelque jour vos naissances latentes:
A, noir corset velu des mouches éclatantes
Qui bombinent autour des puanteurs cruelles,   4

Golfes d'ombre; E, candeurs des vapeurs et des tentes,
Lances des glaciers fiers, rois blancs, frissons d'ombelles;
I, pourpres, sang craché, rire des lèvres belles
Dans la colère ou les ivresses pénitentes;   8

U, cycles, vibrements divins des mers virides,
Paix des pâtis semés d'animaux, paix des rides
Que l'alchimie imprime aux grands fronts studieux;   11

O, suprême Clairon plein des strideurs étranges,
Silences traversés des Mondes et des Anges:
– O l'Oméga, rayon violet de Ses Yeux!   14

Le Bateau ivre

Comme je descendais des Fleuves impassibles,
Je ne me sentis plus guidé par les haleurs:
Des Peaux-Rouges criards les avaient pris pour cibles,
Les ayant cloués nus aux poteaux de couleurs.   4

J'étais insoucieux de tous les équipages,
Porteur de blés flamands ou de cotons anglais.
Quand avec mes haleurs ont fini ces tapages,
Les Fleuves m'ont laissé descendre où je voulais.   8

Dans les clapotements furieux des marées,
Moi, l'autre hiver, plus sourd que les cerveaux d'enfants,
Je courus! Et les Péninsules démarrées
N'ont pas subi tohu-bohus plus triomphants.   12

La tempête a béni mes éveils maritimes.
Plus léger qu'un bouchon j'ai dansé sur les flots
Qu'on appelle rouleurs éternels de victimes,
Dix nuits, sans regretter l'œil niais des falots!   16

Plus douce qu'aux enfants la chair des pommes sures,
L'eau verte pénétra ma coque de sapin
Et des taches de vins bleus et des vomissures
Me lava, dispersant gouvernail et grappin.   20

Et dès lors, je me suis baigné dans le Poème
De la Mer, infusé d'astres, et lactescent,
Dévorant les azurs verts; où, flottaison blême
Et ravie, un noyé pensif parfois descend;   24

Où, teignant tout à coup les bleuités, délires
Et rhythmes lents sous les rutilements du jour,
Plus fortes que l'alcool, plus vastes que nos lyres,
Fermentent les rousseurs amères de l'amour!   28

Je sais les cieux crevant en éclairs, et les trombes
Et les ressacs et les courants : je sais le soir,
L'Aube exaltée ainsi qu'un peuple de colombes,
Et j'ai vu quelquefois ce que l'homme a cru voir !   32

J'ai vu le soleil bas, taché d'horreurs mystiques,
Illuminant de longs figements violets,
Pareils à des acteurs de drames très antiques
Les flots roulant au loin leurs frissons de volets !   36

J'ai rêvé la nuit verte aux neiges éblouies,
Baiser montant aux yeux des mers avec lenteurs,
La circulation des sèves inouïes,
Et l'éveil jaune et bleu des phosphores chanteurs !   40

J'ai suivi, des mois pleins, pareille aux vacheries
Hystériques, la houle à l'assaut des récifs,
Sans songer que les pieds lumineux des Maries
Pussent forcer le mufle aux Océans poussifs !   44

J'ai heurté, savez-vous, d'incroyables Florides
Mêlant aux fleurs des yeux de panthères à peaux
D'hommes ! Des arcs-en-ciel tendus comme des brides
Sous l'horizon des mers, à de glauques troupeaux !   48

J'ai vu fermenter les marais énormes, nasses
Où pourrit dans les joncs tout un Léviathan !
Des écroulements d'eaux au milieu des bonaces,
Et les lointains vers les gouffres cataractant !   52

Glaciers, soleils d'argent, flots nacreux, cieux de braises !
Echouages hideux au fond des golfes bruns
Où les serpents géants dévorés des punaises
Choient, des arbres tordus, avec de noirs parfums !   56

J'aurais voulu montrer aux enfants ces dorades
Du flot bleu, ces poissons d'or, ces poissons chantants.
– Des écumes de fleurs ont bercé mes dérades
Et d'ineffables vents m'ont ailé par instants.   60

Parfois, martyr lassé des pôles et des zones,
La mer dont le sanglot faisait mon roulis doux
Montait vers moi ses fleurs d'ombre aux ventouses jaunes
Et je restais, ainsi qu'une femme à genoux...   64

Presque île, ballottant sur mes bords les querelles
Et les fientes d'oiseaux clabaudeurs aux yeux blonds.
Et je voguais, lorsqu'à travers mes liens frêles
Des noyés descendaient dormir, à reculons !   68

Or moi, bateau perdu sous les cheveux des anses,
Jeté par l'ouragan dans l'éther sans oiseau,
Moi dont les Monitors et les voiliers des Hanses
N'auraient pas repêché la carcasse ivre d'eau;   72

Libre, fumant, monté de brumes violettes,
Moi qui trouais le ciel rougeoyant comme un mur
Qui porte, confiture exquise aux bons poètes,
Des lichens de soleil et des morves d'azur;   76

Qui courais, taché de lunules électriques,
Planche folle, escorté des hippocampes noirs,
Quand les juillets faisaient crouler à coups de triques
Les cieux ultramarins aux ardents entonnoirs;   80

Moi qui tremblais, sentant geindre à cinquante lieues
Le rut des Béhémots et les Maelstroms épais,
Fileur éternel des immobilités bleues,
Je regrette l'Europe aux anciens parapets!   84

J'ai vu des archipels sidéraux! et des îles
Dont les cieux délirants sont ouverts au vogueur:
– Est-ce en ces nuits sans fonds que tu dors et t'exiles,
Million d'oiseaux d'or, ô future Vigueur?   88

Mais, vrai, j'ai trop pleuré! Les Aubes sont navrantes.
Toute lune est atroce et tout soleil amer:
L'âcre amour m'a gonflé de torpeurs enivrantes.
O que ma quille éclate! O que j'aille à la mer!   92

Si je désire une eau d'Europe, c'est la flache
Noire et froide où vers le crépuscule embaumé
Un enfant accroupi plein de tristesses, lâche
Un bateau frêle comme un papillon de mai.   96

Je ne puis plus, baigné de vos langueurs, ô lames,
Enlever leur sillage aux porteurs de cotons,
Ni traverser l'orgueil des drapeaux et des flammes,
Ni nager sous les yeux horribles des pontons.   100

Chanson de la plus haute tour

Oisive jeunesse
A tout asservie,
Par délicatesse
J'ai perdu ma vie.
Ah! Que le temps vienne
Où les cœurs s'éprennent.   6

Je me suis dit: laisse,
Et qu'on ne te voie:
Et sans la promesse
De plus hautes joies.
Que rien ne t'arrête,
Auguste retraite.   12

J'ai tant fait patience
Qu'à jamais j'oublie;
Craintes et souffrances
Aux cieux sont parties.
Et la soif malsaine
Obscurcit mes veines.   18

Ainsi la Prairie
A l'oubli livrée,
Grandie, et fleurie
D'encens et d'ivraies
Au bourdon farouche
De cent sales mouches.   24

Ah! Mille veuvages
De la si pauvre âme
Qui n'a que l'image
De la Notre-Dame!
Est-ce que l'on prie
La Vierge Marie?   30

Oisive jeunesse
A tout asservie,
Par délicatesse
J'ai perdu ma vie.
Ah! Que le temps vienne
Où les cœurs s'éprennent!   36

L'Eternité

Elle est retrouvee.
Quoi? – L'Eternité.
C'est la mer allée
Avec le soleil.   4

Ame sentinelle,
Murmurons l'aveu
De la nuit si nulle
Et du jour en feu.   8

Des humains suffrages,
Des communs élans
Là tu te dégages
Et voles selon.   12

Puisque de vous seules,
Braises de satin,
Le Devoir s'exhale
Sans qu'on dise : enfin.   16

Là pas d'espérance,
Nul orietur.
Science avec patience,
Le supplice est sûr.   20

Elle est retrouvée.
Quoi ? – L'Eternité.
C'est la mer allée
Avec le soleil.   24

O saisons, ô châteaux..

O saisons, ô châteaux,
Quelle âme est sans défauts ?

O saisons, ô châteaux,

J'ai fait la magique étude   4
Du Bonheur, que nul n'élude.

O vive lui, chaque fois
Que chante son coq gaulois.

Mais ! je n'aurai plus d'envie,   8
Il s'est chargé de ma vie.

Ce Charme ! il prit âme et corps,
Et dispersa tous efforts.

Que comprendre à ma parole ?   12
Il fait qu'elle fuie et vole !

O saisons, ô châteaux !

Après le déluge

Aussitôt que l'idée du Déluge se fut rassise,

Un lièvre s'arrêta dans les sainfoins et les clochettes mouvantes et dit sa prière à l'arc-en-ciel à travers la toile de l'araignée.

Oh! les pierres précieuses qui se cachaient, – les fleurs qui regardaient déjà.   4

Dans la grande rue sale les étals se dressèrent, et l'on tira les barques vers la mer étagée là-haut comme sur les gravures.

Le sang coula, chez Barbe-Bleue, aux abattoirs, – dans les cirques, où le sceau de Dieu blêmit les fenêtres. Le sang et le lait coulèrent.   8

Les castors bâtirent. Les "mazagrans" fumèrent dans les estaminets.   12

Dans la grande maison de vitres encore ruisselante les enfants en deuil regardèrent les merveilleuses images.

Une porte claqua, – et sur la place du hameau, l'enfant tourna ses bras, compris des girouettes et des coqs des clochers de partout, sous l'éclatante giboulée.   16

Madame*** établit un piano dans les Alpes. La messe et les premières communions se célébrèrent aux cent mille autels de la cathédrale.   20

Les caravanes partirent. Et le Splendide-Hôtel fut bâti dans le chaos de glaces et de nuit du pôle.

Depuis lors, la Lune entendit les chacals piaulant par les déserts de thym, – et les églogues en sabots grognant dans le verger. Puis, dans la futaie violette, bourgeonnante, Eucharis me dit que c'était le printemps.   24

Sourds, étang, – Ecume, roule sur le pont et par-dessus les bois; – draps noirs et orgues, – éclairs et tonnerre, – montez et roulez; – Eaux et tristesses, montez et relevez les Déluges.   28

Car depuis qu'ils se sont dissipés, – oh les pierres précieuses s'enfouissant, et les fleurs ouvertes! – c'est un ennui! et la Reine, la Sorcière qui allume sa braise dans le pot de terre, ne voudra jamais nous raconter ce qu'elle sait, et que nous ignorons.   32

Aube

J'ai embrassé l'aube d'été.

Rien ne bougeait encore au front des palais. L'eau était morte. Les camps d'ombres ne quittaient pas la route du bois. J'ai marché, réveillant les haleines vives et tièdes, et les pierreries regardèrent, et les ailes se levèrent sans bruit.   4

La première entreprise fut, dans le sentier déjà empli de frais et blêmes éclats, une fleur qui me dit son nom.

Je ris au wasserfall blond qui s'échevela à travers les sapins : 8 à la cime argentée je reconnus la déesse.

Alors je levai un à un les voiles. Dans l'allée, en agitant les bras. Par la plaine, où je l'ai dénoncée au coq. A la grand'ville elle fuyait parmi les clochers et les dômes, et courant comme un 12 mendiant sur les quais de marbre, je la chassais.

En haut de la route, près d'un bois de lauriers, je l'ai entourée avec ses voiles amassés, et j'ai senti un peu son immense corps. L'aube et l'enfant tombèrent au bas du bois. 16

Au réveil il était midi.

Jules Laforgue

(1860–1887)

Laforgue is the most original and technically accomplished member of the so-called 'Decadent' school of poets whose thinking is characterized by a superior disenchantment and a perverse artificial refinement. Baudelaire's influence on this 'Decadent' mood can be clearly felt. It inherits from him the cult of the dandy who elegantly sets himself against the grain of nature as a semblance of moral salvation; the taste for ambiguous sensual pleasures, spiced with eccentric imaginings; the mortal malady of *ennui* which condemns the poet to a self-exhausting neurasthenia and would happily destroy the world in a yawn.

At the root of Laforgue's sensitivity are a crisis of faith and an utter disgust with the vulgarity and futility of the created world: its tawdry cycles of love and procreation giving no relief from the mediocre and the bestial and leading nowhere but to death (the poet himself was tubercular and died at the age of twenty-seven). Life he sees as governed by a blind, impersonal Unconscious, in which human will is a useless foreign body. All that there remains for it to do, therefore, is to annihilate itself and be diluted back into the infallible but irrational universal indifference. It is this conversion to a religion of Nothingness which gives Laforgue's work its bleak cosmic colouring: the belief that all in the world is illusion; the impotent aspiration to Nirvana. This 'pessimiste mystique' is caught between 'la mort de la terre', rolling to its death in infinite space like a blind eye-ball, and what he calls 'la céleste éternullité'. How, in such a situation, can he be anything but 'si cosmiquement désespéré', as one of his earliest *complaintes* puts it?

Laforgue's essential answer is to adopt the posture of an artistic Buddha, an ironic dilettante, sailing impassively above an ocean of degradation and vanity. He guarantees himself a measure of detachment from the universal illusion by lucid self-mockery, and a remnant of sincerity by toying ironically with a world which is a lie. He puts himself in parentheses, as it were, by means of fantasy, casual juggling and stylistic acrobatics. But the despair and the evasive comic masks never cease to reflect each other, setting up a play of tortured grimaces and inscrutable smiles; and the sceptic clowning is only the consequence of a terrible confrontation, reminiscent of that of Mallarmé, with the void. As he writes in a letter in

1885, 'Je tiens à dire (...) qu'avant d'être dilettante et pierrot, j'ai séjourné dans le cosmique'.

Laforgue's earliest collection *Le Sanglot de la Terre* (poems written between 1878 and 1883 an envisaged title for which was *Les Spleens cosmiques*) expresses the themes of planetary disillusionment, meaningless death, the glacial deserts of space, the pitiful comedy of human life, the empty forms of religion, exile and curdled love in a style heavy with demonstrative rhetoric, clumsy and grating articulations, eccentric vocabulary and melodramatic cries. There is little here to remind one of the contemporary Symbolist taste for delicate fleeting impressions and the quiet music of 'songs without words'. In *Les Complaintes* (1885), on the other hand, Laforgue finds a more authentic and versatile manner, still not musical in the Verlainean sense, but combining the easy appeal of familiar street-ballads and the vulgarity of music-hall songs with an ironic lucidity, a spirit of parody, a deliberate intermingling of disparate tones and conflicting rhythms, and all the mocking caprices of an art which refuses to stand still and be grasped. The difference between the poems of 1878 – 83 and the *Complaintes* is neatly resumed in these statements: 'Avant j'étais bouddhiste tragique, et maintenant je suis bouddhiste dilettante' and 'Je trouve stupide de faire la grosse voix et de jouer de l'éloquence. Aujourd'hui (...) je suis plus sceptique et je m'emballe moins aisément (...) je possède ma langue d'une façon plus minutieuse, plus clownesque'. The pieces from *L'Imitation de Notre-Dame la Lune* (1886) are even more meticulously controlled. Pruned, sharp and slightly precious, these studies of clowns and of the moon present a charming but deathly world, elegantly dressed for the mortuary. His *Derniers vers*, finally, represent another, more radical change of style in that they abandon verse-form, proceed by an energetic, unpredictable play of association and are a crucial stepping-stone into the free verse of the twentieth century. For the poet, they constitute a new way of abandoning the will and joining the blind force of the Unconscious. (One should add that Laforgue's standing in the English-speaking world has often been higher than in France. T. S. Eliot was much influenced by him: in Eliot's early Prufrock poems, for instance, one can see the same parodic mastery of verse-form and urbane irony playing with the themes of spiritual dereliction and the tawdriness of modern life, to say nothing of a cluster of anti-Romantic 'moon' poems.)

Were one to leave a picture to summarize Laforgue, one could well choose the triple image of a Buddha, clown and skeleton dressed in topper and tails.

SELECT BIBLIOGRAPHY

M.-J. Durry, *Jules Laforgue*, (Poètes d'aujourd'hui, 30), Seghers, 1952.

L. Guichard, *Jules Laforgue et ses poésies*, Presses universitaires de France, 1950.

P. Newman-Gordon, *Corbière, Laforgue et Apollinaire ou le rire en pleurs*, Nouvelles Editions Debresse, 1964.

W. Ramsey, *Jules Laforgue and the ironic inheritance*, Oxford University Press, 1953.

P. Reboul, *Laforgue*, (Connaissance des lettres), Hatier, 1960.

F. Ruchon, *Jules Laforgue, sa vie, son œuvre*, Editions Albert Ciana, 1924.

Complainte à Notre-Dame des Soirs

L'Extase du soleil, peuh! La Nature, fade
Usine de sève aux lymphatiques parfums.
Mais les lacs éperdus des longs couchants défunts
Dorlotent mon voilier dans leurs plus riches rades,   4
    Comme un ange malade ...
    O Notre-Dame des Soirs,
    Que Je vous aime sans espoir!   7

Lampes des mers! blancs bizarrants! mots à vertiges!
Axiomes *in articulo mortis* déduits!
Ciels vrais! Lune aux échos dont communient les puits!
Yeux des portraits! Soleil qui, saignant son quadrige,   11
    Cabré, s'y crucifige!
    O Notre-Dame des Soirs,
    Certes, il.vont haut vos encensoirs!   14

Eux sucent des plis dont le frou-frou les suffoque;
Pour un regard, ils battraient du front les pavés;
Puis s'affligent sur maint sein creux, mal abreuvés;
Puis retournent à ces vendanges sexciproques.   18
    Et moi, moi, Je m'en moque!
    Oui, Notre-Dame des Soirs,
    J'en fais, paraît-il, peine à voir.   21

En voyage, sur les fugitives prairies,
Vous me fuyez; ou du ciel des eaux m'invitez;
Ou m'agacez au tournant d'une vérité;
Or vous ai-je encor dit votre fait, je vous prie?   25
    Ah! coquette Marie,
    Ah! Notre-Dame des Soirs,
    C'est trop pour vos seuls Reposoirs!   28

Vos Rites, jalonnés de sales bibliothèques,
Ont voûté mes vingt ans, m'ont tari de chers goûts.
Verrai-je l'oasis fondant au rendez-vous,
Où...vos lèvres (dit-on!) à jamais nous dissèquent?   32

O Lune sur la Mecque!
Notre-Dame, Notre-Dame des Soirs,
De *vrais* yeux m'ont dit: au revoir!   35

Complainte de la lune en province

Ah! la belle pleine Lune,
Grosse comme une fortune!

La retraite sonne au loin,
Un passant, monsieur l'adjoint;   4

Un clavecin joue en face,
Un chat traverse la place:

La province qui s'endort!
Plaquant un dernier accord,   8

Le piano clot sa fenêtre.
Quelle heure peut-il bien être?

Calme Lune, quel exil!
Faut-il dire: ainsi soit-il?   12

Lune, ô dilettante Lune,
A tous les climats commune,

Tu vis hier le Missouri,
Et les remparts de Paris,   16

Les fiords bleus de la Norvège,
Les pôles, les mers, que sais-je?

Lune heureuse! ainsi tu vois,
A cette heure, le convoi   20

De son voyage de noce!
Ils sont partis pour l'Ecosse.

Quel panneau, si, cet hiver,
Elle eût pris au mot mes vers!   24

Lune, vagabonde Lune,
Faisons cause et mœurs communes?

O riches nuits! je me meurs,
La province dans le cœur!   28

Et la lune a, bonne vieille,
Du coton dans les oreilles.

Complainte du Roi de Thulé

Il était un roi de Thulé
    Immaculé,
Qui loin des jupes et des choses,
Pleurait sur la métempsychose
    Des lys en roses,
    Et quel palais!   6

Ses fleurs dormant, il s'en allait,
    Traînant des clés,
Broder aux seuls yeux des étoiles,
Sur une tour, un certain Voile
    De vive toile,
    Aux nuits de lait!   12

Quand le voile fut bien ourlé,
    Loin de Thulé,
Il rama fort sur les mers grises,
Vers le soleil qui s'agonise,
    Féerique Eglise!
    Il ululait: 18

"Soleil-crevant, encore un jour,
Vous avez tendu votre phare
Aux holocaustes vivipares,
Du culte qu'ils nomment l'Amour.   22

"Et comme, devant la nuit fauve,
Vous vous sentez défaillir,
D'un dernier flot d'un sang martyr
Vous lavez le seuil de l'Alcôve!   26

"Soleil! Soleil! moi je descends
Vers vos navrants palais polaires,
Dorloter dans ce Saint-Suaire
    Votre cœur bien en sang,
    En le berçant!"   31

Il dit, et, le Voile étendu,
    Tout éperdu,
Vers les coraux et les naufrages,
Le roi raillé des doux corsages,
    Beau comme un Mage
    Est descendu!   37

Braves amants! aux nuits de lait,
    Tournez vos clés!
Une ombre, d'amour pur transie,
Viendrait vous gémir cette scie:
  "Il était un roi de Thulé
    Immaculé..."   43

Complainte du soir des comices agricoles

Deux royaux cors de chasse ont encore un duo
    Aux échos,
Quelques fusées reniflent s'étouffer là-haut!   3

    Allez, allez, gens de la noce,
    Qu'on s'en donne une fière bosse!   5

Et comme le jour naît, que bientôt il faudra,
    A deux bras,
Peiner, se recrotter dans les labours ingrats,   8

    Allez, allez, gens que vous êtes,
    C'est pas tous les jours jour de fête!   10

Ce violon incompris pleure au pays natal,
    Loin du bal,
Et le piston risque un appel vers l'Idéal...   13

    Mais le flageolet les rappelle
    Et allez donc, mâl's et femelles!   15

Un couple erre parmi les rêves des grillons,
    Aux sillons;
La fille écoute en tourmentant son médaillon.   18

    Laissez, laissez, ô cors de chasse,
    Puisque c'est le sort de la race.   20

Les beaux cors se sont morts; mais cependant qu'au loin,
    Dans les foins,
Crèvent deux rêves niais, sans maire et sans adjoint.   23

    Pintez, dansez, gens de la Terre,
    Tout est un triste et vieux Mystère.   25

– Ah! le Premier que prit ce besoin insensé
    De danser
Sur ce monde enfantin dans l'Inconnu lancé!   28

O Terre, ô terre, ô race humaine,
Vous me faites bien de la peine. 30

Pierrots

I

C'est, sur un cou qui, raide, émerge
D'une fraise empesée *idem*,
Une face imberbe au cold-cream,
Un air d'hydrocéphale asperge. 4

Les yeux sont noyés de l'opium
De l'indulgence universelle,
La bouche clownesque ensorcèle
Comme un singulier géranium. 8

Bouche qui va du trou sans bonde
Glacialement désopilé,
Au transcendental en-allé
Du souris vain de la Joconde. 12

Campant leur cône enfariné
Sur le noir serre-tête en soie,
Ils font rire leur patte d'oie
Et froncent en trèfle leur nez. 16

Ils ont comme chaton de bague
Le scarabée égyptien,
A leur boutonnière fait bien
Le pissenlit des terrains vagues. 20

Ils vont, se sustentant d'azur,
Et parfois aussi de légumes,
De riz plus blanc que leur costume,
De mandarines et d'œufs durs. 24

Ils sont de la secte du Blême,
Ils n'ont rien à voir avec Dieu,
Et sifflent: 'Tout est pour le mieux
Dans la meilleur' des mi-carême!' 28

Locutions de Pierrots

XII

Encore un livre; ô nostalgies
Loin de ces très goujates gens,

Loin des saluts et des argents,
Loin de nos phraséologies!   4

Encore un de mes pierrots mort;
Mort d'un chronique orphelinisme;
C'était un cœur plein de dandysme
Lunaire, en un drôle de corps.   8

Les dieux s'en vont; plus que des hures;
Ah! ça devient tous les jours pis;
J'ai fait mon temps, je déguerpis
Vers l'Inclusive Sinécure!   12

Locutions de Pierrots

XVI

Je ne suis qu'un viveur lunaire
Qui fait des ronds dans les bassins,
Et cela, sans autre dessein
Que devenir un légendaire.   4

Retroussant d'un air de défi
Mes manches de mandarin pâle,
J'arrondis ma bouche et – j'exhale
Des conseils doux de Crucifix.   8

Ah! oui, devenir légendaire,
Au seuil des siècles charlatans!
Mais où sont les Lunes d'antan?
Et que Dieu n'est-il à refaire?   12

L'Hiver qui vient

Blocus sentimental! Messageries du Levant!...
Oh, tombée de la pluie! Oh! tombée de la nuit,
Oh! le vent!...
La Toussaint, la Noël et la Nouvelle Année,   4
Oh, dans les bruines, toutes mes cheminées!...
D'usines...

On ne peut plus s'asseoir, tous les bancs sont mouillés;
Crois-moi, c'est bien fini jusqu'à l'année prochaine, 8
Tous les bancs sont mouillés, tant les bois sont rouillés,
Et tant les cors ont fait ton ton, ont fait ton taine!...

Ah! nuées accourues des côtes de la Manche,
Vous nous avez gâté notre dernier dimanche.   12

Il bruine;
Dans la forêt mouillée, les toiles d'araignées
Ploient sous les gouttes d'eau, et c'est leur ruine.
Soleils plénipotentiaires des travaux en blonds Pactoles   16
Des spectacles agricoles,
Où êtes-vous ensevelis?
Ce soir un soleil fichu gît au haut du coteau,
Gît sur le flanc, dans les genêts, sur son manteau.   20
Un soleil blanc comme un crachat d'estaminet
Sur une litière de jaunes genêts,
De jaunes genêts d'automne.
Et les cors lui sonnent!   24
Qu'il revienne...
Qu'il revienne à lui!
Taïaut! Taïaut et hallali!
O triste antienne, as-tu fini!...   28
Et font les fous!
Et il gît là, comme une glande arrachée dans un cou,
Et il frissonne, sans personne!...

Allons, allons, et hallali!   32
C'est l'Hiver bien connu qui s'amène;
Oh! les tournants des grandes routes,
Et sans petit Chaperon Rouge qui chemine!...
Oh! leurs ornières des chars de l'autre mois,   36
Montant en don quichottesques rails
Vers les patrouilles des nuées en déroute
Que le vent malmène vers les transatlantiques bercails!...
Accélérons, accélérons, c'est la saison bien connue, cette fois. 40
Et le vent, cette nuit, il en a fait de belles!
O dégâts, ô nids, ô modestes jardinets!
Mon cœur et mon sommeil: ô échos des cognées!...

Tous ces rameaux avaient encor leurs feuilles vertes,   44
Les sous-bois ne sont plus qu'un fumier de feuilles mortes;
Feuilles, folioles, qu'un bon vent vous emporte
Vers les étangs par ribambelles,
Ou pour le feu du garde-chasse,   48
Ou les sommiers des ambulances
Pour les soldats loin de la France.

C'est la saison, c'est la saison, la rouille envahit les masses,
La rouille ronge en leurs spleens kilométriques   52
Les fils télégraphiques des grandes routes où nul ne passe.

Les cors, les cors, les cors – mélancoliques!...
Mélancoliques!
S'en vont, changeant de ton,   56
Changeant de ton et de musique,
Ton ton, ton taine, ton ton!...
Les cors, les cors, les cors!...
S'en sont allés au vent du Nord.   60

Je ne puis quitter ce ton: que d'échos!...
C'est la saison, c'est la saison, adieu vendanges!...
Voici venir les pluies d'une patience d'ange,
Adieu vendanges, et adieu tous les paniers,   64
Tous les paniers Watteau des bourrées sous les marronniers.
C'est la toux dans les dortoirs du lycée qui rentre,
C'est la tisane sans le foyer,
La phtisie pulmonaire attristant le quartier,   68
Et toute la misère des grands centres.

Mais, lainages, caoutchoucs, pharmacie, rêve,
Rideaux écartés du haut des balcons des grèves
Devant l'océan de toitures des faubourgs,   72
Lampes, estampes, thé, petits-fours,
Serez-vous pas mes seules amours!...
(Oh! et puis, est-ce que tu connais, outre les pianos,
Le sobre et vespéral mystère hebdomadaire   76
Des statistiques sanitaires
Dans les journaux?)

Non, non! c'est la saison et la planète falote!
Que l'autan, que l'autan   80
Effiloche les savates que le temps se tricote!
C'est la saison, oh déchirements! c'est la saison!
Tous les ans, tous les ans,
J'essaierai en chœur d'en donner la note.   84

Paul Valéry

(1871–1945)

One of the great intellectuals of modern French culture, Paul Valéry is celebrated for the lucidity with which he analyses the workings of his own mind and the spell of poetry. Although nurtured in the climate of Symbolism (and taking from Mallarmé, whose famous salon he frequented, the search for a purified poetic atmosphere and a suggestivity poised on the very edge of absence), he shows little interest in the possibility of a transcendent *au-delà*; the two realms which fascinate him are the inner universe of his intellect and the 'univers poétique', the complex state of perception and feeling which poetry can conjure up (the title of his major anthology, *Charmes*, suggests both sorcerer's spells and *carmina*, the Latin word for songs). The process of writing poetry stimulates both concerns since he can at the same time observe his brain at work and explore the intricacies and suggestive potential of poetic language. This simultaneity of observation is especially clear in those pieces which seem to propose a symbolic image of the act of poetic creation *(Le Sylphe, L'Abeille, L'Insinuant* and even *Les Pas)*. The reservation implied in the phrase 'seem to' is necessary because of Valéry's use of the inexplicit metaphor: one is often unsure as to how many levels of meaning there are in a poem. But it would be unfair to accuse Valéry of deliberate obscurity or some mischievous game, for he is primarily interested in the making of the creative poem, and not in leaving it attached for the rest of its days to his own or any one single correct interpretation, an invalid concept in his eyes: 'Mes vers ont le sens qu'on leur prête'.

In Valéry the intellect does not exclude the emotions. Indeed these two modes of human consciousness are seen in terms of each other, so much so that one often wonders whether the poet is intellectualizing the emotions or giving erotic and sensual expression to what is basically an intellectual observation. The development of some poems depends on this ambiguity: in *L'Abeille*, there is a hinted intellectual significance in the concluding stanza after a poem of languorous desire; in *Les Grenades* the bursting pomegranates, after a luscious appeal to the senses, finally provoke in the poet an inward reflection on his soul's architecture; in *Le Sylphe*, the suggestions that the sylph is a spirit of poetry and the allusion to poetic obscurity give way to the teasing eroticism of a glimpsed breast. Both *Les Pas* and *L'Insinuant*, poems of anticipated love, also yield to an intellectual interpretation. Perhaps *Le Cimetière marin*, the most lyrical of Valéry's poems, achieves the greatest fusion between the thinking and the feeling consciousness; it is hard to imagine two more contrasting stanzas than those beginning 'Les cris aigus des filles chatouillées' and 'Zénon! Cruel Zénon! Zénon d'Elée!', yet both express the poet's fear of immobility, first a sensual apprehension, then philosophical.

The fact that Valéry prized above all else the intellectual inventiveness and self-searching of the human mind is reflected in the poet's preference for a demanding poetic form. Free verse offers no mirror to the creative Narcissus; strict metre, on the other hand, forces the mind back on itself, the structures of the rhymes and rhythms bringing to light the poet's own hidden structures. Form is thus not a halt to inspiration but an active encouragement, an obstacle which incites poetic ingenuity and can even be said to control idea and image (Valéry tells us that the form of *Le Cimetière marin* preceded and necessitated its subject). The exigencies of form are essential to the creation of the authentic 'univers poétique': they set poetry apart from prose, suggesting to the reader or listener that he is entering a system of language in which 'les pensées énoncées ou suggérées...ne sont pas du tout l'objet unique et capital du discours, – mais des *moyens* qui concourent *également* avec les sons, les cadences, le nombre et les ornements, à provoquer, à soutenir une certaine tension ou exaltation, à engendrer en nous un *monde* – ou un *mode d'existence* – tout harmonique'. Perhaps the most characteristic feature of Valéry's method of evoking this 'monde tout harmonique' is his beautifully blended patternings of alliteration, assonance, internal rhymes and rich rhymes. Between sound and sense the poet forges a link which seems necessary and unalterable, this being another provocative fusion of emotion and intellect. In the composition of these lines from *Le Cimetière marin*:

> Ce lieu me plaît, dominé de flambeaux
> Composé d'or, de pierre et d'arbres sombres
> Où tant de marbre est tremblant sur tant d'ombres

one might wonder whether the pleasing repetition of sound has carried almost as much sway as the demands of the sense; and the listener's response to the meaning is bound to be affected by the charm of the verbal music.

Valéry's poetry in *Charmes* (1922) is different in many ways from that of other twentieth-century poets: it is more discreet, unified and fluent in tone than Apollinaire's and does not indulge in the heterogeneous surprises and *collages* of the Cubist aesthetic; more intellectual in its inquiry than Supervielle's whose inspiration turns to pictures, fables and childlike expression; and more controlled than Surrealist poetry of which, in its taste for lucidity, meticulous prosody, Classical balance and euphony, it is the very antithesis. It asserts the independence of a mind which observes itself thinking, which circles back to itself via the subject and form of poems and which leaves us, the readers, with the refined and highly evocative by-product of its far-reaching intellectual adventure.

SELECT BIBLIOGRAPHY

J. Charpier, *Paul Valéry*, (Poètes d'aujourd'hui, 51), Seghers, 1958.
C. M. Crow, *Paul Valéry: consciousness and nature*, Cambridge University Press, 1972.
J. Duchesne-Guillemain, *Etude de 'Charmes' de Paul Valéry*, Brussels, L'Ecran du monde, 1947.
W. N. Ince, *The Poetic Theory of Paul Valéry: inspiration and technique*, Leicester University Press, 1961.
J. R. Lawler, *Lecture de Valéry: une étude de 'Charmes'*, Presses Universitaires de France, 1963.
P.-O. Walzer, *La poésie de Valéry*, Geneva, Cailler, 1953; repr. Slatkine, 1966.
C. G. Whiting, *Charmes ou Poèmes*, (Athlone French Poets), Athlone Press, 1973.

L'Abeille

Quelle, et si fine, et si mortelle,
Que soit ta pointe, blonde abeille,
Je n'ai, sur ma tendre corbeille,
Jeté qu'un songe de dentelle. 4

Pique du sein la gourde belle,
Sur qui l'Amour meurt ou sommeille,
Qu'un peu de moi-même vermeille
Vienne à la chair ronde et rebelle! 8

J'ai grand besoin d'un prompt tourment:
Un mal vif et bien terminé
Vaut mieux qu'un supplice dormant! 11

Soit donc mon sens illuminé
Par cette infime alerte d'or
Sans qui l'Amour meurt ou s'endort! 14

Les Pas

Tes pas, enfants de mon silence,
Saintement, lentement placés,
Vers le lit de ma vigilance
Procèdent muets et glacés. 4

Personne pure, ombre divine,
Qu'ils sont doux, tes pas retenus!
Dieux!...tous les dons que je devine
Viennent à moi sur ces pieds nus!　　　　　　8

Si, de tes lèvres avancées,
Tu prépares pour l'apaiser,
A l'habitant de mes pensées
La nourriture d'un baiser,　　　　　　　　12

Ne hâte pas cet acte tendre,
Douceur d'être et de n'être pas,
Car j'ai vécu de vous attendre,
Et mon cœur n'était que vos pas.　　　　　16

La Ceinture

Quand le ciel couleur d'une joue
Laisse enfin les yeux le chérir
Et qu'au point doré de périr
Dans les roses le temps se joue,　　　　　4

Devant le muet de plaisir
Qu'enchaîne une telle peinture,
Danse une Ombre à libre ceinture
Que le soir est près de saisir.　　　　　　8

Cette ceinture vagabonde
Fait dans le souffle aérien
Frémir le suprême lien
De mon silence avec ce monde...　　　　12

Absent, présent...Je suis bien seul,
Et sombre, ô suave linceul.　　　　　　14

Le Sylphe

Ni vu ni connu
Je suis le parfum
Vivant et défunt
Dans le vent venu!　　　　　　　　　4

Ni vu ni connu,
Hasard ou génie?
A peine venu
La tâche est finie!　　　　　　　　　8

Ni lu ni compris?
Aux meilleurs esprits
Que d'erreurs promises!   11

Ni vu ni connu,
Le temps d'un sein nu
Entre deux chemises!   14

L'Insinuant

O Courbes, méandre,
Secrets du menteur,
Est-il art plus tendre
Que cette lenteur?   4

Je sais où je vais,
Je t'y veux conduire,
Mon dessein mauvais
N'est pas de te nuire...   8

(Quoique souriante
En pleine fierté,
Tant de liberté
La désoriente!)   12

O Courbes, méandre,
Secrets du menteur,
Je veux faire attendre
Le mot le plus tendre.   16

Les Grenades

Dures grenades entr'ouvertes
Cédant à l'excès de vos grains,
Je crois voir des fronts souverains
Eclatés de leurs découvertes!   4

Si les soleils par vous subis,
O grenades entre-bâillées,
Vous ont fait d'orgueil travaillées
Craquer les cloisons de rubis,   8

Et que si l'or sec de l'écorce
A la demande d'une force
Crève en gemmes rouges de jus,   11

Cette lumineuse rupture
Fait rêver une âme que j'eus
De sa secrète architecture.   14

Le Cimetière marin

Ce toit tranquille, où marchent des colombes,
Entre les pins palpite, entre les tombes;
Midi le juste y compose de feux
La mer, la mer, toujours recommencée!
O récompense après une pensée
Qu'un long regard sur le calme des dieux!   6

Quel pur travail de fins éclairs consume
Maint diamant d'imperceptible écume,
Et quelle paix semble se concevoir!
Quand sur l'abîme un soleil se repose,
Ouvrages purs d'une éternelle cause,
Le Temps scintille et le Songe est savoir.   12

Stable trésor, temple simple à Minerve,
Masse de calme, et visible réserve,
Eau sourcilleuse, Œil qui gardes en toi
Tant de sommeil sous un voile de flamme,
O mon silence!... Edifice dans l'âme,
Mais comble d'or aux mille tuiles, Toit!   18

Temple du Temps, qu'un seul soupir résume,
A ce point pur je monte et m'accoutume,
Tout entouré de mon regard marin;
Et comme aux dieux mon offrande suprême,
La scintillation sereine sème
Sur l'altitude un dédain souverain.   24

Comme le fruit se fond en jouissance,
Comme en délice il change son absence
Dans une bouche où sa forme se meurt,
Je hume ici ma future fumée,
Et le ciel chante à l'âme consumée
Le changement des rives en rumeur.   30

Beau ciel, vrai ciel, regarde-moi qui change!
Après tant d'orgueil, après tant d'étrange
Oisiveté, mais pleine de pouvoir,
Je m'abandonne à ce brillant espace,

Sur les maisons des morts mon ombre passe
Qui m'apprivoise à son frêle mouvoir.   36

L'âme exposée aux torches du solstice,
Je te soutiens, admirable justice
De la lumière aux armes sans pitié!
Je te rends pure à ta place première:
Regarde-toi!... Mais rendre la lumière
Suppose d'ombre une morne moitié.   42

O pour moi seul, à moi seul, en moi-même,
Auprès d'un cœur, aux sources du poème,
Entre le vide et l'événement pur,
J'attends l'écho de ma grandeur interne,
Amère, sombre et sonore citerne,
Sonnant dans l'âme un creux toujours futur!   48

Sais-tu, fausse captive des feuillages,
Golfe mangeur de ces maigres grillages,
Sur mes yeux clos, secrets éblouissants,
Quel corps me traîne à sa fin paresseuse,
Quel front l'attire à cette terre osseuse?
Une étincelle y pense à mes absents.   54

Fermé, sacré, plein d'un feu sans matière,
Fragment terrestre offert à la lumière,
Ce lieu me plaît, dominé de flambeaux,
Composé d'or, de pierre et d'arbres sombres,
Où tant de marbre est tremblant sur tant d'ombres;
La mer fidèle y dort sur mes tombeaux!   60

Chienne splendide, écarte l'idolâtre!
Quand solitaire au sourire de pâtre,
Je pais longtemps, moutons mystérieux,
Le blanc troupeau de mes tranquilles tombes,
Éloignes-en les prudentes colombes,
Les songes vains, les anges curieux!   66

Ici venu, l'avenir est paresse.
L'insecte net gratte la sécheresse;
Tout est brûlé, défait, reçu dans l'air
A je ne sais quelle sévère essence...
La vie est vaste, étant ivre d'absence,
Et l'amertume est douce, et l'esprit clair.   72

Les morts cachés sont bien dans cette terre
Qui les réchauffe et sèche leur mystère.
Midi là-haut, Midi sans mouvement
En soi se pense et convient à soi-même...
Tête complète et parfait diadème,
Je suis en toi le secret changement.   78

Tu n'as que moi pour contenir tes craintes!
Mes repentirs, mes doutes, mes contraintes
Sont le défaut de ton grand diamant...
Mais dans leur nuit toute lourde de marbres,
Un peuple vague aux racines des arbres
A pris déjà ton parti lentement.   84

Ils ont fondu dans une absence épaisse,
L'argile rouge a bu la blanche espèce,
Le don de vivre a passé dans les fleurs!
Où sont des morts les phrases familières,
L'art personnel, les âmes singulières?
La larve file où se formaient des pleurs.   90

Les cris aigus des filles chatouillées,
Les yeux, les dents, les paupières mouillées,
Le sein charmant qui joue avec le feu,
Le sang qui brille aux lèvres qui se rendent,
Les derniers dons, les doigts qui les défendent,
Tout va sous terre et rentre dans le jeu!   96

Et vous, grande âme, espérez-vous un songe
Qui n'aura plus ces couleurs de mensonge
Qu'aux yeux de chair l'onde et l'or font ici?
Chanterez-vous quand serez vaporeuse?
Allez! Tout fuit! Ma présence est poreuse,
La sainte impatience meurt aussi!   102

Maigre immortalité noire et dorée,
Consolatrice affreusement laurée,
Qui de la mort fais un sein maternel,
Le beau mensonge et la pieuse ruse!
Qui ne connaît, et qui ne les refuse,
Ce crâne vide et ce rire éternel!   108

Pères profonds, têtes inhabitées,
Qui sous le poids de tant de pelletées,
Etes la terre et confondez nos pas,

Le vrai rongeur, le ver irréfutable
N'est point pour vous qui dormez sous la table,
Il vit de vie, il ne me quitte pas!   114

Amour, peut-être, ou de moi-même haine?
Sa dent secrète est de moi si prochaine
Que tous les noms lui peuvent convenir!
Qu'importe! Il voit, il veut, il songe, il touche!
Ma chair lui plaît, et jusque sur ma couche,
A ce vivant je vis d'appartenir!   120

Zénon! Cruel Zénon d'Elée!
M'as-tu percé de cette flèche ailée
Qui vibre, vole, et qui ne vole pas!
Le son m'enfante et la flèche me tue!
Ah! le soleil... Quelle ombre de tortue
Pour l'âme, Achille immobile à grands pas!   126

Non,,non!... Debout! Dans l'ère successive!
Brisez, mon corps, cette forme pensive!
Buvez, mon sein, la naissance du vent!
Une fraîcheur, de la mer exhalée,
Me rend mon âme... O puissance salée!
Courons à l'onde en rejaillir vivant!   132

Oui! Grande mer de délires douée,
Peau de panthère et chlamyde trouée
De mille et mille idoles du soleil,
Hydre absolue, ivre de ta chair bleue,
Qui te remords l'étincelante queue
Dans un tumulte au silence pareil,   138

Le vent se lève!... Il faut tenter de vivre!
L'air immense ouvre et referme mon livre,
La vague en poudre ose jaillir des rocs!
Envolez-vous, pages tout éblouies!
Rompez, vagues! Rompez d'eaux réjouies
Ce toit tranquille où picoraient des focs!   144

La Caresse

Mes chaudes mains, baigne-les
Dans les tiennes... Rien ne calme
Comme d'amour ondulés
Les passages d'une palme.   4

Tout familiers qu'ils me sont,
Tes anneaux à longues pierres
Se fondent dans le frisson
Qui fait clore les paupières   8

Et le mal s'étale, tant,
Comme une dalle est polie,
Une caresse l'étend
Jusqu'à la mélancolie.   12

Guillaume Apollinaire

(1880–1918)

Apollinaire is generally looked upon as a poet caught between contrasting worlds. By birth he was a hybrid, the son of a Polish adventuress and an Italian army officer, but receiving most of his education in France. In time, he was at a crossroads, rooted in the late nineteenth century, but thrown into the frenetic innovations of the early years of the twentieth century (the surge of scientific discoveries, the widespread use of electricity and the development of the aeroplane, expanding communications networks and a growing sense of cosmopolitanism, the re-shaping of philosophy and moral outlooks). In the history of French poetry, he stands as an ungainly and genial Colossus, with one foot in an established order and the other in adventure (a duality summed up in the poem *La jolie rousse*): fondly attached to the oldest lyrical traditions (singing ballads of lost love and faithless hearts or laments on the passage of time), but allying himself fervently with all the artistic experiments of the Cubist period (the shattering of reality and its recomposition in surprising shapes and angular juxta-positions). He is at the same time a poet belonging to a bygone age and the most dynamic symbol of his own era. He shows a fascination with the past, its myths and legends, its quaint anecdotes and old wives' tales, its strange little bits of erudition; and a desire to be at the forefront of the *avant-garde*, shaping the future and the new vision of things.

It is not surprising that one critic should have greeted Apollinaire's first major collection, *Alcools* (1913) by describing it as a bric-à-brac shop. Its hallmark is its heterogeneous quality. Patent little love-songs appear alongside the most weird and obscure dream-poems, entertaining picture post-cards of the Rhineland scenery and folklore alongside misty and melancholic lyricism, a city-scene from modern Amsterdam alongside ancient palaces, or the most earthy and concrete 'slice of life' alongside poetry of an abstract and metaphysical significance. Even more typical is the way in which these various styles are often welded together in the same poem. The crude and truculent nestles with the pure and tender. Traditional rhetoric interweaves with offhand colloquialism. Genuine sentimentalism wears a falsely gay or ironic mask. The mythological makes friends with the modern (Icarus and the aeroplane, the lyre and the barrel organ, triremes and trams). But what many critics have overlooked is that the bringing together of the disparate is not an accident, but an essential principle, of Apollinaire's aesthetics; and that what may appear to be slapdash composition is, in fact, a truly experimental art, based on the belief that everything in life, ancient or modern, erudite or coarse, portentous or banal, rural or urban, can be compounded in the crucible of poetry to create a new and surprising artistic explosion. Similarly, the suppression of all punctuation in *Alcools* or the innovating techniques employed in his later collection *Calligrammes* (1918), especially the 'picture-poems' in which the words are laid out on the page to represent in pictorial form the actual subject, are not simply the cheap tricks of a self-conscious modernist. They are a genuine attempt to extend poetic suggestiveness, to bring about a new kind of synthesis (either between disparate material or between the pictorial and verbal arts), and to move poetic appreciation on to a more relevant foundation.

Time is the main theme of Apollinaire's work: time the arch-executioner which severs all links, time moving at a pace of its own and leaving the wishful poet abandoned and impotent in a solitary world, time which throws up its flotsam from the depths of the past and preys dictatorially on the conscience of the present. It is a theme accompanied by images of the seasons and the movements of the stars, and by a preoccupation with the cyclic pattern of lives, deaths and resurrections. It goes hand in hand with the theme of rootlessness. One sees the poet as a perennial wanderer in time and space, passing from country to country, walking the city streets alone, pacing the corridors of the museum of history and his own private gallery of memories and subconscious images, or giving himself as a propitiatory offering to the flames which will forge the future.

Apollinaire's poetry breaks with the rarefied climate of French Symbolism. Instead of pursuing an eternal ideal of Beauty or a metaphysical goal, spiritualized and intangible, he finds beauty in modern city street-scenes, everyday human dramas and picturesque anecdotes. Instead of the musical vagueness and unobtrusive fluid forms of a Verlaine, he introduces bold colour, shock-effects and irregular shapes. Instead of the high seriousness of a Mallarmé, he introduces an off-beat and casual humour, marked by a gentle self-mockery and a love of the incongruous.

SELECT BIBLIOGRAPHY

A. Billy, *Guillaume Apollinaire*, (Poètes d'aujourd'hui, 8), Seghers, 1954.
C. Bonnefoy, *Apollinaire*, (Classiques du xxe siècle, 100), Editions universitaires, 1969.
L. C. Breunig, *Guillaume Apollinaire*, (Columbia essays on modern writers, 46), Columbia University Press, 1969.
M. Davies, *Apollinaire*, Oliver and Boyd, 1964.

M.-J. Durry, *Guillaume Apollinaire: Alcools*, 3 vols., S.E.D.E.S., 1956–65.
P. Pia, *Apollinaire par lui-même*, Seuil, 1954.
G. Rees, *Alcools*, (Athlone French Poets), Athlone Press, 1975.
Ph. Renaud, *Lecture d'Apollinaire*, L'Age d'Homme, 1969.
A. Rouveyre, *Amour et poésie de Guillaume Apollinaire*, Seuil, 1955.
F. Steegmuller, *Apollinaire: poet among the painters*, Penguin, 1974.

Le Pont Mirabeau

Sous le pont Mirabeau coule la Seine
    Et nos amours
  Faut-il qu'il m'en souvienne
La joie venait toujours après la peine   4

    Vienne la nuit sonne l'heure
    Les jours s'en vont je demeure   6

Les mains dans les mains restons face à face
    Tandis que sous
  Le pont de nos bras passe
Des éternels regards l'onde si lasse   10

    Vienne la nuit sonne l'heure
    Les jours s'en vont je demeure   12

L'amour s'en va comme cette eau courante
    L'amour s'en va
  Comme la vie est lente
Et comme l'Espérance est violente   16

    Vienne la nuit sonne l'heure
    Les jours s'en vont je demeure   18

Passent les jours et passent les semaines
    Ni temps passé
  Ni les amours reviennent
Sous le pont Mirabeau coule la Seine   22

    Vienne la nuit sonne l'heure
    Les jours s'en vont je demeure   24

Marie

    Vous y dansiez petite fille
    Y danserez-vous mère-grand
    C'est la maclotte qui sautille
    Toutes les cloches sonneront
    Quand donc reviendrez-vous Marie   5

Les masques sont silencieux
Et la musique est si lointaine
Qu'elle semble venir des cieux
Oui je veux vous aimer mais vous aimer à peine
Et mon mal est délicieux   10

Les brebis s'en vont dans la neige
Flocons de laine et ceux d'argent
Des soldats passent et que n'ai-je
Un cœur à moi ce cœur changeant
Changeant et puis encor que sais-je   15

Sais-je où s'en iront tes cheveux
Crépus comme mer qui moutonne
Sais-je où s'en iront tes cheveux
Et tes mains feuilles de l'automne
Que jonchent aussi nos aveux   20

Je passais au bord de la Seine
Un livre ancien sous le bras
Le fleuve est pareil à ma peine
Il s'écoule et ne tarit pas
Quand donc finira la semaine   25

La Tzigane

La tzigane savait d'avance
Nos deux vies barrées par les nuits
Nous lui dîmes adieu et puis
De ce puits sortit l'Espérance   4

L'amour lourd comme un ours prive
Dansa debout quand nous voulûmes
Et l'oiseau bleu perdit ses plumes
Et les mendiants leurs *Ave*   8

On sait très bien que l'on se damne
Mais l'espoir d'aimer en chemin
Nous fait penser main dans la main
A ce qu'a prédit la tzigane   12

L'Emigrant de Landor Road

Le chapeau à la main il entra du pied droit
Chez un tailleur très chic et fournisseur du roi
Ce commerçant venait de couper quelques têtes
De mannequins vêtus comme il faut qu'on se vête   4

La foule en tous les sens remuait en mêlant
Des ombres sans amour qui se traînaient par terre
Et des mains vers le ciel plein de lacs de lumière
S'envolaient quelquefois comme des oiseaux blancs   8

Mon bateau partira demain pour l'Amérique
Et je ne reviendrai jamais
Avec l'argent gagné dans les prairies lyriques
Guider mon ombre aveugle en ces rues que j'aimais   12

Car revenir c'est bon pour un soldat des Indes
Les boursiers ont vendu tous mes crachats d'or fin
Mais habillé de neuf je veux dormir enfin
Sous des arbres pleins d'oiseaux muets et de singes   16

Les mannequins pour lui s'étant déshabillés
Battirent leurs habits puis les lui essayèrent
Le vêtement d'un lord mort sans avoir payé
Au rabais l'habilla comme un millionnaire   20

Au-dehors les années
Regardaient la vitrine
Les mannequins victimes
Et passaient enchaînées   24

Intercalées dans l'an c'étaient les journées veuves
Les vendredis sanglants et lents d'enterrements
De blancs et de tout noirs vaincus des cieux qui pleuvent
Quand la femme du diable a battu son amant   28

Puis dans un port d'automne aux feuilles indécises
Quand les mains de la foule y feuillolaient aussi
Sur le pont du vaisseau il posa sa valise
Et s'assit   32

Les vents de l'Océan en soufflant leurs menaces
Laissaient dans ses cheveux de longs baisers mouillés
Des émigrants tendaient vers le port leurs mains lasses
Et d'autres en pleurant s'étaient agenouillés   36

Il regarda longtemps les rives qui moururent
Seuls des bateaux d'enfant tremblaient à l'horizon
Un tout petit bouquet flottant à l'aventure
Couvrit l'Océan d'une immense floraison   40

Il aurait voulu ce bouquet comme la gloire
Jouer dans d'autres mers parmi tous les dauphins
   Et l'on tissait dans sa mémoire
   Une tapisserie sans fin
   Qui figurait son histoire   45

   Mais pour noyer changées en poux
Ces tisseuses têtues qui sans cesse interrogent
   Il se maria comme un doge
Aux cris d'une sirène moderne sans époux   49

Gonfle-toi vers la nuit O Mer Les yeux des squales
Jusqu'à l'aube ont guetté de loin avidement
Des cadavres de jours rongés par les étoiles
Parmi le bruit des flots et les derniers serments   53

Rosemonde

Longtemps au pied du perron de
La maison où entra la dame
Que j'avais suivie pendant deux
Bonnes heures à Amsterdam
Mes doigts jetèrent des baisers   5

Mais le canal était désert
Le quai aussi et nul ne vit
Comment mes baisers retrouvèrent
Celle à qui j'ai donné ma vie
Un jour pendant plus de deux heures   10

Je la surnommai Rosemonde
Voulant pouvoir me rappeler
Sa bouche fleurie en Hollande
Puis lentement je m'en allai
Pour quêter la Rose du Monde   15

Les Sapins

Les sapins en bonnets pointus
De longues robes revêtus
   Comme des astrologues

Saluent leurs frères abattus
Les bateaux qui sur le Rhin voguent   5

Dans les sept arts endoctrinés
Par les vieux sapins leurs aînés
    Qui sont de grands poètes
Ils se savent prédestinés
A briller plus que des planètes   10

A briller doucement changés
En étoiles et enneigés
    Aux Noëls bienheureuses
Fêtes des sapins ensongés
Aux longues branches langoureuses   15

Les sapins beaux musiciens
Chantent des noëls anciens
    Au vent des soirs d'automne
Ou bien graves magiciens
Incantent le ciel quand il tonne   20

Des rangées de blancs chérubins
Remplacent l'hiver les sapins
    Et balancent leurs ailes
L'été ce sont de grands rabbins
Ou bien de vieilles demoiselles   25

Sapins médecins divagants
Ils vont offrant leurs bons onguents
    Quand la montagne accouche
De temps en temps sous l'ouragan
Un vieux sapin geint et se couche   30

Les Femmes

Dans la maison du vigneron les femmes cousent
Lenchen remplis le poêle et mets l'eau du café
Dessus – Le chat s'étire après s'être chauffé
– Gertrude et son voisin Martin enfin s'épousent   4

Le rossignol aveugle essaya de chanter
Mais l'effraie ululant il trembla dans sa cage
Ce cyprès là-bas a l'air du pape en voyage
Sous la neige – Le facteur vient de s'arrêter   8

Pour causer avec le nouveau maître d'école
– Cet hiver est très froid le vin sera très bon

– *Le sacristain sourd et boiteux est moribond*
– *La fille du vieux bourgmestre brode une étole*   12

Pour la fête du curé La forêt là-bas
Grâce au vent chantait à voix grave de grand orgue
Le songe Herr Traum survint avec sa sœur Frau Sorge
Kaethi tu n'as pas bien raccommodé ces bas   16

– *Apporte le café le beurre et les tartines*
La marmelade le saindoux un pot de lait
– *Encore un peu de café Lenchen s'il te plaît*
– *On dirait que le vent dit des phrases latines*   20

– *Encore un peu de café Lenchen s'il te plaît*
– *Lotte es-tu triste O petit cœur – Je crois qu'elle aime*
– *Dieu garde – Pour ma part je n'aime que moi-même*
– *Chut A présent grand-mère dit son chapelet*   24

– *Il me faut du sucre candi Leni je tousse*
– *Pierre mène son furet chasser les lapins*
Le vent faisait danser en rond tous les sapins
Lotte l'amour rend triste – Ilse la vie est douce   28

La nuit tombait Les vignobles aux ceps tordus
Devenaient dans l'obscurité des ossuaires
En neige et repliés gisaient là des suaires
Et des chiens aboyaient aux passants morfondus   32

Il est mort écoutez La cloche de l'église
Sonnait tout doucement la mort du sacristain
Lise il faut attiser le poêle qui s'éteint
Les femmes se signaient dans la nuit indécise   36

1909

La dame avait une robe
En ottoman violine
Et sa tunique brodée d'or
Etait composée de deux panneaux   4
S'attachant sur l'épaule

Les yeux dansants comme des anges
Elle riait elle riait
Elle avait un visage aux couleurs de France   8
Les yeux bleus les dents blanches et les lèvres très rouges
Elle avait un visage aux couleurs de France

Elle était décolletée en rond
Et coiffée à la Récamier   12
Avec de beaux bras nus

N'entendra-t-on jamais sonner minuit

La dame en robe d'ottoman violine
Et en tunique brodée d'or   16
Décolletée en rond
Promenait ses boucles
Son bandeau d'or
Et traînait ses petits souliers à boucles   20

Elle était si belle
Que tu n'aurais pas osé l'aimer

J'aimais les femmes atroces dans les quartiers énormes
Où naissaient chaque jour quelques êtres nouveaux   24
Le fer était leur sang la flamme leur cerveau
J'aimais j'aimais le peuple habile des machines
Le luxe et la beauté ne sont que son écume
Cette femme était si belle   28
Qu'elle me faisait peur

Liens

Cordes faites de cris

Sons de cloches à travers l'Europe
Siècles pendus

Rails qui ligotez les nations   4
Nous ne sommes que deux ou trois hommes
Libres de tous liens
Donnons-nous la main

Violente pluie qui peigne les fumées   8
Cordes
Cordes tissées
Câbles sous-marins
Tours de Babel changées en ponts   12
Araignées-Pontifes
Tous les amoureux qu'un seul lien a liés

D'autres liens plus ténus
Blancs rayons de lumière   16
Cordes et Concorde

J'écris seulement pour vous exalter
O sens ô sens chéris
Ennemis du souvenir   20
Ennemis du désir

Ennemis du regret
Ennemis des larmes
Ennemis de tout ce que j'aime encore   24

Fête

Feu d'artifice en acier
Qu'il est charmant cet éclairage
   Artifice d'artificier
Mêler quelque grâce au courage   4

Deux fusants
Rose éclatement
Comme deux seins que l'on dégrafe
Tendent leurs bouts insolemment
IL SUT AIMER
     quelle épitaphe   10

Un poète dans la forêt
Regarde avec indifférence
   Son revolver au cran d'arrêt
Des roses mourir d'espérance   14

Il songe aux roses de Saadi
Et soudain sa tête se penche
Car une rose lui redit
La molle courbe d'une hanche   18

L'air est plein d'un terrible alcool
Filtré des étoiles mi-closes
Les obus caressent le mol
Parfum nocturne où tu reposes
   Mortification des roses   23

Jules Supervielle

(1884–1960)

Like Laforgue, Supervielle was born in Montevideo, close to the vast South American pampas, and, curiously, both are poets with an acute and highly imaginative sense of space. Both have the ability to see the earth in a cosmic perspective, gyrating among the planets, suffering vertigo and abandonment, and seeking some inkling of its purpose and justification. Coming to France from the outside (and in Supervielle's case making the slow journey across the Atlantic numerous times in the span of a few years), neither poet is imprisoned in a purely Parisian or local vision of things: Laforgue's French provincial scene is set against the corrective mirror of the moon and kept in proportion by comparison with the Missouri and the polar seas, while Supervielle's Boulevard Lannes suddenly finds itself transported lock, stock and barrel into the celestial realm, to tremble as it looks down through the chinks in its paving-stones to see the galloping stars below, and wonder in bewilderment if it should be switching its street-lamps on or off. It is perhaps their awareness of double roots and a kind of homelessness which prompts the theme of exile in their work, encouraging in Laforgue his easy ironic detachment from his own person, and in Supervielle a constant uncertainty as to the boundaries between *l'espace du dedans* and *l'espace du dehors* and a tendency to see himself projected from the outside.

But in other respects the poetic worlds of Laforgue and Supervielle are poles apart. Supervielle is a genial spirit, full of warmth and sympathy for his fellow-men and linked by a bond of solicitude and humour to all aspects of the created world, animals, rocks and plants. If one feels in his work the occasional horror of the cold reaches of space and a planet thrown from its bearings, it is an infinity domesticated and made livable by the family portraits which are hung from star to star and by the chink of milk-bottles. If death is a constant image, eating its way deep into the poet's bones and organs and provoking a disquieting sense of presence – absence, it is rarely a cause for despair, for the dead make the transition to-and-fro as if there were no obstacle, still imagine that they are breathing and bump into the living as they might on a street corner. If there is a certain alienation from the spectacle of the world, it is the alienation of perpetual surprise and wonderment, and not of *ennui* or supercilious satire. If Supervielle favours a playful, evasive style, it is not the irony of the literary dandy, a polished veneer over pessimism or a means of disguising and protecting his own personality, but a gentle self-mockery, a love of fable and story such as that by which a grandfather might win over a child, and a simple picturesqueness of vision which makes him human, harmless and approachable.

Most of Supervielle's main themes emerge in his early collection *Gravitations* (1925), which is the most accessible, varied and colourful introduction to his work as a whole: the origins of life, primeval innocence and moments of first vision; childhood and memory; the giddy movements of the Earth in an incomprehensible pattern of things; the frontiers between different realms or strata of existence (life and death, the human and the divine, body and spirit, air and water, the real and the surreal); wandering looks and detached gestures seeking a focus or a totality; apparitions and disappearances; the quest for a communication with only limited or inappropriate means. The essentials of his poetic vision and style are also established by this time: the surprisingly concrete imagination which stitches together material objects and abstractions, reality and dream, with a dainty needle; the childlike naivety; the ability to create miniature parables and legends; the humour which exploits incongruity and paradox and so draws the sting of the discrepancies of life. Supervielle's subsequent collections, *Le Forçat innocent* (1930) and *Les Amis inconnus* (1934) turn the attention more on the inner space, listening to all the disturbing foreign notes within the self, and have a more sombre tone; while *La Fable du Monde* (1938), another summit, is the poet's most unified and ambitious attempt to explore the totality of Man's position in the universe, in relation to the animals, the elements, divinity, destiny and himself.

SELECT BIBLIOGRAPHY

D. Blair, *Jules Supervielle, a modern fabulist*, Blackwell, 1960.
E. Etiemble, *Supervielle*, (Bibliothèque idéale), Gallimard, 1960.
T. W. Greene, *Jules Supervielle*, Droz et Minard, 1958.
J. A. Hiddleston, *L'Univers de Supervielle*, Corti, 1965.
C. Roy, *Jules Supervielle*, (Poètes d'aujourd'hui, 15), Seghers, 1949.
P. Villaneix, *Le Hors-venu, ou le personnage poétique de Supervielle*, Klincksieck, 1972.
R. Vivier, *Lire Supervielle*, Corti, 1971.

Prophétie

Un jour la Terre ne sera
Qu'un aveugle espace qui tourne,
Confondant la nuit et le jour.
Sous le ciel immense des Andes
Elle n'aura plus de montagnes,
Même pas un petit ravin. 6

De toutes les maisons du monde
Ne durera plus qu'un balcon
Et de l'humaine mappemonde
Une tristesse sans plafond.
De feu l'Océan Atlantique
Un petit goût salé dans l'air,
Un poisson volant et magique
Qui ne saura rien de la mer. 14

D'un coupé de mil-neuf-cent-cinq
(Les quatre roues et nul chemin!)
Trois jeunes filles de l'époque
Restées à l'état de vapeur
Regarderont par la portière
Pensant que Paris n'est pas loin
Et ne sentiront que l'odeur
Du ciel qui vous prend à la gorge. 22

A la place de la forêt
Un chant d'oiseau s'élèvera
Que nul ne pourra situer,
Ni préférer, ni même entendre,
Sauf Dieu qui, lui, l'écoutera
Disant: 'C'est un chardonneret'. 28

Montévidéo

Je naissais, et par la fenêtre
Passait une fraîche calèche. 2

Le cocher réveillait l'aurore
D'un petit coup de fouet sonore.

Flottait un archipel nocturne
Encor sur le liquide jour. 6

Les murs s'éveillaient et le sable
Qui dort écrasé dans les murs.

Un peu de mon âme glissait
Sur un rail bleu, à contre-ciel, 10

Et un autre peu, se mêlant
A un bout de papier volant

Puis, trébuchant sur une pierre,
Gardait sa ferveur prisonnière. 14

Le matin comptait ses oiseaux
Et toujours il recommençait.

Le parfum de l'eucalyptus
Se fiait à l'air étendu. 18

Dans l'Uruguay sur l'Atlantique,
L'air était si liant, facile,
Que les couleurs de l'horizon
S'approchaient pour voir les maisons. 22

C'était moi qui naissais jusqu'au fond sourd des bois
Où tardent à venir les pousses
Et jusque sous la mer où l'algue se retrousse
Pour faire croire au vent qu'il peut descendre là. 26

La Terre allait, toujours recommençant sa ronde,
Reconnaissant les siens avec son atmosphère,
Et palpant sur la vague ou l'eau douce profonde
La tête des nageurs et les pieds des plongeurs. 30

Haute mer

Parmi les oiseaux et les lunes
Qui hantent le dessous des mers
Et qu'on devine à la surface
Aux folles phases de l'écume, 4

Parmi l'aveugle témoignage
Et les sillages sous-marins
De mille poissons sans visage
Qui cachent en eux leur chemin, 8

Le noyé cherche la chanson
Où s'était formé son jeune âge,
Ecoute en vain les coquillages
Et les fait choir au sombre fond. 12

Sous le large

Les poissons des profondeurs
Qui n'ont d'yeux ni de paupières
Inventèrent la lumière
Pour les besoins de leur cœur. 4

Ils en mandent une bulle,
Loin des jours et des années,
Vers la surface où circule
L'océane destinée.   8

Un navire coule à pic,
Houle dans les cheminées,
Et la coque déchirée
Laisse la chaudière à vif.   12

Dans le fond d'une cabine
Une lanterne enfumée
Frappe le hublot fermé
Sur les poissons de la nuit.   16

Le Sillage

On voyait le sillage et nullement la barque,
Une menace errait, comme cherchant la place.

Ils s'étaient regardés dans le fond de leurs yeux,
Apercevant enfin la clairière attendue   4

Où couraient de grands cerfs dans toute leur franchise.
Les chasseurs n'entraient pas dans ce pays sans larmes.

Ce fut le lendemain, après une nuit froide,
Qu'on reconnut en eux des noyés par amour.   8

Mais ce que l'on pouvait prendre pour leur douleur
Nous faisait signe à tous de ne pas croire en elle.

Un peu de leur voilure errait encore en l'air
Toute seule, prenant le vent pour son plaisir,   12

Loin de la barque et des rames à la dérive.

Le Nuage

Il fut un temps où les ombres
A leur place véritable
N'obscurcissaient pas mes fables.
Mon cœur donnait sa lumière.   4

Mes yeux comprenaient la chaise de paille,
La table de bois,
Et mes mains ne rêvaient pas
Par la faute des dix doigts.   8

Mais maintenant le temps se désagrège
Comme sous mille neiges;
Plus je vais et je viens,
Moins je suis sûr de rien.   12

Ecoute-moi, Capitaine de mon enfance,
Faisons comme avant,
Montons à bord de ma première barque
Qui passait la mer quand j'avais dix ans.   16

Elle ne prend pas l'eau du songe
Et sent sûrement le goudron,
Ecoute, ce n'est plus que dans mes souvenirs
Que le bois est encor le bois, et le fer, dur. 20

Depuis longtemps, Capitaine,
Tout m'est nuage et j'en meurs.

Visite de la nuit

Terrasse ou balcon, je posai le pied
A la place exacte où l'on sait toute chose,

J'attendis longtemps, gêné par mon corps,
Il faisait grand jour et l'on approchait.   4

C'était bien la nuit convertie en femme,
Tremblante au soleil comme une perdrix,

Si peu faite encore à son enveloppe
Toute errante en soi, même dans son cœur.   8

Quand il m'arrivait de faire des signes
Elle regardait mais voyait ailleurs.

Je ne bougeais plus pour mieux la convaincre
Mais aucun silence ne lui parvenait.   12

Ses gestes obscurs comme ses murmures
Toujours me voulaient d'un autre côté.

Quand baissa le jour, d'un pas très humain
A jamais déçu, elle s'éloigna.   16

Elle rejoignit au bout de la rue
Son vertige ardent, sa forme espacée.

Comme chaque nuit, elle s'étoila
De ses milliers d'yeux dont aucun ne voit.   20

Et depuis ce jour je cède à mes ombres.

Tristesse de Dieu

(Dieu parle)

Je vous vois aller et venir sur le tremblement de la Terre
Comme aux premiers jours du monde, mais grande est la
    différence,
Mon œuvre n'est plus en moi, je vous l'ai toute donnée.   4
Hommes, mes bien-aimés, je ne puis rien dans vos malheurs,
Je n'ai pu que vous donner votre courage et les larmes;
C'est la preuve chaleureuse de l'existence de Dieu.
L'humidité de votre âme, c'est ce qui vous reste de moi.   8
Je n'ai rien pu faire d'autre.
Je ne puis rien pour la mère dont va s'éteindre le fils
Sinon vous faire allumer, chandelles de l'espérance.
S'il n'en était pas ainsi, est-ce que vous connaîtriez,   12
Petits lits mal défendus, la paralysie des enfants?
Je suis coupé de mon œuvre,
Ce qui est fini est lointain et s'éloigne chaque jour.
Quand la source descend du mont comment revenir là-dessus?   16
Je ne sais pas plus vous parler qu'un potier ne parle à son pot,
Des deux il en est un de sourd, l'autre muet devant son œuvre
Et je vous vois avancer vers d'aveuglants précipices
Sans pouvoir vous les nommer,   20
Et je ne peux vous souffler comment il faudrait s'y prendre,
Il faut vous en tirer tout seuls comme des orphelins dans la neige.
Je ne puis rien pour vous, hélas si je me répète
C'est à force d'en souffrir.   24
Je suis un souvenir qui descend, vous vivez dans un souvenir,
L'espoir qui gravit vos collines, vous vivez dans une espérance.
Secoué par les prières et les blasphèmes des hommes,
Je suis partout à la fois et ne peux pas me montrer,   28
Sans bouger je déambule et je vais de ciel en ciel,
Je suis l'errant en soi-même, le foisonnant solitaire,
Habitué des lointains, je suis très loin de moi-même,
Je m'égare au fond de moi comme un enfant dans les bois,   32
Je m'appelle, je me hale, je me tire vers mon centre.
Homme, si je t'ai créé, c'est pour y voir un peu clair,
Et pour vivre dans un corps, moi qui n'ai mains ni visage.

Je veux te remercier de faire avec sérieux   36
Tout ce qui n'aura qu'un temps sur la Terre bien-aimée,
O mon enfant, mon chéri, ô courage de ton Dieu,
Mon fils qui t'en es allé courir le monde à ma place
A l'avant-garde de moi dans ton corps si vulnérable   40
Avec sa grande misère. Pas un petit coin de peau
Où ne puisse se former la profonde pourriture.
Chacun de vous sait faire un mort sans avoir eu besoin
    d'apprendre,   44
Un mort parfait qu'on peut tourner et retourner dans tous
    les sens,
Où il n'y a rien à redire.
Dieu vous survit, lui seul survit entouré par un grand massacre   48
D'hommes, de femmes et d'enfants.
Même vivants, vous mourez un peu continuellement,
Arrangez-vous avec la vie, avec vos tremblantes amours.
Vous avez un cerveau, des doigts pour faire le monde   52
    à votre goût,
Vous avez des facilités pour faire vivre la raison
Et la folie en votre cage,
Vous avez tous les animaux qui forment la Création,   56
Vous pouvez courir et nager comme le chien et le poisson,
Avancer comme le tigre ou comme l'agneau de huit jours,
Vous pouvez vous donner la mort comme le renne, le scorpion,
Et moi je reste l'invisible, l'introuvable sur la Terre,   60
Ayez pitié de votre Dieu qui n'a pas su vous rendre heureux,
Petites parcelles de moi, ô palpitantes étincelles,
Je ne vous offre qu'un brasier où vous retrouverez du feu.

Paul Eluard

(1895–1952)

Paul Eluard is the most widely recognized poet of Surrealism, a revolutionary artistic movement which has played a major rôle in the development of twentieth-century French thought and vision. Although André Breton (1896 – 1966) was chief spokesman of the Surrealists, Eluard too was an eloquent broadcaster of their ideals. Reacting partly to the crisis of the First World War in which he was involved, he calls for man's total liberation from the shackles of a system of values which could produce and allow the massacre in the trenches. The key to this new world (already apprehended by Rimbaud, with his hatred of a sterile hide-bound moral society, his recreative thirst, and his cry that 'l'amour est à réinventer') lies in freeing man's imaginative vision, in promoting his capacity to dream to the level of a principle for living. Breaking through the sallow, emaciated mask of the goddess Reason, Surrealism seeks to reveal the more colourful and fertile processes of thought which lie underneath; hence its interest in dreams and the subconscious – not just as a source of highly imaged poetry, but as a means of allowing latent ideals to surge into reality with the utmost spontaneity, of kindling life to an awareness of its capacity for joy and luminosity, of reconciling man with the deeper potentialities of his 'other self' and of saving him from his fate as a divided being, a source of conflict. For Eluard, the realm to be attained is that in which apparent opposites can exchange identities, and dreams and pictures of the imagination are recognized to be as much a part of man's reality as his flesh and blood:

> C'est la douce loi des hommes
> De changer l'eau en lumière
> Le rêve en réalité
> Et les ennemis en frères
> *(Bonne justice).*

These four lines stress the close connexion in Surrealist thought between poetic and social ambition. Since everyone possesses 'le trésor inestimable' of a dream-world, everyone is equally capable of turning life into poetry. In poetry and in life as a whole all men are equal, and in this liberation by the imagination there are no élites: 'Le surréalisme travaille à démontrer que la pensée est commune à tous, il travaille à réduire les différences qui existent entre les hommes...' Eluard's deep feeling of fraternity towards his fellow-men lies at the heart of some of his finest poems, such as *Sans âge*.

But, although his devotion to a revolutionary cause and his fight for the simple man against the horrors of war, suffering and injustice have made him the best loved of the 'committed' poets of the twentieth century, Eluard's widest appeal is as a love poet. He has written the purest and most delicate love-poems of the age, expressing in refreshing images, graceful forms, yet commonplace words, the renovating force of this experience. Love is the great destroyer of drabness and the source of new visions; it is the power which shatters the shell of solitude and fuses the world of the self with the world of the other; it is intensely personal and yet universal, shaping a lyricism which is both private and accessible. His loved one, though mysterious and treading the borders of unreality, blends harmoniously with the natural world of water, sun, colours and scents accessible to all. Though untranslatable into the direct language of reason, his love-poems create a compelling atmosphere of pastoral serenity *(Je ne suis pas seul)*, of sheer wonder *(L'Amoureuse)*, or of security and joy *(La courbe de tes yeux...)*. In all of them, the reader is inspired to share, not only the intimacy and exuberance, but the magical transforming power of the poet's feelings.

There is nothing erudite or cerebral in Eluard's poetry. It is written for everyone to read and enjoy. The poet's function, as he defines it, is social and practical; he rejects the idea of a poetry for specialists or 'the happy few' which is 'une sorte de rite sacré' (that of Mallarmé, for instance). For him, 'la poésie est dans la vie'. It is contagious, affecting everyone, opening eyes and offering its simple wonders to all (cf. his title *Donner à voir*).

It is not surprising that, pursuing such an ideal, Eluard should dismiss with the revolutionary's impatience conventional metrical forms: 'Il faut parler une pensée musicale qui n'ait que faire des tambours, des violons, des rythmes et des rimes du terrible concert pour oreilles d'âne'. At the heart of his poetry, instead of the artificial strictures of prosody, is the typically Surrealist feature of the startling image which surges from the poet's subconscious to pierce barriers and shake one's usual view of objects: the image of the stone in *L'Amoureuse* is one conspicuous example, but even this does not equal the audacity of 'La terre est bleue comme une orange' which begins another of his poems. For the reader who needs an exact meaning, such imagery will seem obscure and baffling. But for the mind tired of the utilitarian and prosaic, it offers the exhilaration of a world where grey reality is lit up, overthrown as if by a wave of the wand, and the excitement of an unimpeded journey between the real and the ideal: 'L'imagination change le monde... Cette reine du monde est la mère du progrès'.

SELECT BIBLIOGRAPHY

Europe: Revue mensuelle, no. 403 (November, 1962) and no. 525 (January, 1973).
R. Jean, *Paul Eluard par lui-même*, Seuil, 1968.
L. Parrot and J. Marcenac, *Paul Eluard*, (Poètes d'aujourd'hui, 1), Seghers, 1969.
L. Perche, *Paul Eluard*, (Classiques du xxe siècle, 63), Editions universitaires, 1964.
G. Poulet, 'Eluard' in *Le Point de départ* (Etudes sur le temps humain, III), Plon, 1964.
J.-P. Richard, 'Paul Eluard' in *Onze études sur la poésie moderne*, Seuil, 1964.

L'Amoureuse

Elle est debout sur mes paupières
Et ses cheveux sont dans les miens,
Elle a la forme de mes mains,
Elle a la couleur de mes yeux,
Elle s'engloutit dans mon ombre
Comme une pierre sur le ciel.   6

Elle a toujours les yeux ouverts
Et ne me laisse pas dormir.
Ses rêves en pleine lumière
Font s'évaporer les soleils,
Me font rire, pleurer et rire,
Parler sans avoir rien à dire.   12

La courbe de tes yeux...

La courbe de tes yeux fait le tour de mon cœur,
Un rond de danse et de douceur,
Auréole du temps, berceau nocturne et sûr,
Et si je ne sais plus tout ce que j'ai vécu
C'est que tes yeux ne m'ont pas toujours vu.   5

Feuilles de jour et mousse de rosée,
Roseaux du vent, sourires parfumés,
Ailes couvrant le monde de lumière,
Bateaux chargés du ciel et de la mer,
Chasseurs des bruits et sources des couleurs,   10

Parfums éclos d'une couvée d'aurores
Qui gît toujours sur la paille des astres,
Comme le jour dépend de l'innocence
Le monde entier dépend de tes yeux purs
Et tout mon sang coule dans leurs regards.   15

Tu te lèves l'eau se déplie...

Tu te lèves l'eau se déplie
Tu te couches l'eau s'épanouit

Tu es l'eau détournée de ses abîmes
Tu es la terre qui prend racine   4
Et sur laquelle tout s'établit

Tu fais des bulles de silence dans le désert des bruits
Tu chantes des hymnes nocturnes sur les cordes de l'arc-en-ciel
Tu es partout tu abolis toutes les routes   8

Tu sacrifies le temps
A l'éternelle jeunesse de la flamme exacte
Qui voile la nature en la reproduisant

Femme tu mets au monde un corps toujours pareil   12
Le tien

Tu es la ressemblance.

Sans âge

Nous approchons
Dans les forêts
Prenez la rue du matin
Montez les marches de la brume   4

Nous approchons
La terre en a le cœur crispé

Encore un jour à mettre au monde.

                              *
Le ciel s'élargira   8
Nous en avions assez
D'habiter dans les ruines du sommeil
Dans l'ombre basse du repos
De la fatigue de l'abandon   12

La terre reprendra la forme de nos corps vivants
Le vent nous subira
Le soleil et la nuit passeront dans nos yeux
Sans jamais les changer   16

Notre espace certain notre air pur est de taille
A combler le retard creusé par l'habitude
Nous aborderons tous une mémoire nouvelle

Nous parlerons ensemble un langage sensible.   20

*

O mes frères contraires gardant dans vos prunelles
La nuit infuse et son horreur
Où vous ai-je laissés
Avec vos lourdes mains dans l'huile paresseuse   24
De vos actes anciens
Avec si peu d'espoir que la mort a raison
O mes frères perdus
Moi je vais vers la vie j'ai l'apparence d'homme   28
Pour prouver que le monde est fait à ma mesure

Et je ne suis pas seul
Mille images de moi multiplient ma lumière
Mille regards pareils égalisent la chair   32
C'est l'oiseau c'est l'enfant c'est le roc c'est la plaine
Qui se mêlent à nous
L'or éclate de rire de se voir hors du gouffre
L'eau le feu se dénudent pour une seule saison   36
Il n'y a plus d'éclipse au front de l'univers.

*

Mains par nos mains reconnues
Lèvres à nos lèvres confondues
Les premières chaleurs florales   40
Alliées à la fraîcheur du sang

Le prisme respire avec nous
Aube abondante
Au sommet de chaque herbe reine   44
Au sommet des mousses à la pointe des neiges
Des vagues des sables bouleversés
Des enfances persistantes
Hors de toutes les cavernes   48
Hors de nous-mêmes.

Je ne suis pas seul

Chargée
De fruits légers aux lèvres
Parée
De mille fleurs variées   4
Glorieuse

Dans les bras du soleil
Heureuse
D'un oiseau familier   8
Ravie
D'une goutte de pluie
Plus belle
Que le ciel du matin   12
Fidèle

Je parle d'un jardin
Je rêve

Mais j'aime justement.   16

Critique de la poésie

Le feu réveille la forêt
Les troncs les cœurs les mains les feuilles
Le bonheur en un seul bouquet
Confus léger fondant sucré   4
C'est toute une forêt d'amis
Qui s'assemble aux fontaines vertes
Du bon soleil du bois flambant

Garcia Lorca a été mis à mort   8

Maison d'une seule parole
Et des lèvres unies pour vivre
Un tout petit enfant sans larmes
Dans ses prunelles d'eau perdue   12
La lumière de l'avenir
Goutte à goutte elle comble l'homme
Jusqu'aux paupières transparentes

Saint-Pol-Roux a été mis à mort   16
Sa fille a été suppliciée

Ville glacée d'angles semblables
Où je rêve de fruits en fleur
Du ciel entier et de la terre   20
Comme à de vierges découvertes
Dans un jeu qui n'en finit pas
Pierres fanées murs sans écho
Je vous évite d'un sourire   24

Decour a été mis à mort.

Paul Eluard

Bonne justice

C'est la chaude loi des hommes
Du raisin ils font du vin
Du charbon ils font du feu
Des baisers ils font des hommes   4

C'est la dure loi des hommes
Se garder intact malgré
Les guerres et la misère
Malgré les dangers de mort   8

C'est la douce loi des hommes
De changer l'eau en lumière
Le rêve en réalité
Et les ennemis en frères   12

Une loi vieille et nouvelle
Qui va se perfectionnant
Du fond du cœur de l'enfant
Jusqu'à la raison suprême.   16

Semaine

1

Les flots de la rivière
La croissance du ciel
Le vent la feuille et l'aile
Le regard la parole   4
Et le fait que je t'aime
Tout est mouvement.

2

Une bonne nouvelle
Arrive ce matin   8
Tu as rêvé de moi.

3

Je voudrais associer notre amour solitaire
Aux lieux les plus peuplés du monde
Qu'il puisse laisser de la place   12
A ceux qui s'aiment comme nous

Ils sont nombreux ils sont trop peu.

4

Je m'en prends à mon cœur je m'en prends à mon corps
Mais je ne fais pas mal à celle que j'adore.   16

5

Nous étions deux et nous venions de vivre
Une journée d'amour ensoleillé
Notre soleil nous l'embrassions ensemble
La vie entière nous était visible   20

Quand la nuit vint nous restâmes sans ombre
A polir l'or de notre sang commun
Nous étions deux au cœur du seul trésor
Dont la lumière ne s'endort jamais.   24

6

Le brouillard mêle sa lumière
A la verdure des ténèbres
Toi tu mêles ta chair tiède
A mes désirs acharnés.   28

7

Tu te couvres tu t'éclaires
Tu t'endors et tu t'éveilles
Au long des saisons fidèles

Tu bâtis une maison   32
Et ton cœur la mûrit
Comme un lit comme un fruit

Et ton corps s'y réfugie
Et tes rêves s'y prolongent   36
C'est la maison des jours tendres

Et des baisers dans la nuit.

Henri Michaux

(1899–   )

Although one of the grand 'unclassifiables' of contemporary poetry, Michaux is one of its most significant and symptomatic figures. He represents a poetry not concerned with beauty or aesthetic order but with efficacy: that is to say, a poetry not content to contemplate or ornament, but which works for its living and becomes a practical act in his *problème d'être*, his difficult relations with reality. Hence his theory of poetry as 'exorcism', the purpose of which is to lay the innumerable ghosts which lurk menacingly in the recesses of the poet's sensitive interior or to 'tenir en échec les puissances environnantes du monde hostile'. His fascinating imaginary countries, 'Grande Garabagne', the 'Pays de la Magie' and 'Poddema', elaborately described in the prose poetry of *Ailleurs*, are not escapist lands but what he calls 'buffer-states', thrown up by the imagination in the endless war between himself and reality, absorbing the shocks from both sides, and acting as a psychic necessity in what would otherwise be an irreconcilable situation. It is also a poetry which comes very close to scientific exploration, and in this, too, it is highly modern. Michaux's attitude in this respect is summed up in his epigraph to the collection, *Connaissance par les gouffres*, in which one could substitute the word 'poetry' for 'drugs':

> Les drogues nous ennuient avec leur paradis.
> Qu'elles nous donnent plutôt un peu de savoir.
> Nous ne sommes pas un siècle à paradis.

His work, in fact, takes the form of a long process of self-exploration, guided partly by the principle that to liberate the unknown in oneself is to liberate oneself from the unknown (one could say, by the same token, that he is an inheritor of Rimbaud, a twentieth-century 'horrible travailleur' working the tool of poetry deeply and violently into the seams of *l'inconnu*). Not only is Michaux's writing a curious amalgam of the scientific and the poetic, the documentary and the imaginative (thus illustrating his deep-rooted suspicion of poetry as an idle mandarin pastime in a realm apart), but it also crosses the frontiers of prose and poetry with the utmost facility as if they were purely arbitrary. So, paradoxically, one could say that his essential poetry is to be found in his prose texts like *Au pays de la magie* or *Portrait des*

Meidosems, rather than in those which stay more or less within a formal poetic tradition as free verse (though these are mainly the ones we have printed here).

A neat way to collect revealing insights into the thematic and visionary texture of Michaux's work is to study the implications of some of his major titles. *Qui je fus* (1927) touches on the question of identity and the divided nature of the self, caught between various expressions and tendencies of its own nature; while *Mes propriétés* (1929) poses the problem, not only of the definition of the self ('properties' almost in the chemical sense: just what elements go to make that contradictory and turbulent compound which is the human person?), but also of autonomy and ownership (to what extent does one possess one's own domain, clearly contoured and reliable, or must there be constant encroachment, by the individual into realms which are alien to him, and by external forces, beneficent or pernicious, into the pretended sanctity of the person?). These themes are all relevant to the poem *Clown*. Then one has *La Nuit remue* (1935) or *Apparitions* (1946), titles which speak of the dreams and nightmares, images and energies, which animate or disturb the poet's inner obscurity. The 'jeune fille de Budapest' and the 'jeune magicienne' spring from such sources as these to set in motion his mental 'cinema'. *Je vous écris d'un pays lointain* (1942), the collective title *Ailleurs* (1948) and *Nouvelles de l'étranger* (1952) tell how he is drawn as an explorer into foreign zones and further reaches of perception where things are subject to a new order, causing one to revalue one's own. His 'Meidosems' are compelled by a similar yearning to be 'elsewhere', beyond their own nature and cured of its limitations. This searching spiritual dimension (though always coupled in Michaux with an unsuperstitious lucidity) is hinted at in titles such as *Misérable miracle* (1956) and *L'Infini turbulent* (1957): another expression of it is seen in the poems *Dans la nuit* and *Icebergs*.

One should emphasize, finally, words like *Liberté d'action* (1945), *Passages* (1950) and *Mouvements* (1951). For Michaux stands apart above all as a poet of energy and turbulence, a poet of penetrations between worlds and dynamic transitions, and his poetry is almost invariably an expression of liberation.

SELECT BIBLIOGRAPHY

R. Bellour, *Henri Michaux ou une mesure de l'être*, Gallimard, 1965.
R. Bertelé, *Henri Michaux*, (Poètes d'aujourd'hui, 5), Seghers, 1963.
A. Bosquet, 'Henri Michaux' in *Verbe et vertige*, Hachette, 1961.
M. Bowie, *Henri Michaux: a study of his literary works*, Oxford University Press, 1973.
R. Bréchon, *Michaux*, (Bibliothèque idéale), Gallimard, 1959.
Cahiers de l'Herne, No. 8: *Henri Michaux*, 1966.
N. Murat, *Michaux*, (Classiques du xxe siècle, 88), Editions universitaires, 1967.

Emportez-moi

Emportez-moi dans une caravelle,
Dans une vieille et douce caravelle,
Dans l'étrave, ou si l'on veut, dans l'écume,
Et perdez-moi, au loin, au loin.　　　　　　　　　　　　　4

Dans l'attelage d'un autre âge.
Dans le velours trompeur de la neige.
Dans l'haleine de quelques chiens réunis.
Dans la troupe exténuée des feuilles mortes.　　　　　　8

Emportez-moi sans me briser, dans les baisers,
Dans les poitrines qui se soulèvent et respirent,
Sur les tapis des paumes et leur sourire,
Dans les corridors des os longs et des articulations.　　12

Emportez-moi, ou plutôt enfouissez-moi.

La jeune fille de Budapest

Dans la brume tiède d'une haleine de jeune fille, j'ai pris place.
Je me suis retiré, je n'ai pas quitté ma place.
Ses bras ne pèsent rien. On les rencontre comme l'eau.
Ce qui est fané disparaît devant elle. Il ne reste que ses yeux.　4
Longues belles herbes, longues belles fleurs croissaient dans notre
　　champ.
Obstacle si léger sur ma poitrine, comme tu t'appuies maintenant.
Tu t'appuies tellement, maintenant que tu n'es plus.　　　　8

Dans la nuit

Dans la nuit
Dans la nuit
Je me suis uni à la nuit
A la nuit sans limites　　　　　　　　　　　　　　　4
A la nuit.
Mienne, belle, mienne.
Nuit
Nuit de naissance　　　　　　　　　　　　　　　　8
Qui m'emplis de mon cri
De mes épis
Toi qui m'envahis
Qui fais houle houle　　　　　　　　　　　　　　　12
Qui fais houle tout autour

Et fumes, es fort dense
Et mugis
Es la nuit.   16
Nuit qui gît, Nuit implacable.
Et sa fanfare, et sa plage,
Sa plage en haut, sa plage partout,
Sa plage boit, son poids est roi, et tout   20
    ploie sous lui
Sous lui, sous plus ténu qu'un fil,
Sous la nuit
La Nuit.   24

Icebergs

Icebergs, sans garde-fou, sans ceinture, où de vieux cormorans
abattus et les âmes des matelots morts récemment viennent
s'accouder aux nuits enchanteresses de l'hyperboréal.

Icebergs, Icebergs, cathédrales sans religion de l'hiver éternel, 4
enrobés dans la calotte glaciaire de la planète Terre.
Combien hauts, combien purs sont vos bords enfantés par le
froid.

Icebergs, Icebergs, dos du Nord-Atlantique, augustes Boud- 8
dhas gelés sur des mers incontemplées, Phares scintillants de la
Mort sans issue, le cri éperdu du silence dure des siècles.

Icebergs, Icebergs, Solitaires sans besoin, des pays bouchés,
distants, et libres de vermine. Parents des îles, parents des sources, 12
comme je vous vois, comme vous m'êtes familiers...

Clown

Un jour.
Un jour, bientôt peut-être.
Un jour j'arracherai l'ancre qui tient mon navire loin des mers.
Avec la sorte de courage qu'il faut pour être rien et rien que rien, 4
je lâcherai ce qui paraissait m'être indissolublement proche.
Je le trancherai, je le renverserai, je le romprai, je le ferai
dégringoler.
D'un coup dégorgeant ma misérable pudeur, mes misérables 8
combinaisons et enchaînements 'de fil en aiguille'.
Vidé de l'abcès d'être quelqu'un, je boirai à nouveau l'espace
nourricier.

A coups de ridicules, de déchéances (qu'est-ce que la déché- 12
ance?), par éclatement, par vide, par une totale dissipation-
dérision-purgation, j'expulserai de moi la forme qu'on croyait
si bien attachée, composée, coordonnée, assortie à mon entourage
et à mes semblables, si dignes, si dignes, mes semblables.   16
Réduit à une humilité de catastrophe, à un nivellement parfait
comme après une intense trouille.
Ramené au-dessous de toute mesure à mon rang réel, au
rang infime que je ne sais quelle idée-ambition m'avait fait 20
déserter.
Anéanti quant à la hauteur, quant à l'estime.
Perdu en un endroit lointain (ou même pas), sans nom, sans
identité.   24

Clown, abattant dans la risée, dans le grotesque, dans l'esclaffe-
ment, le sens que contre toute lumière je m'étais fait de mon
importance.
Je plongerai.   28
Sans bourse dans l'infini-esprit sous-jacent ouvert à tous,
ouvert moi-même à une nouvelle et incroyable rosée
à force d'être nul
et ras...   32
et risible...

Portrait des Meidosems

C'est aujourd'hui l'après-midi du délassement des Meidosemmes. Elles montent dans les arbres. Pas par les branches, mais
par la sève.
Le peu de forme fixe qu'elles avaient, fatiguées à mort, elles 4
vont la perdre dans les rameaux, dans les feuilles et les mousses et
dans les pédoncules.
Ascension ivre, douce comme savon entrant dans la crasse.
Vite dans l'herbette, lentement dans les vieux trembles. Suavement 8
dans les fleurs. Sous l'infime mais forte aspiration des trompes
de papillons, elles ne bougent plus.
Ensuite, elles descendent par les racines dans la terre amie,
abondante en bien des choses, quand on sait la prendre.   12
Joie, joie qui envahit comme envahit la panique, joie comme
sous une couverture.
Il faut ensuite ramener à terre les petits des Meidosems qui,
perdus, éperdus dans les arbres, ne peuvent s'en détacher.   16

Les menacer, ou encore les humilier. Ils s'en reviennent alors, on les détache sans peine et on les ramène, emplis de jus végétal et de ressentiment.

*   *   *

Il se mue en cascades, en fissures, en feu. C'est être Meidosem   20
que de se muer ainsi en moires changeantes.
Pourquoi?
Au moins, ce ne sont pas des plaies. Et va le Meidosem. Plutôt
reflets et jeux du soleil et de l'ombre que souffrir, que méditer.   24
Plutôt cascades.

*   *   *

Sur une grande pierre pelée, qu'est-ce qu'il attend, ce Meidosem? Il attend des tourbillons. Dans ces tourbillons de Meidosems
emmêlés, frénétiques, est la joie; or la germination meidosem   28
augmente avec l'exaltation.

D'autres Meidosems attendent plus loin, fils légers qui désirent
s'emmêler à d'autres fils, qui attendent des effilochés du même
genre, qui passent en flocons emportés par le vent, qui eux-   32
mêmes attendent un courant qui les soulève, les ascende et
leur fasse rejoindre ou des isolés ou une troupe plus grosse de
'Meidosems de l'air'.

La chance fait parfois qu'ils rencontrent les algues d'âmes.   36
Mystérieux est leur commerce, mais il existe.

Tremblements, emportement cyclonique, ce sont les risques
de l'air. Ce sont les joies de l'air. Comment ne pas se laisser
emporter par la haute bourrasque meidosem?   40
Sans doute elle a une fin.

Il y a en effet constamment dans le ciel des chutes de Meidosems.
On y devient presque indifférent. Il faut être parmi les proches
pour y faire attention. Certains ont les yeux en l'air seulement   44
pour voir tomber.

*   *   *

Des ailes sans têtes, sans oiseaux, des ailes pures de tout corps
volent vers un ciel solaire, pas encore resplendissant, mais qui
lutte fort pour le resplendissement, trouant son chemin dans   48
l'empyrée comme un obus de future félicité.
Silence. Envols.
Ce que ces Meidosems ont tant désiré, enfin ils y sont arrivés.
Les voilà.   52

Dans le cercle brisant de la jeune magicienne

Jamais ostensoir plus clair n'apparut dans les prières et les
adorations
Jamais soucoupe volante, plus démente, ne tourna magnésienne,
aluminiée dans un ciel déchiré   4
Comme une goutte brûlante apparaissant à la fleur de nerfs
désarmés, surarmés aussitôt qui voudraient renverser le monde,
tu parais et tu pars, lumière qui m'as transpercé.

Jamais tête folle draguée dans la carrière de la nuit   8
Jamais halètement et grincement de dragonne, rêvée dans
l'égarement des sabbats
Jamais cinglement des fusées, des éléments éclatés, des évi-
dences extraordinaires, plus torrentiellement ne dévala contre 12
moi.

Jamais surprise et admiration d'enfants, braillant dans une
barrique, ne réunit joie gonflée de tant d'échos, de ronflements,
de renflements d'orage, de senteurs, de retours à d'autres âges, 16
de vrilles, de ravages dans les lignes droites, de brassages, de
retours à la caverne. . .là où Phou lance ses troupes, où déboulent
les meutes, où les cathédrales sont liquides et en formation. . .
mais tu pars, amour, et tu disparais. . .   20

Ainsi, ce jour-là fut . . .

Ainsi, ce jour-là fut celui de la grande ouverture. Oubliant
les images de pacotille qui du reste disparurent, cessant de lutter,
je me laissai traverser par le fluide qui, pénétrant par le sillon,
paraissait venir du bout du monde. Moi-même j'étais torrent,   4
j'étais noyé, j'étais navigation. Ma salle de la constitution, ma
salle des ambassadeurs, ma salle des cadeaux et des échanges
où je fais entrer l'étranger pour un premier examen, j'avais
perdu toutes mes salles avec mes serviteurs. J'étais seul, tumul- 8
tueusement secoué comme un fil crasseux dans une lessive éner-
gique. Je brillais, je me brisais, je criais jusqu'au bout du monde.
Je frissonnais. Mon frissonnement était un aboiement. J'avançais,
je dévalais, je plongeais dans la transparence, je vivais cristalline- 12
ment.

Parfois un escalier de verre, un escalier en échelle de Jacob,
un escalier de plus de marches que je n'en pourrais gravir en
trois vies entières, un escalier aux dix millions de degrés, un   16
escalier sans paliers, un escalier jusqu'au ciel, l'entreprise la

plus formidable, la plus insensée depuis la tour de Babel, montait
dans l'absolu. Tout à coup je ne le voyais plus. L'escalier qui allait
jusqu'au ciel avait disparu comme bulles de champagne, et je   20
continuais ma navigation précipitée, luttant pour ne pas rouler,
luttant contre des succions et des tiraillements, contre des infini-
ment petits qui tressautaient, contre des toiles tendues et des
pattes arquées.   24

Par moments, des milliers de petites tiges ambulacraires d'une
astérie gigantesque se fixaient sur moi si intimement que je ne
pouvais savoir si c'était elle qui devenait moi, ou moi qui étais
devenu elle. Je me serrais, je me rendais étanche et contracté,   28
mais tout ce qui se contracte ici promptement doit se relâcher,
l'ennemi même se dissout comme sel dans l'eau, et de nouveau
j'étais navigation, navigation avant tout, brillant d'un feu pur et
blanc, répondant à mille cascades, à fosses écumantes et à rav-   32
inements virevoltants, qui me pliaient et me plissaient au passage.
Qui coule ne peut habiter.

Le ruissellement qui en ce jour extraordinaire passa par moi
était quelque chose de si immense, inoubliable, unique que je   36
pensais, que je ne cessais de penser: 'Une montagne malgré son
inintelligence, une montagne avec ses cascades, ses ravins, ses
pentes de ruissellements serait dans l'état où je me trouve, plus
capable de me comprendre qu'un homme...'   40

Robert Desnos

(1900–1945)

Robert Desnos is one of the early adherents of Surrealism, a movement from which he broke away in 1929. He shared with other Surrealists an interest in dreams, 'second states' and the subconscious; of all the group, he was the most gifted at drawing inspiration from the experiments in hypnosis and 'automatic writing', conducted with the hope of releasing the mind's imaginative potential and the wonders of the *insolite*. He discovered his own method of linking the surprises of the subconscious and the world of language. In *Rrose Sélavy* (1922 – 3), for example, a collection of word-games apparently suggested to Desnos during his *séances*, it is the sounds and orthography of words which are left to generate the idea and the image, so that the rational process of shaping thoughts is abandoned and the colourful, but perfectly valid, unreason of language and the subconscious allowed to take flight. There are some surprisingly poetic results:

O mon crâne, étoile de nacre qui s'étiole.

or

Les lois de nos désirs sont des dés sans loisir.

But such cultivation of gratuitousness has its limits. His adeptness with language and his taste for the irrational develop very differently in *A la Mystérieuse* (1926) in which they are wedded to a more traditional and moving inspiration. An urgent love, and not some artificial mechanism, becomes the major force. Whether reciprocated or not, whether tender or cruel, it opens and closes the door easily into the poet's subconscious, spanning the frontiers between dream and reality, absence and presence, illusion and truth, confusing them as if they were one and the same thing, sometimes producing a refreshing 'surreality', sometimes a nebula of doubts. The constant shuttling between these states creates much of the tension and uncertainty of *A la Mystérieuse*, a tension aggravated by the poet's disturbed sense of time, for not only are many of the poems balanced at a critical moment in a love-relationship, but his own time-factor seems problematical and his personality dispersed to different points of the temporal compass. Unlike Eluard's poems, those of *A la Mystérieuse* strike a note of solitary and divided lyricism: Desnos dreams of the woman rather than holds her; he affirms that his love is alive and unique, and yet admits its passing; and it is not only in *A la faveur de la nuit* that one feels that he is gazing lovingly at a closed window.

The Desnos of *A la Mystérieuse* achieves an unusual combination of two different styles: the familiar language of love, and the challenging language of the unexplained image; a simple and fluent sentimental lyricism open to all, and the jerky apparition of the flotsam and jetsam of the imagination, the subconscious or the private memory. It is a combination with a special appeal: later in his career, Desnos writes that an ideal of poetry would be to unite 'le langage populaire, le plus populaire, à une atmosphère inexprimable, à une imagerie aiguë'. But this curious blending of styles, while undoubtedly an enriching feature of much of his work, gives a hint of a man who is unsure of his poetry's value (perhaps unsure of the kind of poetry to which he belongs) and who even says so: in *Non, l'amour n'est pas mort*, he begins by rejecting the decorative aspects of his style; in *Comme une main à l'instant de la mort*, he talks dismissively of his imagery as irrelevant 'paysages'; in another poem he admits his 'rhétorique facile où le flot meurt sur les plages, où la corneille vole dans des usines en ruines...'; and even in *La Voix de Robert Desnos* his words, creating an incantatory spell and apparently all-powerful, are impotent to recall the presence of the loved one. So, one is aware again of the poet's uncertain stance at the boundary between real experience and verbal experience, the genuine and the figurative.

But to think of Desnos primarily as a melancholic and self-doubting love-poet would be false. Quite apart from the bounding verbal humour and spirit of linguistic liberation of *Rrose Sélavy*, his work contains some of the most spontaneous and unselfconscious lyricism of the century: ardent, joyful, magically creative, warmly human, boyish in its effervescence and openness. It would be wrong, too, to adopt the poet's doubts about the efficacy of his own style. Desnos is masterly in his handling of free verse, his exploitation of litanic rhythm, his juxtaposition of clipped phrases and long developments, his adjustments of pace and mood, and his sense of overall form (seen especially in *J'ai tant rêvé de toi*). Even when the poet is expressing the passion of his experience, there is a controlling mind perceptible in the ordered structure of the verse, exerting only an instinctive control perhaps, but riding the surge of feelings and imagination with an almost uncanny balance. The poems selected here are fine illustrations of his search for a poetry which would be simultaneously 'délirante et lucide'. The passionate lover and the conscious poet, the surrealist dreamer and the plain speaker meet in Desnos.

SELECT BIBLIOGRAPHY

P. Berger, *Robert Desnos*, (Poètes d'aujourd'hui, 16), Seghers, 1970.

R. Buchole, *L'Evolution poétique de Robert Desnos*, Académie royale de langue et de littérature françaises de Belgique, 1956.

M. A. Caws, 'Robert Desnos' in *The Poetry of Dada and Surrealism*, Princeton University Press, 1970.

Europe: Revue mensuelle, Nos. 517–18 (May-June, 1972).

I. D. McFarlane, 'Love and the "accessoire poétique" in the Poetry of Robert Desnos' in *Order and Adventure in Post-Romantic French Poetry*, (eds. E. M. Beaumont, J. M. Cocking and J. Cruickshank), Blackwell, 1973.

J. H. Matthews, 'Robert Desnos (1900–1945)' in *Surrealist Poetry in France*, Syracuse University Press, 1969.

J'ai tant rêvé de toi

J'ai tant rêvé de toi que tu perds ta réalité.

Est-il encore temps d'atteindre ce corps vivant et de baiser sur cette bouche la naissance de la voix qui m'est chère?

J'ai tant rêvé de toi que mes bras habitués en étreignant ton   4
ombre à se croiser sur ma poitrine ne se plieraient pas au contour de ton corps, peut-être.

Et que, devant l'apparence réelle de ce qui me hante et me gouverne depuis des jours et des années, je deviendrais une   8
ombre sans doute.

O balances sentimentales.

J'ai tant rêvé de toi qu'il n'est plus temps sans doute que je m'éveille. Je dors debout, le corps exposé à toutes les apparences   12
de la vie et de l'amour et toi, la seule qui compte aujourd'hui pour moi, je pourrais moins toucher ton front et tes lèvres que les premières lèvres et le premier front venu.

J'ai tant rêvé de toi, tant marché, parlé, couché avec ton fantôme   16
qu'il ne me reste plus peut-être, et pourtant, qu'à être fantôme parmi les fantômes et plus ombre cent fois que l'ombre qui se promène et se promènera allégrement sur le cadran solaire de
ta vie.   20

Non, l'amour n'est pas mort

Non, l'amour n'est pas mort en ce cœur et ces yeux et cette bouche qui proclamait ses funérailles commencées.

Ecoutez, j'en ai assez du pittoresque et des couleurs et du charme.   4

J'aime l'amour, sa tendresse et sa cruauté.

Mon amour n'a qu'un seul nom, qu'une seule forme.

Tout passe. Des bouches se collent à cette bouche.
Mon amour n'a qu'un nom, qu'une forme.   8
Et si quelque jour tu t'en souviens
O toi, forme et nom de mon amour,
Un jour sur la mer entre l'Amérique et l'Europe,
A l'heure où le rayon final du soleil se réverbère sur la surface   12
ondulée des vagues, ou bien une nuit d'orage sous un arbre dans la
campagne ou dans une rapide automobile,
Un matin de printemps boulevard Malesherbes,
Un jour de pluie,   16
A l'aube avant de te coucher,
Dis-toi, je l'ordonne à ton fantôme familier, que je fus seul
à t'aimer davantage et qu'il est dommage que tu ne l'aies pas
connu.   20
Dis-toi qu'il ne faut pas regretter les choses: Ronsard avant
moi et Baudelaire ont chanté le regret des vieilles et des mortes
qui méprisèrent le plus pur amour.
Toi quand tu seras morte   24
Tu seras belle et toujours désirable.
Je serai mort déjà, enclos tout entier en ton corps immortel,
en ton image étonnante présente à jamais parmi les merveilles
perpétuelles de la vie et de l'éternité, mais si je vis   28
Ta voix et son accent, ton regard et ses rayons,
L'odeur de toi et celle de tes cheveux et beaucoup d'autres
choses encore vivront en moi,
En moi qui ne suis ni Ronsard ni Baudelaire,   32
Moi qui suis Robert Desnos et qui pour t'avoir connue et
aimée,
Les vaux bien.
Moi qui suis Robert Desnos, pour t'aimer   36
Et qui ne veux pas attacher d'autre réputation à ma mémoire
sur la terre méprisable.

Comme une main à l'instant de la mort

Comme une main à l'instant de la mort et du naufrage se
dresse comme les rayons du soleil couchant, ainsi de toutes
parts jaillissent tes regards.
Il n'est plus temps, il n'est plus temps peut-être de me voir,   4
Mais la feuille qui tombe et la roue qui tourne te diront que
rien n'est perpétuel sur terre,
Sauf l'amour,
Et je veux m'en persuader.   8

Des bateaux de sauvetage peints de rougeâtres couleurs,
Des orages qui s'enfuient,
Une valse surannée qu'emportent le temps et le vent durant
les longs espaces du ciel.   12
Paysages.
Moi je n'en veux pas d'autres que l'étreinte à laquelle j'aspire,
Et meure le chant du coq.
Comme une main à l'instant de la mort se crispe, mon cœur   16
se serre.
Je n'ai jamais pleuré depuis que je te connais.
J'aime trop mon amour pour pleurer.
Tu pleureras sur mon tombeau,   20
Ou moi sur le tien.
Il ne sera pas trop tard.
Je mentirai. Je dirai que tu fus ma maîtresse
Et puis vraiment c'est tellement inutile,   .   24
Toi et moi, nous mourrons bientôt.

A la faveur de la nuit

Se glisser dans ton ombre à la faveur de la nuit.
Suivre tes pas, ton ombre à la fenêtre,
Cette ombre à la fenêtre c'est toi, ce n'est pas une autre, c'est
toi.   4
N'ouvre pas cette fenêtre derrière les rideaux de laquelle tu
bouges.
Ferme les yeux.
Je voudrais les fermer avec mes lèvres.   8
Mais la fenêtre s'ouvre et le vent, le vent qui balance bizarrement
la flamme et le drapeau entoure ma fuite de son manteau.
La fenêtre s'ouvre: ce n'est pas toi.
Je le savais bien.   12

La Voix de Robert Desnos

Si semblable à la fleur et au courant d'air
au cours d'eau aux ombres passagères
au sourire entrevu ce fameux soir à minuit
si semblable à tout au bonheur et à la tristesse   4
c'est le minuit passé dressant son torse nu au-dessus des beffrois
    et des peupliers
j'appelle à moi ceux-là perdus dans les campagnes
les vieux cadavres les jeunes chênes coupés   8

les lambeaux d'étoffe pourrissant sur la terre et le linge séchant aux
    alentours des fermes
j'appelle à moi les tornades et les ouragans
les tempêtes les typhons les cyclones   12
les raz de marée
les tremblements de terre
j'appelle à moi la fumée des volcans et celle des cigarettes
les ronds de fumée des cigares de luxe   16
j'appelle à moi les amours et les amoureux
j'appelle à moi les vivants et les morts
j'appelle les fossoyeurs j'appelle les assassins
j'appelle les bourreaux j'appelle les pilotes les maçons et les 20
    architectes
les assassins
j'appelle la chair
j'appelle celle que j'aime   24
j'appelle celle que j'aime
j'appelle celle que j'aime
le minuit triomphant déploie ses ailes de satin et se pose sur mon
    lit   28
les beffrois et les peupliers se plient à mon désir
ceux-là s'écroulent ceux-là s'affaissent
les perdus dans la campagne se retrouvent en me trouvant
les vieux cadavres ressuscitent à ma voix   32
les jeunes chênes coupés se couvrent de verdure
les lambeaux d'étoffe pourrissant dans la terre et sur la terre
claquent à ma voix comme l'étendard de la révolte
le linge séchant aux alentours des fermes habille d'adorables 36
    femmes que je n'adore pas
qui viennent à moi
obéissent à ma voix et m'adorent
les tornades tournent dans ma bouche   40
les ouragans rougissent s'il est possible mes lèvres
les tempêtes grondent à mes pieds
les typhons s'il est possible me dépeignent
je reçois les baisers d'ivresse des cyclones   44
les raz de marée viennent mourir à mes pieds
les tremblements de terre ne m'ébranlent pas mais font tout crouler
    à mon ordre
la fumée des volcans me vêt de ses vapeurs   48
et celle des cigarettes me parfume
et les ronds de fumée des cigares me couronnent
les amours et l'amour si longtemps poursuivis se réfugient en moi

les amoureux écoutent ma voix 52
les vivants et les morts se soumettent et me saluent les premiers
    froidement les seconds familièrement
les fossoyeurs abandonnent les tombes à peine creusées et déclarent
    que moi seul puis commander leurs nocturnes travaux 56
les assassins me saluent
les bourreaux invoquent la révolution
invoquent ma voix
invoquent mon nom 60
les pilotes se guident sur mes yeux
les maçons ont le vertige en m'écoutant
les architectes partent pour le désert
les assassins me bénissent 64
la chair palpite à mon appel

celle que j'aime ne m'écoute pas
celle que j'aime ne m'entend pas
celle que j'aime ne me répond pas. 68

Ombres des arbres dans l'eau...

Ombres des arbres dans l'eau
Si nette si claire si propre
Est-il possible qu'un tel miroir si sale et lourd de vase et
    lourd de nuages et lourd de mort 4
Vous reflète si correctement
Martin pêcheur
Je distingue tes couleurs
Je distingue celle des fleurs 8
Et celle des péniches qui passent
Et tout ça n'est que reflets
Dans une eau sale et vaseuse et malsaine.

NOTES

Victor Hugo

Souvenir de la nuit du 4

After Napoleon III's *coup d'état* in 1851, Hugo went into exile in Jersey where he wrote *Les Châtiments*, a collection of poems into which he poured all his contempt for 'monsieur Bonaparte' and his regime. This poem recalls the death of a child on the streets of Paris on December 4th, two days after the *coup*. Seething with scorn, the poet unleashes an attack on the established order, an attack based on essential human emotions rather than any political doctrine. He lets the scene speak for itself and, until the last twelve lines, Hugo the polemicist is quite self-effacing.

Study the initial description and the way in which the accumulation of short sentences suggests a grief which has numbed expression (only one sentence breaks the deliberately monotonous order of presentation to give vivid exposure to the figure of the dead boy). The reader is drawn dramatically into the scene by the violent image of the gashed blackberry in line 10 (one of the very few images in the poem) and by the question which demands commitment, and he joins the poet and his companions as a witness of the old woman's pathetic attempts to bring light and warmth to the child's corpse. The scene is narrowed down to the circle of lamplight or firelight (lines 13 and 20), reminding one of those paintings of Mary's lamentation for Christ which use a similar technique to focus attention (the parallel is strengthened by the 'Jésus' of line 36). Notice the particularity of detail which strikes an authentic note (e.g. the symbolic palm-branch on the holy picture which evokes the simple faith of the household); the variety of emotions implicit in the grandmother's outburst (bewilderment, protest, ingenuousness, helplessness). Hugo shows a masterly ability to capture the rhythms of common speech and the high emotion of the old woman's words which in their pure humanity and grief are a disarming indictment of indiscriminate violence. Which do you think the more effective method of fighting brutal injustice: the documentary approach of the first section or the bitter satire of the poet's closing remarks? Would something essential be missing without the last twelve lines? Why does Hugo mention specifically Saint-Cloud, a fashionable suburb of Paris which used to boast a fine château, the scene of many historic events? Throughout the poem, Hugo handles his verse-form with great subtlety: study, for example, the occasional initial and seventh-syllable stress, and the contrasting use of end-stopped and run-on lines.

Compare this piece with Rimbaud's *Le Dormeur du val* in aims, techniques and artistic effects: which do you find the more successful? Compare also the depiction of two radically separate worlds as shown here with that in Hugo's *Je suis fait d'ombre et de marbre*...

L'Homme a ri

This piece of violent invective from *Les Châtiments* was written in response to a report in the *Journaux élyséens*, part of which Hugo uses as his epigraph. From his exile, the poet launched his searing counter-thrust. The glorious leader of the *coup d'état* is reduced to a common criminal, condemned by history, jeered by the mob and fit for branding. Study the sustained development of this image and its climax in the dramatic personal confrontation of accuser and accused. Hugo's scorn and bitterness are burnt deep into every line; they are found in the throaty rhyming of 'misérable' and 'exécrable', in the ironic use of 'triomphe', the abrupt, arresting *rejet* ('Je t'ai saisi'), the contemptuous 'toi', and in the sonority of the terrifying last line. The whole poem demands to be read aloud and with an orator's vigour. How easily do the sounds and rhythms lend themselves to strong, expressive articulation?

Notice how in *Je suis fait d'ombre et de marbre...*, although not from the collection *Les Châtiments*, there is also an ominous warning issued to kings of the world, the self-appointed demi-gods of an illusory temporal power.

Demain, dès l'aube...

This is one of the shortest and most poignant of Hugo's lyrical poems. The expression of emotion is uncomplicated and follows a neat linear development, but behind the direct simplicity is a sure artistic touch imparting subtlety to the poem's mood. Notice, for instance, the delicate blending of the four sentences in the first stanza: the mixture of strongly-articulated decisiveness ('Je partirai', carefully isolated for stress) and a more plaintive need on the part of the poet to justify his impulse ('Vois-tu...'); the movement between future and present tenses, between reference to landscape and insight into his emotions; the reciprocity between the expectations of the 'tu' figure ('je sais que tu m'attends') and his own inner compulsion ('Je ne puis demeurer'). The vigour and syntactical variety of the first stanza is replaced in the second by a single long sentence with a heavy enumeration (note the sad monotony created by the accumulated repetitive forms) dependent on the initial verb. How do the descriptions of mental state and physical posture combine to produce a picture of a self-enclosed *promeneur solitaire*, oblivious of the outside world? How is the metrical arrangement used to emphasize aspects of the poet's mood? The first two lines of the final stanza, reiterating his unresponsiveness to the splendour of nature, also mark a progression of time from dawn to sunset, which takes place in three dramatically brief movements (although the poet sees himself in a continual night): how appropriate at this point is the idea of oncoming night? In what way does the reference to 'ta tombe' take one by surprise, adding depth to the details of the first two stanzas? In September 1843, soon after her marriage, Hugo's young daughter, Léopoldine, was drowned with her husband in a boating accident and buried at Villequier (near Harfleur): how necessary is this information to a full appreciation of the poem? The revelation of the actual purpose of the journey is withheld until the last line. Note the unpretentiousness of the poet's gesture, the contrast between these humble offerings and the earlier references to the more grandiose ('la campagne... la forêt... l'or du soir'); study the musicality of this line, the symbolic connotations of holly and heather and their appropriateness as tributes on a tomb. What is the effect of writing the poem predominantly in the future tense? Note how the second stanza forms the dark meditative heart of the poem, broodingly intercalated between intention and action, decision and destination.

Compare the image of the poet as a solitary figure in a landscape with that in *Pasteurs et troupeaux*.

Paroles sur la dune

This poem, like *Demain, dès l'aube...*, comes from *Les Contemplations* and shares with it (as with *Pasteurs et troupeaux* and *J'ai cueilli cette fleur...*) the picture of the poet as a lonely thinker in a natural landscape, burdened by sombre thoughts. Here, he reflects on an irrevocable past, a present barrenness and dereliction and a swiftly approaching death; and meditates on man's place in the universe and the possible absurdity of human destiny.

The opening rhetorical repetition (supported by emphatic sound-patterns) sets a tone of heavy, trailing melancholy; the images are all funereal. Scene and mental state, the visual eye and the inner eye, are fused by the close parallel between the personal image of the second stanza and the descriptive image of the fourth: both depict dispersion and the persecution of helpless victims (cf. the implications of the word 'toison' with its use in *Pasteurs et troupeaux*). The poet's meditation deepens ('J'entends' becomes 'J'écoute'). The pattern becomes one of confrontation and query: confrontation between powerful forces of nature and humble mankind pursuing its industrious functions and seeking to bring life to fruition and order, between the firmament with its enigmatic purposes and the tormented question-mark of human life, between the sense of something eternal and the brief, seemingly illusory passage of man's existence. Study the themes of life as mere appearances, the loss of personal identity, the lack of a firm centre: how effectively does Hugo express his feelings in terms of the landscape? The figurative image of line 3 ('je touche au tombeau') is transformed in this crisis of despair into a real hallucination, as the earth seems to become a tomb and the poet, emptied of life, sees himself as a ghost; death becomes a tangible presence to be addressed in a chilling image of unyielding finality ('noir verrou') which contrasts with the flux and tenuousness of life. Study the effect of the return to description in the final stanza; the ironic introduction of a smiling summer scene; and the symbolic significance of the 'chardon bleu des sables' (is this comparable to the value of the flower in *J'ai cueilli cette fleur...* which follows?). One looks back finally upon the title to realize that its suggestion of a bare, eroded landscape was a premonition of the state of the poet's soul.

How well has Hugo used his shorter and longer lines for special effects? Note the balance of abstraction and concrete imagery, philosophical generality and personal searching.

For a very different view of a face-to-face confrontation between moon and poet ('Elle qui brille et moi qui souffre'), see Laforgue's *Complainte de la lune en province*.

Pasteurs et troupeaux

For a guided commentary on this poem, see *The Appreciation of Modern French Poetry*, pp. 64–7.

J'ai cueilli cette fleur pour toi sur la colline...

This poem shows Hugo at his descriptive best; outer scene and inner emotion become as one, so that the picking of the flower from the chasm becomes a symbolic act of salvation and love in the face of overpowering melancholy. The initial description is one of menace: the flower lives precariously on the cliffs, sailing boats hurry home to port, human activity seems to cower before the advancing night (cf. the description of the onset of night in *Pasteurs et troupeaux*: the 'chaume croulant qui s'étoile le soir', the opposition between 'la lune triomphale' and 'l'ombre' etc.). Study the use of contrast here (especially in the choice of adjectives) and the ambiguity of the simile (lines 6–9) in which the differences might seem more significant than the similarities. Does the sea-imagery here and throughout the poem have the same value as in *Paroles sur la dune* and *Pasteurs et troupeaux*? The dangerous situation of the flower and the threat of oncoming darkness enhance the value of the poet's act, so that, when he repeats 'J'ai cueilli cette fleur pour toi...', the words mean so much more; the poet's love appears strong enough to stand its ground against the black forces of nightfall. Compare Hugo's token of love with the traditional sweet-smelling red rose; what is the importance of the contrast? (Note that the only scent the flower has is that imposed on it by the blue-green seaweed, the harsh-sounding 'glauques goëmons'.)

Faced with images of flight and dispersion (lines 18–19), the poet decides to change the flower's destiny by endowing it with human significance. He gives it to love and the human heart which, in its depth and mystery, surpasses Nature. But the defiant act of saving the flower from a meaningless death is as incapable of stemming the poet's sadness as it is of pushing back the march of night and the poem ends with the triumph of 'le gouffre noir' (cf. the final image of the invaded soul with similar ones in Baudelaire's *Chant d'automne* and *Quand le ciel bas et lourd...*). After this conclusion, how successful do you consider the poet's act of salvation to have been? (Again one could make a significant comparison with Baudelaire's *Harmonie du soir*.)

From the stylistic point of view, study the use of tenses (the dominant imperfects throwing into relief the less frequent past perfect and present); the harmony and sound structure of certain lines (e.g. lines 1, 2, 15–16, 19), the rhythm and positioning of effects in others (e.g. lines 3, 4, 8, 17, 23 and especially the last line).

A celle qui est voilée

During his years of exile in Jersey, Hugo developed a passionate interest in spiritualism, partly awakened by the ghostly presence of 'la Dame Blanche' who traditionally haunted the Marine Terrace near Hugo's house. It is to this symbol of the unknown that he addresses this poem from *Les Contemplations*: a plea for illumination of the divine mystery, for some shining apparition to dispel the darkness which surrounds him in his groping search for knowledge of 'l'Idéal'. The very nature of this plea provokes images of light and dark which predominate in a piece remarkable for its sustained wealth of figurative language (used to give substance to intangible concepts).

In the opening stanzas (lines 1–20), a succession of images helps to establish between poet and spirit a mysterious relationship built on contrast and affinity. Their affinity (a common spiritual essence, a shared state of exile in a material world) is crystallized in the questions of the fifth stanza. In what way can one speak of contrast? Note how the poet can only define himself in seemingly endless complementary metaphors, and in terms of a variety of natural elements. The poet then makes his first exhortation (lines 21–40), accumulating in brilliant fashion images of light ('phare...rayon... blancheur...l'aurore...lumière') and communication ('regard...chant...sourire mystérieux') in order to persuade the woman to alleviate his solitary brooding. How well do the different expressions which he imagines she might assume correspond to the images he has given of his own definition and destiny? In lines 41–64, the poet intuitively senses the unknown, tantalizingly close, ebbing and flowing like the tides. He recognizes once again a kindred being and this affinity between himself and the feminine presence is stressed by a curious reversal of rôles: she becomes the meditator, the inquiring eye, the maker of comparisons, the link between microcosm and macrocosm (cf. Hugo's position in *Pasteurs et troupeaux*), while he becomes the observed, the unknown (line 49), associated with ghostliness and light ('blêmes...spectre blanc... lampe'). Notice how the excitement of being in contact with the 'Idéal' is accompanied by a greater poetic density (felt in the images forged by concise apposition in lines 54–5 and 60 and in the tightly-knit expressive sound-patterns of lines 57–60). As elsewhere, there is emphasis here on love, sensual contact, and the beyond taking on humanized expression. The poet's renewed plea (lines 65–88) is all the more intense now that we know the distance between him and his enlightenment is so small ('fais un pas de plus!'). In what ways are the images here similar to, or different from, those which characterized his first plea? It is noticeable that he has returned to the multiple metaphors of himself, trying them one after the other as if in search of the magic rôle which will ensure communication. But still total revelation is held back and the glimpse of divine truths through dream and vision (cf. Rimbaud) only aggravates by contrast the poet's awareness of his human condition (lines 89–116). The quest for communion with 'la Dame Blanche' has failed and the plea peters out in the desperate misanthropy of a man who suffers from humanity's fallen state and the acute memory of a lost paradise. Study in this concluding section the boldly expressed images of degraded man, the self-deprecating final image of contact with the apparition (lines 97–100), the emotive use of repetition and contrast, and the almost exasperated sonority of the concluding stanza.

Pursue the links between the imagery here and in other poems by Hugo in the selection (e.g. 'l'arbre intérieur', 'gouttes de sueur' and *Je suis fait d'ombre et de marbre...*).

Booz endormi

This poem of Biblical inspiration is taken from one of the early sections of Hugo's *La Légende des siècles*, a huge epic undertaking in which the poet aims to trace humanity's progress towards enlightenment. Here, he takes the story of Boaz and Ruth from the Old Testament (Ruth 2–4), modifies it and adds to it (notably the idea of the dream which recalls Abraham's experience in Genesis 17, and the tree of Jesse, a concept often found in medieval iconography). The result is a poem which captures the serene dignity and wisdom of ancient mankind and the innocent vision of an ordered and unified world.

Study firstly the measured development of the poem, noting the particular significance of each of the four divisions, which Hugo insisted should be indicated by a star. The opening description of Boaz sets him firmly and totally in a natural landscape as an ordinary hard-working man, spending his day on the threshing-floor and his night amidst the bushels which are the reward reaped from this simple life of honest toil. The character study is marked by the mixture of literal, abstract vocabulary and the figurative language which is so frequently found in the Bible (most obviously in the Old Testament Proverbs and the New Testament parables). So the simple statements of lines 7 and 8, coming after the abstract judgment of line 6, take on a figurative value, and reflect the character of Boaz (godliness, a chastened purity, serenity); in a more explicit way the simile of line 9 uses concrete elements to epitomize inner qualities (his closeness to nature and his essential youthfulness). Note a similar use of the figurative in line 13 and especially the ultimate fusion of abstract and concrete in the syllepsis of line 14. How artistically has Hugo used the images of fire and water? How has he exploited the balance of his verse to suggest the order and equilibrium of Boaz's world?

The intermezzo (stanzas 7 and 8) concentrates the scene, stressing its dark, somnolent, rustic atmosphere, and then dramatically widens the perspective, showing Boaz in relation to time and to his race and pushing the mind back to the lurking dangers of earlier epochs. Why does Hugo introduce this glimpse of nomadic man? Notice that the reference to the Flood (Genesis 6–9) and to the ruling judges of Israel (Book of Judges; Ruth 1 : 1) compresses within a single stanza the time-scale of the first seven books of the Old Testament; this ability to take in vast dimensions at a swift glance is typical of Hugo's epic vision.

The third section unfolds in careful order: introduction, the dream, Boaz's interpretation and his questioning of God, conclusion and preparation for the final section. The Biblical echoes are again taken from various sources outside the specific story of

Boaz and Ruth. The mention of Jacob preludes the idea of a link between man and the heavens (in Jacob's dream in Genesis 28 : 12, the link is represented as a ladder). The comparison of Boaz with Judith (the heroine of the book of *The Apocrypha* which bears her name) is less precise in its function, but it does elevate Boaz's stature and thus prepares the way for the rather special event which will ensure his greatness. Study the imagery here, especially the significance of the recurrent tree-image (cf. the earlier 'Laissez tomber exprès des épis' or the picture of 'Ses sacs de grains...'). Note the contrast between Boaz's self-deprecating reflections on youth and old age (lines 49–56) and the poet's own more flattering comments (lines 19–24).

In the final part, the quiet presence of Ruth (herself a 'pauvre glaneuse') already promises fulfilment of Boaz's dream. It is here that all the themes of fertility and abundance (cf. man as the seed of the earth and 'As thou sowest therefore shalt thou reap'), youth and age and the great cycles of life are consummated. This closing nocturne is justly celebrated. It evokes a magical scene in which scent, sound, movement and light are muted by the general aura of serenity; in which any doubts raised by Boaz's anguish are evaporated by the fragrant night breeze; and in which the action of the poem moves almost imperceptibly to its close, culminating in the magnificent expansive image of the God-harvester which unifies the whole poem, links microcosm and macrocosm and emphasizes the poetic coherence of the universe, glimpsed by an innocent mind ignorant of reason, theology and civilization. Study the variety of evoked sensations which are contained in the nocturne. What is the effect of introducing proper names into this scene of universal peace? (Galgala was in Judea, Ur in Mesopotamia, and Jérimadeth seems to be a name of Hugo's invention.)

In this poem, Hugo has succeeded in giving the effect of Biblical style. One notices the short simple sentences, often confined to a single line (cf. the verse structure of the Bible); the consequent simplicity of certain rhetorical devices (chiasmus, parallelism, antitheses); the use of balanced phonetic patterns (e.g. lines 33–4); the frequency of the reassuring generalized comment, sometimes showing proverbial wisdom, sometimes a calm confidence in the vast routine of God's world. All these stylistic features (and others) contribute to the uncomplicated solemnity of a Biblical event, an event of immense importance in the history of humanity in that one branch of Boaz's family by Ruth produced King David ('Un roi chantait en bas') and Jesus ('en haut mourait un Dieu').

Jean Gaudon sees in poems such as *Booz endormi* Hugo's desire to '[faire] éclore l'objet dans une féerie verbale... manifester la beauté... faire du poème un objet de beauté'. Do you agree that this is the case with *Booz endormi*? Do you prefer the impersonality of this poem or the lyricism of those pieces taken from *Les Contemplations*?

Jour de fête aux environs de Paris

Les Chansons des rues et des bois from which this lively poem is taken is a collection of poems written in light, jaunty rhythms and, for the first half *(Jeunesse)* at least, in a gay, joyous mood. Here Hugo captures the holiday atmosphere of a summer's scene; the cares and inhibitions of life in the capital are forgotten in the pleasures of the outdoors (that most inhibiting of institutions, the 'donjon de saint Louis' – part of the present-day Palais de Justice – is thankfully 'à l'horizon', as are the chimneys and domes mentioned in the last stanza). The poem is alive with impressionistic details, each deftly touched upon in the short octosyllabic lines. Yet the description, for all its flitting details, has a definite pictorial unity with Paris in the background, the fields in the middleground and the 'fête' in the foreground. Notice how also, from the structural point of view, the picture of the carousing farm-workers dominates the centre of the poem as it does the centre of the 'canvas'.

The opening description can be compared to some by Verlaine (e.g. in *L'échelonne-ment des haies*): with an eye for suggestive imprecision, Hugo delights in the shimmering heat-haze which blurs contours ('lueur douce...groupes vagues'), softens the sharp face of reality and encourages the metaphor of the poppies as glowing embers. And well before Verlaine he makes full use of those characteristics of the *chanson*: allite-ration, assonance and internal rhyme (the most conspicuous examples being 'chauffe... sèche...champs', 'pleins...tambourins', 'l'horizon...donjon', 'Accable...éblouis', 'fournaise...braise...brebis'). How does each detail of the scene contribute to the general impression of heat, colour and serene gaiety?

The noisy introduction of the farm-workers changes the tone. How would you describe this new tone? Is it meant to jar with what has preceded? (Look at line 24, for instance.) The drinkers' disrespect for the constraint of law is neatly summed up in the image of the vine-prop ('l'échalas') and toll-gate post. In mid-nineteenth-century France, this would have had particular significance. The wine-tax imposed by Paris (and indeed by each large town) at its toll-gates meant that wine was always cheaper in the country (in out-lying Suresnes, for example) than in the capital; 'le poteau de l'octroi' was understandably a symbolic target of resentment for the topers of Paris.

The portrait of the ass is gently whimsical; the animal, in spite of (or perhaps because of) his traditional dim-wittedness (of which long ears are supposedly the sign), is able to accept the world and himself for what they are and to enjoy the simple pleasures of life. This fable-like stanza brings one away from the rowdy drinkers and back to a quieter scene, but one now more animated than before. What possible process of association might have made Hugo switch from the children running 'par volée' to the description of the walls of Clichy? The sight of the trundling cart leads the eye along the road back towards Paris with its skyline mixture of pomp and industry. How suitable is the rag-picker image? (Hugo specializes in personifying concepts of vast dimension; look elsewhere for examples of this facet of his imagination.) The poem closes in a series of contrasts to underline Hugo's theme: between the sinister 'chiffonnier' and the merry-making 'filles'; between the tatters of French monarchy which he carries on his back and the blossoming crown of flowers which the girls wear royally in their hair; between the distant architecture of the city and the simple features of the country-side.

Compare the zest for the outdoor life found in this poem with that shown by Rimbaud in *Roman*.

– Va-t'en, me dit la bise...

This poem is another from *Les Chansons des rues et des bois* but this time from the second part, *Sagesse*, which, according to Hugo, is the verso side of *Jeunesse*, the 'apaisement du soir' as compared to the 'frais tumulte du matin'. So, although the same short, lightweight metres are still present (here the hexasyllabic), the tone in *Sagesse* tends to be more sombre, more wintry. The context tells us that this poem is the first of four under the heading *Nivôse*, the fourth month of the French Republican calendar (December–January): why do you think Hugo preferred this term to the normal name for the month? (Compare this choice with Baudelaire's 'Pluviôse' in his *Spleen* poem.)

The brutal, ungracious opening hits one like the first blast of winter. The very curtness of the sentences contrasts with the long six-line development given to the reaction of 'ma chanson'; how does this formal and rhythmic contrast highlight the very different natures of 'la bise' (a virago is a boisterous, overbearing woman) and the delicate, timorous 'chanson'? In what way does the choice of vocabulary contribute? (*'Quos ego*', an expression taken from Vergil's *Aeneid* I, 135, is defined by Larousse as 'paroles qui expriment, dans la bouche d'un supérieur, la colère et la menace.')

The third and fourth stanzas both begin with biting conciseness, a horrified recognition that winter is here and getting worse; the surprise has yielded to acceptance ('Fin de la comédie/Hirondelles, partons.'). The season is over and, like a summer busker, Hugo leaves with the swallows. In what way do the bare descriptions of lines 13–19 help to suggest a winter scene? The conclusion is perhaps ambiguous: is the keyhole the promise of domestic warmth for the home-coming poet? or is the poet already at home feeling the draught whistling in?

What effect has Hugo succeeded in evoking through his use of the six-syllable line in this poem? For a glimpse of the variation of treatment given to cognate themes, compare this poem of winter with Baudelaire's *Chant d'automne* and Laforgue's *L'Hiver qui vient*.

Je suis fait d'ombre et de marbre...

For a guided commentary on this poem, see *The Appreciation of Modern French Poetry*, pp. 68–70.

Qui sait si tout n'est pas un pourrissoir immense?...

The literature of horror was an offshoot of the Romantics' search for intensity of feeling, and the vogue of Satanism and vampirism went hand in hand with the more sentimental forms of their movement. This poem is a good example of this morbid and grotesque strand, spun out by Hugo's imagination to cosmic dimensions. By adopting a type of Pyrrhonism, a doctrine which maintains that certainty of knowledge is unattainable, Hugo shakes our accepted view of the universe and suggests a frightening alternative.

The first stanza follows its provocative opening questions with a direct address to the 'contemplateur' who might be Hugo himself (cf. his rôle in *Paroles sur la dune*). Study here and in the rest of the poem the use of lengthened vowels to support the doom-laden stress of the poet's words (as, too, the predominance of resonant feminine rhymes). The idea of decomposition and death continues in the second stanza, this time accompanied by an unpleasant insect image and a macabre parody of the conventional poetic picture of dawn as the bringer of new life (cf. the final line of the poem which has a similar effect of parody). The relentless doubting is taken up in the second half by the repeated 'Peut-être'. What is the effect of the direct addresses, 'O vivants pleins de bruits', 'O mortels'? In what way is the final anthropomorphic vision of space a terrifying climax to the poem? As with horror films, the danger of this type of writing is that it becomes ludicrous; do you think that Hugo has avoided this danger?

SUBJECTS FOR DISCUSSION

1. 'Victor Hugo était, dès le principe, l'homme le mieux doué (...) pour exprimer par la poésie ce que j'appellerai le *mystère de la vie*' (BAUDELAIRE). Discuss.
2. 'Hugo's imagination embraces the picturesque and the profound, the tiny and the sublime, the personal and the universal, the contemporary and the eternal; his is a truly complete genius.' Discuss.
3. It has been said that Hugo is a master of dramatic antithesis. What evidence is there of this, in the structure of his poems, in his vision, in his phrase-making?

4. G.-E. Clancier speaks of 'son imagerie a la fois naïve et prodigieuse', Baudelaire of his 'images orageuses'. Study Hugo's use of imagery: are there any images or types of image for which he shows a predilection, and what main functions does imagery fulfil in his work?
5. Examine Hugo's vision of nature; death; human destiny; the divine.
6. Study the expressive variations (changes of rhythm, dramatic *rejets*, flexibilities of arrangement etc.) that Hugo brings into his verse-form. How true is his famous claim: 'J'ai disloqué ce grand niais d'alexandrin'?

Gérard de Nerval

El Desdichado

If some of the details of this poem escape interpretation, then at least its overall tension is not too difficult to sense. The mood wavers between poles of feeling (desolation and hope, certainty and doubt, defeat and victory) until the last two lines suggest a mysterious reconciliation.

What is the initial effect of the title which means 'the disinherited one' in Spanish? The first stanza is weighted with suggestions of darkness, death and dispossession. After the dolefully rhythmic self-definition (what part do the definite articles play?), every line carries an image of despoliation (the demolished tower, the dead star, the eclipsed sun). What might 'mon luth' symbolize? How has Nerval ennobled his melancholy? What era of time is evoked? Draw a detailed comparison between the second verse and the whole of *Myrtho*, showing how the reading of one adds to the understanding of the other. After such a comparison, one is tempted to identify 'toi qui m'as consolé' as Myrtho; but examine the possibility that the poet is speaking to his 'luth constellé'. Whereas the opening picture was blackness itself, the plea for a return of a happier time (cf. similar hopes in *Delfica*) sheds a welcome light 'dans la nuit du tombeau'. How do you account for Nerval's use of italics? The thought of the brilliant home of the ancient gods and the love experienced there reminds the poet that there was, and might again be, an alternative to his present dereliction; the example of harmony ('le pampre à la rose s'allie'), cryptic as it is, intimates an alliance and equilibrium to be regained, and this in turn prompts the questioning style of a man severed from unity and seeking his own true personality. Very typically, Nerval cloaks his personal inquiry in allusions. 'Amour' (Eros, the god of love) and 'Phébus' (Apollo, the god of light) represent the Golden Age. Lusignan, a king of Cyprus descended from the dukes of Aquitaine, married Mélusine, a fairy, whom he left when she betrayed his trust; this figure thus fuses France and the Mediterranean, history and legend, the themes of love and separation. 'Biron' poses different problems: the Biron family (linked also with Aquitaine) achieved a legendary reputation for valour in the sixteenth century (one of them is the dancing hero of a popular song); but Biron could also be (simultaneously, as it were) Lord Byron, idol of the French Romantics, a figure of revolt (cf. *Antéros*), a famed Don Juan and closely associated with the Mediterranean (he died at Missolonghi). The spelling need not disqualify this interpretation because Nerval elsewhere, in a clear reference to the English poet, mis-spelt the name. Is the reader any closer to understanding the significance of line 9 after the allusions have been explained? Do you see any vague pattern (connected with the ideas of love, light, different epochs, different places) which would link the two sets of allusions with the first two stanzas? Lines 10 and 11 not only expand the theme of love and that of a now-lost royalty, but also contribute to the confusion between two times (in which things are simultaneously past and intensely present). In *Myrtho*, there are hints of a duplicity in the girl–divinity; here, 'la syrène' is by legend both fascinating and fatal, and the queen's kiss may, as well as symbolizing love, presage danger and retribution (cf. line 6 of *Antéros*). But in a line of surprising self-assurance, Nerval dismisses such possible perils; he has descended into 'la nuit du tombeau' and returned victorious over his melancholy, and over the duality of woman ('reine...syrène'; 'sainte... fée'). What part has poetry (and, indeed, this poem) played in the victory? Does line 13 affect your reading of line 5? (Orpheus descended into the underworld in his search for Eurydice, crossing the river Acheron and overcoming all obstacles by the charm of his music. Having found her and then forfeited his right to bring her back to life by disobeying the one condition laid down, he was refused a second passage across the Acheron.)

Study the changing progression of mood throughout the poem; the evocation and merging of two different eras; the play of contrasts, alternatives and harmonies; the theme of dubious personal identity. In spite of the opening stanza, is *El Desdichado* more optimistic than the title might suggest? Alexandre Dumas seems to have thought that the only explanations for the poem's obscurity were that Nerval was mad when he wrote it or that the poet was not being serious: how would you refute these insinuations?

Myrtho

For a guided commentary on this poem, see *The Appreciation of Modern French Poetry*, pp. 71–4.

Antéros

The theme of this poem is twofold: inner revolt against Man's exclusion from a paradisiac age and defiant hope in the re-emergence of a primitive pre-Christian harmony. Nerval, the *déshérité*, seeks to give his dissatisfaction a certain grandeur and closer definition by providing himself with a mythological and Biblical ancestry. The protest is against Jehovah, the conqueror of paganism (cf. the 'duc normand' of *Myrtho* and 'Constantin' in *Delfica*) who is responsible for the passing of the Golden Age ('l'ordre des anciens jours' in *Delfica*).

The poem opens with a pattern of query and explanation: the 'tu' (the reader, a feminine figure as in other poems, Jehovah, or just a deliberately vague second person?) asks why, though physically vanquished ('col flexible'), the poet is inwardly rebellious ('rage au cœur...tête indomptée'); the answer lasts until the end of the first tercet. 'Antée' (associated in the mind – as is the first syllable of Antéros – with the prefix *anti*- and, therefore, with the 'contre' of line 4) is the son of Gaea (goddess of the earth) and Poseidon (god of the sea) and is thus linked with the terrestrial rather than the celestial, with the human abode rather than the vast heavens of Christianity. Study the suggestions in the second stanza that the revolt is the result, not of perverse desire, but of irresistible necessity and that the poet is fatally impelled. There is an ambiguity in the use of the Cain and Abel story: since, in the Bible, it is the retributive God of the Old Testament who puts a mark on Cain, one might think of God as 'le Vengeur'; or 'le Vengeur' might be Cain himself whom the French Bible describes as being 'irrité' and as having a 'visage ... abattu' when he learns that his offering to God has been refused while Abel's has been accepted, a description which links him closely with 'sa lèvre irritée'; or, thirdly, the avenger might be a symbolic Lucifer who fans revolt in both Cain and the poet. How does this Biblical reference complement the mythological allusion to Antéros, the avenger of unrequited love? The first tercet continues the explanatory tone; the poet's lineage now includes Baal ('Bélus') and Dagon, the 'false' gods whom Jehovah destroyed and banished to the underworld. As in *Delfica*, the final tercet takes a new direction; the violence ('rage au cœur'), the anger ('implacable rougeur'), the protest ('O tyrannie!') are muted and replaced by a quieter, more patient attitude. The poet's ancestors have initiated him in the rites of the underworld (Cocytus is one of its rivers; cf. line 12 of *El Desdichado*) and his solitary task is to protect the genitrix of the rebellious race to which he belongs (Exodus 17:8–17 recounts the disinheritance of the Amalekites). Note how the rare rhymes ('Cocyte...Amalécyte') yoke together the mythological and the Biblical and how swiftly Nerval changes from one to the other (the last line refers to the legend of Cadmus who, after slaying a dragon, planted its teeth out of which grew the founders of Thebes). The poet is to ensure the eventual resurgence of the Golden Age; the 'dragon vaincu' of *Delfica* will be reawakened and will breathe its legendary fire once again, as the dormant volcano does in *Myrtho*. The earth will slowly nurture the dragon's teeth: where else in this poem and in other poems by Nerval does one find the idea of the earth as the source of reinvigoration? Is this why Nerval attaches so much importance to plants? How does Cain's story (in Genesis 4) support the connection between revolt and the soil of the earth?

How complex is the mood of the poem? Would you agree with Norma Rinsler's comment on the allusions in *Antéros*: 'So tight is the construction of the poem that the emotion aroused by each of these names is determined by the sonnet itself, and not by any previous significance they may have had for the reader'?

Delfica

The poet, a female presence, a Mediterranean landscape, an atmosphere of legend and antiquity are the ingredients of *Delfica*, as they are of *Myrtho*. The title of the poem gives the clue that it concerns prophecy; the temple at Delphi was the place where Apollo uttered his ambiguous oracles. The poet and his mistress (herself connected with Apollo who, in myth, failed to catch Daphne before she turned into a laurel tree) regret the passing of the ancient gods; the poet, however, senses their renaissance in the shudder of the earth (cf. the volcano image in *Myrtho*). But that other prophetic figure, 'la sibylle', denies this hope by her continued sleep in the shadow of Constantine's arch in Rome (Constantine, a supporter of Christianity, fulfils the same rôle as the 'duc normand' in *Myrtho*).

For the poet who awaits the return of 'ces dieux que tu pleures', the love-song seems to contain proof of cyclic recurrence: it is old ('ancienne'), yet present ('cette') and everlasting ('toujours recommence'). The eternal theatre of this 'ancienne romance' is in the groves of the Mediterranean where the divinities of myth acted out their adventures. What symbolic associations are attached to the various trees? Study the musical texture of this first stanza, one of the most carefully orchestrated in Nerval's poetry. Notice the significance of the change from 'connais-tu' to 'reconnais-tu'; and the switch in lines 5 and 6 from grandiose architectural observation to the precise detail of human sensual involvement. The last two lines of the second quatrain add the notion of danger to the notion of idyllic love, and the dimension of underground, irrational legends to that of fresh, pastoral romance. How does Nerval suggest in these lines, as in the first stanza, the cyclic continuity of past, present and future? The implications of the two questions to Dafné lead on naturally to the confident assertions of lines 9–11: the Delphic oracle will pronounce once again, the Golden Age will return. Study the punctuation of the first tercet; the way in which it prepares for the change of tone from expectation to disillusion; the remnant of confidence provided by 'encor' which contains the promise that 'la sibylle' will awake some time;

and the cold, conclusive immobility of the last line which brings to a complete halt the excited hopes of the poet.

Compare the rôle of the girl in *Delfica* to that in *Myrtho*. What does Dafné's presence add to the theme?

Vers dorés

For a guided commentary on this poem, see *The Appreciation of Modern French Poetry*, pp. 74–6.

SUBJECTS FOR DISCUSSION

1. Nerval himself said that his sonnets 'perdraient de leur charme à être expliqués, si la chose était possible'. Does elucidation detract from, rather than add to, the pleasure of reading *Les Chimères*?
2. What seem to you to be the dominant themes of Nerval's poetry? Explore the way in which they interpenetrate.
3. J.-P. Richard has said of Nerval, 'A tous les points du temps et de l'espace, il projette des images mythiques de lui-même. Il se veut à la fois total, égal au monde et identique à lui-même, universel et personnel, éternel et temporel'. Does this seem to be so?
4. 'The charm of a poetry which is musical and mythical, sentimental and symbolic, luminous and obscure': is this a charm you feel in *Les Chimères*?
5. The sonnet-form is a highly rigorous and disciplined one, yet Nerval's manner seems exceptionally 'free' and fitful. How effectively does he exploit the sonnet structure (look especially at the patterns of question and answer, the technique of changing direction, the particular use of the final tercet)? Is it a good choice?
6. Supervielle once said, 'Il y a de grands poètes comme Valéry qui se sont beaucoup méfiés du rêve, qui ont mis de la lucidité à peu près partout, mais n'empêche que j'admire aussi, et peut-être davantage, une poésie comme celle de Nerval où il y a une place plus grande pour la folie, l'inattendu et l'inexplicable'. In a comparison of the two poets, would your preference fall in the same direction and for the same reasons?

Charles Baudelaire

Correspondances

This famous poem from *Les Fleurs du mal* (1857) is a useful starting-point for the study of Baudelaire's verse since it reveals several of the poet's characteristic features: his belief in a significant pattern beyond surface reality which links apparently disparate phenomena, his imaginative power which allows him to perceive these 'correspondances' and his sharp sensual awareness of the interrelation of colours, textures, sounds and scents which serves his aspiration for a superior beauty and induces a feeling of transport.

Study the development of the poem from a vision of man overawed by the dwarfing architecture of the natural world to a feeling of man's capacity to soar into realms of infinite freedom; from metaphysical generalizations ('La Nature est un temple...') to the more specific associations evoked by various perfumes ('Il est des parfums...'). How do these two movements within the structure (the first expanding and taking flight, the second narrowing and becoming more precise) complement each other?

(Notice elsewhere in Baudelaire how the particular, the tiny and the enclosed contain magical properties of expansion: e.g. in *La Chevelure* or the second section of *Un Fantôme*.) The opening stanza proposes an animate universe in which man lives only half-aware of the efforts at communication made by an invisible, mysterious reality (note how religious and natural suggestions are fluently linked by two simple interrelated metaphors). Man is conscious however of certain forms of contact emanating from nature: scents, colours, sounds; and from his sensitive reaction to these, Baudelaire postulates 'une ténébreuse et profonde unité' which lies behind the multiplicity of what we see around us. These stimuli may be attached to our different senses but are all part of a mesh of mysterious relationships (examples of which are given in the tercets). How does Baudelaire stress the idea of convergence and unity in the second stanza? Notice that even the sound-patterns (especially the consonantal arrangement of line 5, the internal rhyme 'profonde' and the half-heard repetition in '*une té*nébreuse...*/ unité*') add to the suggestion of a network of echoes. Not only do the tercets stand apart from the octet (which was concerned with a communication expressed mainly in terms of words and looks, sounds and light), but there is also a conspicuous division within them ('des parfums...'/'Et d'autres...'); what exactly are the differences between these two orders of perfumes and between their various associations (amber and musk are body scents, benzoin is used in perfumery and incense in religious ceremonies)? Is the final line a surprising conclusion?

Do you think *Correspondances* important as a statement of metaphysical belief, as an aesthetic manifesto or simply as a poem rich in imaginative vision? Compare this poem with Nerval's *Vers dorés*, Rimbaud's *Voyelles* and Cros's *Hiéroglyphe*.

La Chevelure

Here Baudelaire is inspired by his mistress, Jeanne Duval, a mulatress of striking attraction. *La Chevelure* is a love poem in which the sensuous female is used as a stimulus to the poet's memory, imagination and senses; it is a poem of ecstatic response to animal charm, of intoxication which is at once physical and spiritual.

The texture, perfume, colour, the rhythmic swaying of the hair all affect the poet's senses and provoke a swell of images which surges through the whole poem. Study the various metamorphoses which the hair undergoes ('toison... mouchoir... forêt... houle... océan' etc.); the imagery is impressively mobile, depending on metaphor rather than simile, and switching audaciously from one line to the next. What would you say is the dominant image?

The poem's shifting energy derives partly from the suggestive tensions within it: between future desire ('J'irai... je plongerai... saura... sèmera...') and the thirst for memories of the past; between the idea of escape and easy-flowing movement (notice the metrical stress on 'voguent... nage... houle...') and the idea of peaceful shelter and refreshment ('alcôve... port... pavillon... oasis... gourde...'); between images of land and sea; between light and dark. And yet the poet's imagination resolves all these in a marvellous unity. Examine the use of evocative vocabulary, especially 'moutonnant... encolure... pavillon (two possible meanings – canopy, flag – will give two different images)... crinière...'; and note the unusual juxtapositions ('amoureuse d'ivresse...féconde paresse... Cheveux bleus...'), lines of expressive rhythm (e.g. lines 13, 19, 25), the lilting sound-echoes and subtle internal rhymes. This is a poem which will yield up more of its secrets with each reading, so rich is it in unsuspected patterns of sound, image and suggestion.

Compare *La Chevelure* with the love poems of Eluard and Desnos.

Avec ses vêtements ondoyants et nacrés...

Here is another poem inspired by the same courtesan mistress. Although the physical intimacy of *La Chevelure* is replaced by a majestic aloofness, the description is equally vibrant with impressions of sensuality: the musical sway of her walk, the lissom body under exotic clothes which gleam and glisten with the sheen of mother-of-pearl, snakeskin and sea-swell. Baudelaire's descriptive technique often depends on accumulated images, sometimes echoing an earlier suggestion, sometimes strangely contradicting it by a play of opposites. Notice, for example, how the marine associations of 'ondoyants et nacrés' are taken up in 'la houle des mers'; how the desert image (line 5) is echoed by the mysterious sphinx (and cf. the oasis at the end of *La Chevelure*); how both land and sea images are used to evoke undulating movement; how female suppleness and tropical heat are contrasted with mineral hardness and emotional frigidity.

Examine the resonances set up by the wave of similes and metaphors. In what way is the woman's nature 'symbolique'? How has Baudelaire thrown into prominence his concluding line? What is the poet's attitude towards the woman? By way of explanation of the final word, one critic has pointed out that it was a fairly common belief in nineteenth-century France that courtesans were not capable of bearing children.

Un Fantôme

This poem was one of several added to the second edition (1861) of *Les Fleurs du mal*; it is clearly a late work written when the poet felt the premature oncoming of senility (note the 'déjà' of line 2). He can look only into his memory for consolation in his joyless existence; there he will rediscover the unforgettable beauty of his mistress. The sequence of four sonnets which make up one poem is unique in Baudelaire; normally, he preferred to write short poems in which it is easier to maintain a poetic intensity. The form he adopted here is a compromise. How successful do you think he has been in keeping a balance between the concentration of the sonnet form and the greater scope for development given by the poem's overall length?

The first sonnet's sombre beginning reveals the poet's despair, solitude, frustrated creativity and self-destructive torment. All this delays and prepares the introduction of the 'spectre' which wells up from his memory. What is the effect of the inversion, the repeated 'et' and the enumeration of verbs in lines 9–10? The capital letter of 'Elle' indicates perhaps that the apparition carries a symbolic value and represents the essential power of Woman (cf. 'nature étrange et symbolique' in the previous poem).

In a long poem there is time for the rise and fall of tone and for the leisurely development of a theme; so Baudelaire leaves the description of his 'belle visiteuse' until the tercets of the second sonnet and turns to address the reader. The theme of the digression (the restoration of past time) is nevertheless crucial to the whole poem and serves to implicate the reader by playing on his own associations. What is the link between perfume and memory? The spectre now becomes powerfully real, alive with youthful animality and captivates the poet with its scent. Study the careful choice of words in the tercets, the sound-links and the rhymes, which bring out a subtle duality of attraction.

The third sonnet, with its slow, extended simile born of awestruck contemplation, develops the painting image of lines 5–6. The woman transforms the wretched void of the poet's room into an artistic harmony, her own beauty enhancing, and enhanced by, the light-catching objects which surround her. How does Baudelaire dispel the pictorial immobility initially suggested in the quatrains? What are the main qualities of the description in the tercets? The use of a long adverb ('voluptueusement') in a decasyllable is unusual; is it well-chosen here? Develop the theme of the isolation from nature by means of artifice.

The final movement of the poem strikes quite a different tone. As the vision fades, the poet leaves the slowly-savoured eroticism of the previous stanzas and their memories of a passionate ('feu... fervents... vifs') yet soothing ('tendres... dictame') relationship, and returns, in overt rhetoric, to the anguished reflexions on the passing of time and the prospect of a solitary death. In the gallery of his brain, the radiant and harmonious picture of the woman dims into a skeletal pencil-drawing, paling with time. Trace the images of painting throughout the poem. What attitude towards Art is revealed? The last three lines replace an earlier version which read:

> Comme un manant ivre, ou comme un soudard
> Qui bat les murs et salit et coudoie
> Une beauté frêle, en robe de soie.

Of the two versions, which is the more dramatic? the more poetic? Do you think that the rather colloquial 'manant' (a churl) and 'soudard' (an insulting term for an old soldier) would have been out of place? Study the implications of the version Baudelaire finally chose and compare the conclusion with that of *Harmonie du soir*.

Harmonie du soir

For a guided commentary on this poem, see *The Appreciation of Modern French Poetry*, pp. 77–9.

L'Invitation au voyage

A seductive and beautiful poem, *L'Invitation au voyage* combines the theme of escape to an ideal country (cf. *La Chevelure*) with that of a lover's plea. The fact that from other sources we know that the country is Holland and the woman a certain Marie Daubrun is of minor importance; refusing to descend to the anecdotal, Baudelaire prefers to leave the identities poetically vague. The gentle musicality of the poem is the result of careful artistic choice: the sonorous rhymes (often rich and drawn close by the short couplets) which have loosely disseminated echoes throughout the whole poem; the fluid run-on lines; the shifting but never jerky rhythm (cf. this use of the *impair* line with its use in Verlaine); the alliterations and assonances (e.g. lines 11–12, 18–20, 29–31) and the restful, reassuring refrain. What is the effect of the seven-syllable line coming after the pentasyllabic couplet? Does the alternating verse-form (long stanza, short refrain) help to make this a two-toned poem?

The address of the first line suggests a calm, almost platonic love-relationship with the woman; but what evidence elsewhere in the poem is there to suggest also that the woman is capricious? Study the different emphases in each stanza (the flattery of the first, the mixture of sensual and spiritual persuasions in the second, the rich, sleepy indolence and the celebration of the woman as a universal queenly figure in the third); the varying qualities of light as the poem unfurls (make sure you have the right meaning of 'hyacinthe'); the changing tenses and the significant development from 'Songe' to 'Vois', the two inviting imperatives. The appealing abstractions of the refrain play their part in the invitation; their very repetition smoothes away all fears of a strange *là-bas* which, by the end of the poem, has become warmly familiar. To what extent are these idealized abstract qualities ('ordre, beauté, luxe, calme, volupté') illustrated in the main stanzas of the poem?

L'Invitation au voyage has often been called a lullaby. Does such a description devalue the poem?

Chant d'automne

Here is another example of Baudelaire's experimentation with poetic form; he fuses together under one title two poems which could very well stand alone. In the first part, the noisy delivery of a load of wood for winter stoves evokes in the poet's mind a dread of winter (the symbol of a foreseen emotional numbness, suggested also by the frozen, insensible heart) and a series of images all associated with hammering sounds (the scaffold being knocked together, the besieged tower being battered, the coffin being made). As elsewhere (e.g. in the *Spleen* poem 'Quand le ciel bas et lourd...'), Baudelaire expresses his anguish imaginatively by the deliberate interpenetration of the inner and outer worlds (lines 5–6); in this vision, his whole being ('mon être... Mon cœur... Mon esprit') is seen to lie vulnerable to the remorseless exigencies of life. Study the progression of images, so essential to the structure of the first part. The fourth stanza which is seemingly the most funereal introduces a change of tone (indicated by the suddenly restless rhythm of the penultimate line); the frightening realization of an approaching death awakens the poet to the lingering, autumnal beauty which precedes winter. What is the significance of the last line of this first part? From the point of view of style, look at the hammering rhythm of the enumeration in lines 5–6; the patterns of sounds with unpleasant associations ('*fr*oides... reten*tiss*ant... *fr*issons... *fr*émi*ss*ant'); the onomatopoeia (what do you make of the extraordinary sequence of 'ch-k-b' sounds in lines 3, 9, 10?); the use of close internal rhyme.

The second part, with its stress on 'douceur' (lines 18, 23, 28) and in spite of the belittling rejection in the first stanza of the mistress's powers (her love, the intimacy of her boudoir, the warmth of her hearth), has as its theme a plea for a calm, consoling love-relationship (even motherly or sisterly) before the poet's death. The volte-face after the first stanza ('Et pourtant...') dramatically conveys the poet's need to clutch at a last *pis aller* in the absence of the ideal, and his reluctance to abandon hope and sink into total melancholy and solitude. In the last stanza, the prospect of imminent death (in fact, Baudelaire died eight years later) again evokes in the poet a determination to savour the mellowed, now fading richness of his life. What has been the development in thought from the opening stanzas of the whole poem? (In this respect, consider the conspicuously parallel sets of adjectives: 'rouge et glacé... blanc et torride... jaune et doux.')

How successful is the fusion of the two parts into a single poem?

The themes of autumn and oncoming winter are not uncommon; compare this poem with Hugo's – *Va-t'en, me dit la bise*..., Verlaine's *Chanson d'automne* and (for a very different treatment) Laforgue's *L'Hiver qui vient*.

La Musique

Rhythm, whether it is that of music, the sea or poetry, is for Baudelaire a constant attraction and source of beauty. As he says, 'la douleur, rythmée et cadencée' can become joy. The enchantments of rhythm excite the non-rational side of his nature, stir within him a concert of emotions and give an enhanced awareness of living. In this poem, as the title might suggest, rhythmical movements and moods are of particular importance. In what ways does Baudelaire exploit the unusual alternation of two different line-lengths (the Alexandrine and the pentasyllable, *pair* and *impair*)? How does he use rhythm expressively? Notice how he accentuates the changes and fluctuations of mood (the matching sense of expansiveness which infuses lines 3 and 5; the sonorous swell, impelled by the alliterations, of line 7; the prolonged run-on effect which precipitates the poem into a precarious ride over the 'gouffre' in lines 11 to 13; and the final, halting sentence).

The swaying surge of music (as elsewhere in Baudelaire's work the rhythm of a woman's walk) acts here as an invitation to the poet: it takes hold of him and launches him on a journey towards the ideal, moulding itself to his sensations and emotions and intensifying them. Notice how elements normally thought of as threatening (mist, night, storm and even the 'immense gouffre') are welcomed as a stimulant and represent escape from the stagnant pools of *ennui*. But musical rhythms are not all turbulent and exhilarating; and the sea can be as still as a mill-pond. At these times, music becomes a passive reflection of the poet's own anchored spirit and despair. How far does the negative tone of the broken, verbless last sentence dispel the euphoria of all that precedes? Perhaps the sea, that deceptive symbol of the infinite, is not a release of the spirit, but a mirror in which one only reads heightened images of oneself.

How good an example is this poem of the way in which Baudelaire sees phenomena in terms of analogy? How effectively has he used the sonnet structure? Compare his use of the metaphor of the poet as a boat (and the broad stages of development of the theme) with that of Rimbaud in *Le Bateau ivre*.

Spleen: '*Pluviôse, irrité contre la ville entière . . .*'

For a guided commentary on this poem, see *The Appreciation of Modern French Poetry*, pp. 80–2.

Spleen: '*Quand le ciel bas et lourd . . .*'

This poem, both lugubrious and violent, depicts a one-sided battle between Spleen and Hope taking place in the poet's spirit. For Baudelaire, the feeling of spleen is one of intense weariness, inertia and stifled aspiration in which the poet, severed from that state of inspiration in which matter becomes vibrant and rhythmically alive, falls victim to some oppressive force; any hope of overthrowing the tyranny of depression is futile and soon crushed, leaving the poet prey to Anguish.

Trace the structural development of the poem: the movement from the vague and trailing 'ennuis' of line 2 to the ruthlessly specific 'Angoisse' of line 19; from the indeterminate 'l'esprit gémissant' to the acute personal reference of 'mon âme' and 'mon crâne'; from claustrophobic impressions of the outside world to morbid inner hallucinations. How are these developments interrelated and drawn together, and how does Baudelaire create the sense of a tightening circle (cf. the implacable narrowing focus in the other *Spleen* poem, '*Pluviôse . . .*')? What part do the repetitive time-clauses (lines 1–12) play in the build-up of atmosphere? Stanza 4 breaks the cumulative tension with a hubbub of revolt: by what means (look at the choice of vocabulary, its positioning, the effects of rhythm, and the grammatical function of this stanza) is the sudden protest of the bells suggested? What makes the final stanza, in contrast to the previous one, so emphatic and fatal?

Would you call this poem dramatic in its presentation? (Compare it with a five-act tragic drama, noticing how its structure differs from that of the poem '*Pluviôse . . .*') Study, finally, the different forms of imagery which combine to make the poem so impressive: the way in which stanzas 1 and 3 suggest inexorable imprisonment (pressed down from above, drawn in from all sides, simultaneously exterior and interior, metallic and liquid), while stanzas 2 and 4 depict a desperate upthrust (at first silent and then in a rage of sound, at first with a certain freedom of movement and then fixed tormentingly to one pivot); the combination of funereal and martial imagery in the finale.

Rêve parisien

Rêve parisien, with its long, excited account of the poet's dream followed by the brutal crash into reality, is a dramatic as well as descriptive poem; the thudding collapse from an ideal world into a tawdry attic could hardly be more sudden. But the retina of Baudelaire's inner eye still bears the picture of his dream which he conjures back in all its sparkling detail. The most striking aspect of the dreamscape is its artificiality and architectural man-made beauty. Baudelaire often claimed the superiority of the artificial, which was the arduous product of man's imagination and will, over the natural, which was out of man's control and an impure part of an evil world. In this poem one notices the repeated emphases on the creative will, even in a dream (lines 9–10 and lines 37–40). Study the elements which make up the dreamscape: the feeling of vastness and serenity; the images of water contained and water sparkling like rich adornments ('rideaux de cristal... le liquide enchâssait sa gloire'); the glittering, metallic richness; objects burning with an inner luminosity and independent of natural light; and finally the timeless silence of the scene. How does Baudelaire sustain the enthusiasm in his account?

The second part is the re-awakening to petty, material cares and the grim passing of time. Pick out the many contrasts which can be drawn between this brief conclusion and the first part. After reading the poem, why do you think Baudelaire chose the title *Rêve parisien*? Compare this piece with Cros's *J'ai bâti dans ma fantaisie...*: are they written in a different spirit; is Baudelaire's imagination tuned to different tastes?

Recueillement

This poem, written after the first two editions of *Les Fleurs du mal*, lacks both the heady sensuality and the desperate anguish of some earlier poems; it is instead a poem of composure and conciliation. After years of mental suffering, torn between an aspiration to a personal sainthood ('Avant tout, être un grand homme et un saint pour soi-même', he said) and the temptations of spiritual and physical vices, between the search for beauty and the nagging pettiness of his daily life, Baudelaire waits for the hushed oblivion of night and death.

The opening lines establish a commanding yet reassuring tone. The sentences are simple and the pace measured. What figure does the personification of 'ma Douleur' suggest? Consider, as a contrast, the picture drawn of the city's pleasure-seekers. There is also a stylistic contrast between the isolated phrases and separate verbs of lines 1–2 and the unchecked, sprawling syntax of lines 5–7; between the quiet, consoling expression of the opening and the extravagance of imagery, sound and moral atmosphere which follows.

How suggestive is the *enjambement* between stanzas 2 and 3? Notice that, while all the rhymes in the quatrains contain the sharp 'i' sound, in the tercets the phonetic quality of the rhymes is much less strident. The imagery, mingling urban details and *états d'âme*, becomes suggestively imprecise and open to the reader's imagination. For example, are the dead years women in faded dresses leaning over balconies silhouetted against the evening sky? or pastel clouds lingering on the Parisian sky-line? Is the 'Regret' which wells up inside the poet seen as a fountain or an under-current rippling the surface of the Seine into a smile? And what image does Baudelaire give to the dying sun (cf. *Harmonie du soir* and *Chant d'automne*)? Study the sonority of the last stanza and the elements which make the last line memorable. What is the effect of so many capital letters used throughout the poem? What are the implications of the 'love-relationship', unobstrusive at first, which becomes prominent in the phrase 'ma chère'?

Paul Valéry thought the opening lines and the closing lines of the poem magical but the rest inept; would you agree?

SUBJECTS FOR DISCUSSION

1. How well does Baudelaire combine the spiritual and the sensual in his verse?
2. Discuss Laforgue's comment on Baudelaire: 'Ni grand cœur, ni grand esprit; mais quels nerfs plaintifs! quelles narines ouvertes à tout! quelle voix magique'.
3. Investigate the theme of time in Baudelaire's poems.
4. How complex is the rôle of the woman in Baudelaire's work?
5. It has been said that Baudelaire brought a new awareness of the possibilities of rhythm and musicality into French verse. Study the rhythmic structure and phonetic texture of any one of Baudelaire's poems, showing how these features add to its suggestive power.
6. With reference to Baudelaire's poetry, consider the relevance of his own definition of artistic creation as 'une magie suggestive, contenant à la fois l'objet et le sujet, le monde extérieur à l'artiste et l'artiste lui-même'.

Stéphane Mallarmé

Brise marine

Brise marine is one of Mallarmé's best known works, perhaps because it is more traditionally lyrical in expression than his later poems, which become increasingly hermetic and impersonal. It replays the Baudelairean themes of creative sterility, *ennui*, the desire to plunge 'Au fond de l'Inconnu pour trouver du *nouveau*', and the attraction of the exotic journey. To what extent is this a poem of contradictory impulses; and is it true to say that the poetic ideal is evoked more in negative than in positive terms? Study Mallarmé's use of the verse to dramatize and give variations of mood and intensity to his themes of spiritual frustration and escape: what does the first line gain from being isolated by its punctuation and broken by the interjection; what effects does he draw from the *enjambements* in such lines as '... des oiseaux sont ivres/D'être parmi l'écume ...' and '... qu'un vent penche sur les naufrages/Perdus'; how well has he patterned the more expansive passages and the brief, heavily stressed exclamations at the beginnings of lines, and, in general, established an alternation between slacker movements and surges of determination? Study the play of contrasts: between images of a relationship at a contemplative distance ('... jardins reflétés par les yeux' and '... le vide papier que la blancheur défend') and the promise of a lyrical immersion ('... parmi l'écume' and '... dans la mer se trempe'); between the confined domestic ideal or the studious pursuits of the literary recluse and the call of limitless, untamed nature. One notices, even in this early poem, the density of Mallarmé's language (phrases such as 'la clarté déserte de ma lampe' and 'le vide papier que la blancheur défend' are, if not symbols, then condensed summaries denoting hidden depths of mental experience); his tendency to project human emotions on to less personal subjects and personify abstractions ('La chair est triste ...', '... que la blancheur défend', 'Un Ennui ... croit encore'); the occasionally tortuous syntax (the fragmented presentation of the subject 'ni les vieux jardins... ni la jeune femme' all dependent on 'Rien' with its singular verb). In what way is the theme of fertility developed in the poem? How do you explain the emphatic reference to 'nuits'? How is the idea of departure progressively intensified? Is there any special significance to be read into the image of 'mâts' which figures so obsessively in the final stages?

Does Mallarmé's treatment of the theme of the sea and the dream of escape strike you as being distinctly different from that of Baudelaire in, say, *La Chevelure* or *La Musique*?

Sainte

Here one imagines an old stained glass window, rich in symbolic depiction, religious suggestion and the aura of the centuries. The poem's original title was *Sainte Cécile jouant sur l'aile d'un chérubin*, indicating that the figure represented there, missal in hand and with ancient instruments at her side, is the patron saint of music: what has been gained by adopting the final abbreviated title? Mallarmé said of this piece, 'C'est un petit poème mélodique et fait surtout en vue de la musique'. Study its exceptionally delicate and widely disseminated musical texture (comparing it with that of a Verlaine poem like *Soleils couchants*): the play of internal rhyme, assonance, alliteration and sound-echo which somehow dissolves the formal structure of the poem and animates it with a more subtle internal music which seems to shimmer and ripple in all parts (cf. 'étincelant...ruisselant'). But it is also an architectural poem: it has the most studied symmetry, in which repeated words and similar parts of speech are set in matching positions, and, on a wider scale, the last two stanzas are placed in perfect apposition to the first two ('A la fenêtre...A ce vitrage'), as if two images or visions of the same scene. Mallarmé delights, in his poetry, in leaving one in doubt as to what is present or absent, real or unreal: in what ways does he do this in the first eight lines (compare 'recélant' with 'étalant', 'se dédore' with 'étincelant'; what is the effect of 'Jadis', and of the repetitions of 'vieux' and 'Jadis' together with so many present participles)? In the second eight lines, where the sentence-structure itself seems to lose its neatly visible contour, the window acquires a mysterious religious vitality (cf. 'ostensoir', with its idea of displaying a sacred symbol and its promise of spiritual communion, in Baudelaire's *Harmonie du soir*), as if touched by the wing of grace: the real instruments recede into the background ('sans le vieux santal'), to be superseded by a more ethereal source of resonance; all that remains of the figure of the saint is the poised finger-tip as an angelic force brushes across the window; and the imagined strains of the Magnificat make way for a supernatural soundless music emanating from a harp-shaped wing (cf. the link of association with the earlier verb 'se déplie'). Note that the whole poem is supported on the one verb 'être': what is the value of this? How suggestively has Mallarmé used a 'run-on' effect between the stanzas? What do you think the window symbolizes? Notice the poet's choice of unusual vocabulary drawn particularly from the realms of art and religion and not sullied with everyday associations ('santal' is sandalwood, 'mandore' is the ancient instrument the mandola, 'vêpre et complie' are the late evening services of vespers and compline).

Autre éventail

For a guided commentary on this poem, see *The Appreciation of Modern French Poetry*, pp. 83–6.

Petit air II

The image of the bird and its relationship to human aspiration is at the centre of this poem, as it is in *Au seul souci de voyager*... and *Le vierge, le vivace*..., as well as having links with the 'blanc vol' of the fan in *Autre éventail*, the 'aile indubitable' in *Quand l'ombre menaça*... and the 'plumage instrumental' of the Angel in *Sainte*, all of which represent the wing of poetry, the means of flight to the Ideal.

One of the most remarkable features of the sonnet is the way in which Mallarmé has used the syntax actually to *imitate* the soaring upward of the bird (Baudelaire has expressed the belief that 'la phrase poétique peut imiter la ligne horizontale, la ligne droite ascendante, la ligne droite descendante... elle peut suivre la spirale, décrire la parabole, ou le zigzag figurant une série d'angles superposés'). Study the development of the two quatrains: the way in which the first line introduces a note of undaunted energy and compulsion, and then links it with the upsurge of the poet's hope, before we know anything of its direction, meaning or subject; the separation of the two parts of the verb 'a dû...éclater' which gives an impression of 'reaching towards'; the long inversion, suspended in turn by adverbial clause, participial phrase and preceding apposition, which stretches up and up before finally meeting its subject 'L'oiseau', beyond which point the dynamism seems to trail away into disappearance and loss. How has Mallarmé made use of paradox in these eight lines? What suggests that this is a supernatural, perhaps even illusory, bird? Does each of the quatrains present a different aspect of mood?

Notice the strictness of the poet's handling of the sonnet form: the octet described an event, real or imagined (the flight of a bird beyond the confines of life and its self-elimination into the supreme nothingness of the beyond); the sestet represents speculation after the event, and doubt: from whose breast did the ultimate cry emanate, in that apparent moment of fulfilment, the bird's or the poet's? If the latter, then it is the poet rather than the bird who is really 'le hagard musicien' (why the word 'hagard'?), and the bird's body will be lying somewhere on a country path, defunct and useless, while his own hope will still be thrusting upwards (note the difference of tenses between 'a dû éclater' and 'qu'on n'ouït' and 's'y lance'). Do you find the isolation of the final couplet effective (cf. a similar division in *Toute l'âme résumée*... and in Valéry's *La Ceinture*)? Could one argue that Mallarmé has deliberately used grammatical obscurity in the last six lines to match the theme of doubt? What features of the poem might justify the title, *Petit air*?

Quand l'ombre menaça de la fatale loi...

This poem has a cosmic grandeur: it sets the individual ('yeux du solitaire') against the vastness of the night sky and the fathomless depths of space and the universe (a confrontation which Hugo often conveys with an awe-inspiring and disturbing power). Its main theme is a kind of crisis of faith: the struggle between a force which threatens to mislead and annihilate human idealism, and man's determined assertion of belief in his own splendour.

The allusive nature of Mallarmé's language, which states nothing but allows almost unlimited scope for interpretation, is most striking ('évoquer, dans une ombre exprès... par des mots allusifs, jamais directs' is one expression of his aim in poetry). What do you see as the meaning of the words 'ombre' and 'Rêve' which are set in opposition as the main symbolic protagonists? Why does 'Rêve' carry a capital letter and why should it be defined as 'vieux'? (Compare this emphasis with the repetition of 'vieux... Jadis' in *Sainte*, and the 'cygne d'autrefois' in *Le vierge, le vivace*...) Note that this dream is not a vague generality but deeply and painfully embedded in his physical substance. How well has the poet combined abstract and concrete images in the first quatrain? Make a detailed comparison between this stanza and Baudelaire's treatment of the dual image of 'aile' and 'plafonds' in *Spleen* ('Quand le ciel bas et lourd...'): in what way do the responses to a threatening situation differ?

The second quatrain offers a stately description of the 'heavenly vault' as a luxurious ebony hall, in which the well-known constellations lie strung out like glinting garlands (cf. the suggested interpretation of 'le Cygne' as a constellation in a state of 'exil inutile' in *Le vierge, le vivace...*). But this apparent magnificence is a deception, as if designed to beguile man into believing that there reigns over him a more prestigious domain than his own. How does Mallarmé suggest this deception? How well chosen is the verb 'Se tordent'? In what ways does the final line of this stanza reinforce the final line of the first? Note how the theme of light is developed: in place of these physical glints in the universe, doomed to die and threatened with blackness, the poet espouses a more reliable, immortal inner or spiritual light (cf. the development of Baudelaire's *Harmonie du soir*).

The tercets switch the emphasis from the vainglorious spectacle of the universe, distant and superfluous, to the luminous mystery of Earth itself and human genius. The tone is affirmative. By what means does the poet stress that the Earth is a centre of radiance and a greater wonder than heaven? (Note that, like the sky, it is a mixture of light and 'ténèbres', its own obscurity being that of time, in which its mystery is imprisoned, but by which it is not doused or negated.) Compare the verb 'roule' with the earlier 'Se tordent'; and the idea of a denial of space with the same idea in *Le vierge, le vivace...* It is important that *ennui*, a state of spiritual sterility, is not attributed here to man (as in Baudelaire's poems or Mallarmé's earlier work), but to the cosmos, coldly impassive, self-contained and self-repetitive, despite its constant metamorphoses and changing cycles. Notice how the final word 'génie' is given a fanfare by the use of prolonged inversion, and how the 'fête' or celebration (which seemed to be prepared by those many impressive 'guirlandes') takes place on earth as this single star radiates outwards as a blaze of light into the universe at large. What is the full significance of the reflexive form 's'est allumé'? Why are the constellations of space 'feux *vils*', and is there an irony that they are now described as 'témoins'? A famous quotation from Mallarmé casts interesting reflections on this sonnet: 'Oui, je le sais, nous ne sommes que de vaines formes de la matière, mais bien sublimes pour avoir inventé Dieu et notre âme'.

Le vierge, le vivace et le bel aujourd'hui...

This sonnet shows Mallarmé's ability to take a single image, in this case the swan imprisoned in the ice, and facet it with the artistry and precision of a diamond-cutter, so that it glistens with a wealth of suggestions. For this reason one cannot interpret the central symbol and sum up the theme in over-simple prosaic terms: Mallarmé wants his poetry, in opening imaginative possibilities, to remain evasive and therefore somehow intact.

The first stanza speculates on whether some new vital force of inspiration will come to tear open the frozen lake's surface. Note that the potential liberating force is described in terms of purity and beauty and as a beating wing (thus creating an affinity with the world of ice and the swan). Compare this with 'Je sens que des oiseaux sont ivres' in *Brise marine* and that outside force of flight which promises to free him from the arduous literary impasse and the world of restrictions. How do you interpret the word 'oublié'? Is there a tinge of despair in the fact that, even below the ice, one would only find the haunting presence of 'vols qui n'ont pas fui'? Compare the vacuous whiteness of the glacier with the image of 'le vide papier que la blancheur défend' in *Brise marine*.

The second stanza is the negative answer to the speculation of the first: the prospect of deliverance only conjures up the remembrance of a swan of yesteryear (note the link between 'oublié' and 'se souvient') who failed, in the past, to conquer a state of exile through its art of song. (The swan, one remembers, is noted for its silent beauty and not for its voice, and its song, so rare, is traditionally associated with the moment of death.) Compare this detail with the final line of *Brise marine*, where the poet's heart reaches out enviously to the facility of song of the mythical sailors, perfectly attuned to the spirit of space and the sea, in whom journeying and lyrical expression are reconciled. Part of the significance of the reference to winter may be explained by Mallarmé's description of it elsewhere as 'saison de l'art serein, l'hiver lucide': in this case, however, it is the season of simultaneous splendour and sterility (in fact the frozen purity, unyielding and unproductive, is the source of splendour).

In what ways does the sestet intensify the themes, especially that of the terrible duality of the bird's position (capable of flight yet trapped in 'Ce lac dur')? Note that, although its graceful neck can shake off the frost and the torment of immobility, its plumage and its wingbeats, which are its true celestial sound (cf. 'plumage instrumental' in *Sainte*), are inexorably imprisoned and earth-bound. Notice the tightly-knit field of reference, with 'blanche agonie' harking back to 'givre', and 'Fantôme' to 'cygne d'autrefois'. Compare the initial promise of the word 'vierge' with the idea of a condemnation imposed by 'son pur éclat'. Assuming that the final words 'le Cygne' refer, in fact, to the constellation of stars known as Cygnus (i.e. the superior symbolic and celestial manifestation of the figure of the swan), develop the implications of the words 'Fantôme', 'songe froid de mépris' and 'l'exil inutile'. This has been called 'le sonnet en *i* majeur': what are the effects of the unrelieved use of this 'i' sound?

Au seul souci de voyager...

For a guided commentary on this poem, see *The Appreciation of Modern French Poetry*, pp. 86–8.

Toute l'âme résumée...

Many of Mallarmé's poems touch on the theme of the nature of poetry, the poet's position and the limits of literary creation. This sonnet is more patently an *art poétique*. But this does not mean that his treatment is over-explicit. The octet presents only a complex metaphor; and it is not until the third verse that this is eventually related to 'le chœur des romances' (itself a suggestive periphrasis which is not necessarily a mere synonym for 'poetry') and then given a falsely simple conclusion in the final couplet which, ironically, has been adopted by critics as a neat summary of Mallarmé's view of art.

The basic image is that of the cigar. Note that the first stanza is concerned solely with the most nebulous aspects: a spirituality breathed into the air, smoke patterns succeeding each other and disappearing into space. What do the words 'résumée' and 'lente' tell us indirectly about Mallarmé's art, and how appropriate to his style (on the basis of your reading of other poems) is the image of the smoke-rings? Is the positioning of the verb 'Atteste' and the transition into the second stanza effective? Here, set at a distance, is the material object from which the ethereal figures have originated, but a material object which is being consumed ('savamment', another word which applies well to Mallarmé) in this artistic act. The success of this carefully controlled artistic transformation, however, depends on the intensity and brightness of the 'clair baiser de feu', the burning tip of the cigar (how do you interpret this 'baiser de feu', this point of union, in terms of poetry and has it any relevance to the kiss of space in *Autre éventail*?), and this in turn depends on the discarding of the useless ash or residue of used matter, so that it is no longer an impediment. The third stanza now establishes the analogy: why do you think Mallarmé has chosen to express this in *musical* rather than poetic terms, leaving the reference to literature at yet a further remove? How closely can you relate the elements here (the idea of flight, the reference to the lip) to the image of the cigar? Study the meticulously neat use of the sonnet form: is the poet flicking off the last two lines of moral or message (which, in being more explicit, are closer to the 'réel' and the 'vil' than any other part of the poem), as a humorous parallel to the flicking off of ash? Is he toying with the reader in that these lines, which many a person will clutch at as something more concrete, are in fact a rather clumsy and redundant 'rature' on what is otherwise an example of 'vague littérature', full of airy *correspondances*?

SUBJECTS FOR DISCUSSION

1. Mallarmé's poems have been described as 'le plus merveilleux prétexte à rêveries' (REMY DE GOURMONT). Would you agree?
2. Few poets have intermingled actual poems and images of the nature of poetry as subtly as Mallarmé. Study the richness of his view of poetry as it emerges from this selection.
3. It has been said that Mallarmé's imagination was obsessed by the fringe-area between presence and absence, being and non-existence. Can this be amply illustrated from the poems here?
4. What (in terms of imagery, vocabulary, handling of verse-form, arrangement of effects) are the most distinctive and significant features of Mallarmé's poetic style?
5. Does Mallarmé's obscurity detract from the appeal of his poetry? Compose a balanced illustrated argument for and against.
6. Analyse the themes of the journey, space, anguish and poetic song in Mallarmé's work. How are they interrelated, and how effectively does he use symbols, rather than intellectual exposition, to give them colour and depth?

Charles Cros

Supplication

This sonnet, written in octosyllabic lines, is built on the studied use of antithesis. Indeed the neatness with which the device recurs might appear too contrived for a piece expressing an all-consuming love; but the poem belongs firmly to a long European tradition of supplicatory verse in which the lover's skill in expression is a token both of the strength of his love and of his mistress' power of inspiration. Analyse the way in which the poet develops the theme of duality in the woman, looking especially at the contrasts between stanzas 1 and 2. Notice the suitable difference between the eyes, so expressive of inner spiritual depth, and the hair, that most atavistic part of the human body, and the most animal (cf. the imagery in Baudelaire's *La Chevelure*). After the dominantly physical description in the quatrains, the first tercet develops the duality on a spiritual level, while the second tercet neatly keeps back until the final line the supplication to the woman's heart, the well of her emotions.

This sonnet derives its polished unity partly from the rigour of its form, partly from its sustained antithesis and partly from the even tenor of its sound-patterns (look at the echo of the A-rhyme, [œ r] in the first tercet, the early internal rhymes in [ɛr] which herald the C-rhyme and, lastly, the reverberation of final [r]'s throughout the poem). The portrait in the octet acquires a particular richness and cohesion from its lavish internal play of sound; and the woman's imperturbable poise is suggested to some extent by the repetitive syntactical patterns of these two stanzas. The first tercet, turning from her physical attributes to her spiritual 'essence', is more condensed: her duality is summed up in these less expansive verbless appositions. The final tercet switches to the poet himself: here the 'je' is in a subordinate position (in contrast to 'Tes... Ta... Ton...') and the rhythm suggested by the syntax and punctuation is less clear-cut and more hesitant, indicating the poet's dependence and comparative powerless-ness. Note Cros's expert use of the *rejet* ('Du rire...', 'A belles dents...'): what is the play on words in this last phrase, and in what way does it help to fuse opposite character-istics in the feminine portrait? It is interesting that in *Conquérant* the octet is devoted to the dominant male and the final tercet to one woman: here the structure is completely reversed.

Compare the picture of the woman in this poem with that in Baudelaire's *Avec ses vêtements ondoyants et nacrés...*

Possession

This poem, which is placed immediately after *Supplication* in all editions of *Le Coffret de santal*, refers perhaps to a successful outcome of the lover's plea. Whereas the supplication demanded words, skilfully wrought, the possession (of the woman physi-cally, and of the lover by his dreams) now calls for silence and secrecy (note the humour of the reason given for his enforced silence). And so the poet, with teasing irony, tries to construct his poem on the theme of saying nothing. The deliberate contradictions in following 'il faut me taire' by another five stanzas, in using long, impressive phrases ('yeux... cabalistiques', 'effluves aromatiques') when he wishes to be tight-lipped, are part of Cros's gentle mockery. The mockery, of course, is also of his own irre-pressible enthusiasm which ignores commands to keep quiet.

The poem is very different from *Supplication* in which the poet could still 'faire... une si savante analyse' and could still exercise his reason. Here, though he has deter-mined to divulge nothing of his dream and to maintain the control of will over words, his 'raison' is progressively taken over by his 'rêves' and the stiff, formal taciturnity is dissolved into a greater fluidity of image. This culminates in suggestions of a swirling feminine power which engulfs, carries away and invades the poet like the sea (cf. *Hiéroglyphe*). But the momentary victory of vertigo over aplomb leads to no disasters, and the final stanza returns to the tone of playful mystification. The poem ends with the private allusion to the almost fantastic figure of 'l'Enchanteresse', made to seem all the more mythical by the third personal form (as opposed to the direct address of the previous poem). The three dots show that the poet is toying with his listeners until the very last line.

What is the value of the four-part structure of the poem: how does Cros give the parts stylistic variation and modifications of mood? Looking at this and other of his poems, what feminine features would you say particularly appeal to him? Is there justification for seeing Cros, in this respect, as a Baudelaire spiced with humour, levity and stylistic acrobatics? If you were reciting this poem, are there places where you would need to give special dramatic effect (intonation, pacing) to the poet's half-reluctance to continue his verse?

Sonnet: *'J'ai bâti dans ma fantaisie...'*

The Cros of *Supplication* and *Possession* might be seen as something of a *poseur*, too aware perhaps of his own skill ('une si savante analyse') and his audience ('on se demandera...') and lacking in true emotional depth. This sonnet shows however that the search for a pose, a rôle to play, may itself be a sign of a rooted melancholy seeking to hide itself (cf. the unhappy theatrical characters in Verlaine's *Clair de lune* and the cult of the clown-figure, the lunar dilettante, in Laforgue). Here the poet weighs up his position: is his poetic world totally unreal? are the women who sway through his poems as perfect as he portrays them? or is he deceiving himself? The lucidity with which Cros answers these questions, distinguishing between reality and fantasy, between the singer and the song, gives this poem its simple power and its unaffected tone. It is a poem of disappointment, and yet it begins positively with the construction of an imaginary theatre in which to stage the poet's verses, verses which have cast Cros in various rôles: the pleading suitor in *Supplication*, the successful lover in *Possession* and the masterful male-lead in *Conquérant*. On the stage are two figures: the poet and the actress who plays his ideal woman.

The mood soon slips into a minor key and bathos. What signs of imperfection creep into the fantasy? The 'Enchanteresse', once she steps onto the boards, loses her magic. Yet the poet's skill as an actor is such that the audience could well believe that, carried away by his part, he is blind to her inadequacy (her reading of lines backward, for example). But Cros reminds us that he is under no illusions; the women of his poetry are given a fictitious, literary perfection created by the poet himself ('Au fard que je lui mets moi-même.'). The rôle of the ideal woman is fashioned in his mind and the leading lady ('la jeune-première') is supposed to fit the part. How does this affect your view of the description of the mistress in *Supplication* and *Possession*? Do you see in the last line the artist's re-assertion of the purity of his make-believe world or a rather sad, lonely acceptance that reality can never match up to his dreams? What effect does the matter-of-fact octosyllabic form (much favoured by Cros, as opposed to the Alexandrine by Baudelaire or imparisyllabic metres by Verlaine) have here? On a much broader plane, what evidence is there, in the work of Baudelaire, Cros, Rimbaud and Laforgue, not only of a remarkable blossoming, but also of a crisis in the literary imagination?

Conquérant

For a guided commentary on this poem, see *The Appreciation of Modern French Poetry*, pp. 89–91.

Hiéroglyphe

For a guided commentary on this poem, see *The Appreciation of Modern French Poetry*, pp. 92–5.

Testament

This moving poem has been called by one critic a 'poignante confession d'un alcoolique'. But the poet, while being aware of his degeneration, is also conscious of a former purity and a future paradise; so it is not so much a confession (there is no regret) as a statement of faith in his own destiny which is to take him to other realms. Is the poem nevertheless poignant? Study the effect of the accumulating 'Si...' clauses, their parallelism (what part do the similes and rhymes play in this?), the juxtaposition of a positive and a negative element in each clause, and the impact of switching from the two-line clauses to the single, climactic 'Et si je meurs, soûl, dans un coin'. How successful do you consider the various images? Notice the curious fact that line 4 has only seven syllables; a mistake? or a subtle piece of evidence to demonstrate the poet's waning powers? The potential decaying of his qualities (spiritual, intellectual and physical) and his obscure, sordid death are due to the alienation between him and this world; he feels he belongs elsewhere (cf. his love of the unreal and rejection of the real in *J'ai bâti dans ma fantaisie*). Just when one might expect some expression of bitterness, the final tercet dispels the gloom of snuffed lamps, fading colours and a drinkers' den (notice how the sparkling adjective 'Matinal' is thrown into prominence just as the similar-sounding 'diamantin' was isolated for effect in a suggestive position). The poet reveals that, on the threshold of death, he has a vision of an ideal, ineffable world. In what way do the final three words (so suitably conclusive in themselves) link up with the theme of inarticulateness touched on in the second stanza?

Study Cros's compact and confident handling of the verse-form: the density of different, and contradictory, impressions in such a spare form, the neat positioning of effects (the 'energizing' of the verb 'Déteint', the stark juxtaposition of opposites in line 5, the suggestive alliterations of lines 7–8, the use of the *rejet* and variations in positioning of punctuation). In your opinion, is there a difference in literary quality and appeal between this poem and the earlier *Supplication*?

SUBJECTS FOR DISCUSSION

1. 'Il se met en son œuvre, comme tout bon lyrique; mais il établit, de lui à la chose qu'il crée, ce que nous appellerions une distanciation: il se regarde écrivant' (L. FORESTIER). Discuss.
2. A critic has detected in Cros's work the eternal tension between the flesh and the spirit, 'le voluptueux' and 'l'idéaliste'. How accurate is this observation?
3. M.-J. Durry says of Cros's poems, 'Ils peuvent être didactiques, frivoles, enlaçants avec quelque chose de voluptueux dans une caresse farouche et musicale. Ils peuvent avoir un goût de légende'. Can you see all these qualities in his work?
4. On the rôle of the woman in Cros's poetry, Louis Forestier notes: 'Tout se passe comme si quelque Circé, maîtresse d'un théâtre imaginaire, exerçait ses maléfices'. Discuss this comment.
5. 'Sa langue très ferme, qui dit haut et loin ce qu'elle veut dire, la sobriété de son verbe et de son discours, le choix toujours rare d'épithètes jamais oiseuses, des rimes excellentes sans l'excès odieux, constituent en lui un versificateur irréprochable qui laisse au thème toute sa grâce ingénue ou perverse' (VERLAINE). Discuss.
6. Analyse Cros's handling of the sonnet form and the octosyllabic line.

Paul Verlaine

Soleils couchants

This poem comes from a section of Verlaine's *Poèmes saturniens* (1866) entitled *Paysages tristes*. One is affected initially by its penetrating musicality, 'la chanson grise/Où l'Indécis au Précis se joint' as the poet puts it in his *Art poétique*: study the repetitive words which create the effect of a chant, the heavy saturation of rhymes (internal and terminal) which make it difficult to know just what *is* the formal framework of the poem, the background monotone of droning nasal sounds ('ch*amps*... mél*an*colie... cou-ch*ants*... ch*ants*... étr*ange*... f*an*tômes... s*ans* trêve... gr*ands*...') which lulls the ear, the use of several particularly rich rhymes. The effect of these is felt all the more intensely in the slender pentasyllabic line, so short that it can be swamped by a single word like 'La mélancolie' and absorbed by *enjambement* into an unbroken musical flow which virtually annihilates it as an independent value.

But the repetition can be deceptive and give one a false sense of 'sameness'. What change of register, tempo or mood takes place from the half-way point? (Look at the displacement of the rhyme, the new sentence-structure, the increased use of the mute 'e', the introduction of consonant endings for the feminine rhymes, and the final switch from *rimes croisées* to *rimes embrassées* which changes the established pattern.) One could easily forget, too, that the poem does not take place at sunset: its 'real' starting-point is a dawn scene. Follow the development of the 'soleils couchants' image (how it is first drawn in by association and the slightly changed context each time that it appears). What aspects of the poet's mind and temperament are revealed?

Chanson d'automne

For a guided commentary on this poem, see *The Appreciation of Modern French Poetry*, pp. 96–8.

Clair de lune

The title of this poem brings to mind Verlaine's taste for pallid settings in which outlines dissolve and become somewhat phantomatic and unreal. The striking image of the first line ('Votre âme est un paysage...') also suggests the extent to which, in Verlaine's poetry, there is no clear division between state of mind and landscape (cf. *Soleils couchants* or 'Il pleure dans mon cœur/Comme il pleut sur la ville'), external scenes and mental fancies: here the stately fountains, the marble statues, the masked revellers in their period costumes are all part of an inner décor, a dreamscape.

The essential feature of the piece is its ambiguity of mood, ultimately crystallized in the words 'triste et beau' and 'sangloter d'extase'. One should note, on the one hand, the affirmative tone of 'choisi' (as if the imagination were a theatre of delights in which one can create *paradis artificiels* at will), the air of enchantment of 'Que vont charmant ...', the gaiety and good humour implicit in the dancing, singing and eccentric masks ('bergamasques' has been taken by critics to mean either of two things: a rustic dance from the town of Bergamo in Italy, or buffoons from the Italian *commedia dell'arte* originally modelled on country bumpkins from Bergamo), the note of optimism about love and life, and in general the delicate play of alliterations throughout which gives the poem such a persuasive musical charm; but, on the other hand, the under-mining effect of the *enjambement* '... quasi/Tristes' (attention being drawn to 'quasi' because of its rhyming position and to 'Tristes' because it carries the only initial stress in the whole poem), the theme of semblances or untrustworthy appearances ('quasi... déguisements... Ils n'ont pas l'air de croire...'), the fact that they are only singing 'sur le mode mineur', and the slight doubt surrounding 'Tout en chantant...' (which can suggest, as well as simultaneity, the concessive idea of 'Even though...'). Why should they not believe their own good fortune? Compare *Clair de lune* with *Colloque sentimental*, the first and last poems of Verlaine's collection *Fêtes galantes* (1869): both set on stage unreal or spectral figures who finally disappear on the night air and leave one with a sense of coldness.

En sourdine

Again the title deserves comment. it shows Verlaine's affection for muted tones, discreet and faint modes of expression. This is a quiet and intimate poem, spoken in a self-effacing way in the name of an unknown 'nous'. It expresses the desire for an ecstasy of perfect union (between person and person, between spirit, emotion and senses, between the lovers and the calm of nature). The setting is characterized, not only by its peace ('calmes... silence'), but by its vague half-light ('le demi-jour... Ferme tes yeux à demi'), the gentle swooning of the surrounding shrubs ('arbousiers' are arbutus bushes, a species of ornamental evergreen plant) induced perhaps by their swaying motions, perhaps by their perfumes, the faintly rippling breeze and its lulling rhythms. One may wonder if the state of contentment which the voice seeks is not a nihilistic or merely quietistic one, involving the extinction of all will, purpose or desire and the loss of the self in an empty oblivion (what impression is given by 'Croise tes bras'?).

What is the full effect of the final stanza? Study the way in which it breaks the preceding syntactical pattern by holding subject and verb in suspense until the final line; the change of tense from wishful imperatives to the more fatalistic futures; the rhyme-link between the words 'soir... noir... désespoir'; the switch to more brutal impressions ('chênes noirs' instead of half-tints, the physical suddenness of nightfall after the delicately poised enchantment); the possible irony of the last line (that nature, after all their entreaties, should be their echo in this). As in *Clair de lune*, one is aware here of a certain pretence ('Laissons-nous persuader...'), of something belied by the appearances.

Colloque sentimental

For a guided commentary on this poem, see *The Appreciation of Modern French Poetry*, pp. 98–100.

C'est l'extase langoureuse...

This, the opening piece of Verlaine's *Romances sans paroles* (1874), is a fine illustration of the poet's intention to create songs without words, that is to say a poetry where music would predominate over meaning, sound over sense, and words would be used not so much to signify as to create a web of suggestion, vague atmosphere and melodic grace. The use of the *vers impair* ('Plus vague et plus soluble dans l'air', says *Art poétique*) gives, not a too firmly balanced rhythm, but one which is variable and less conclusive. Look closely at this subtle play of sound (assonance, alliteration, onomatopoeia) and rhythm.

The whole poem is an attempt to define and grasp some nebulous spirit or impression to which the poet is responsive. But this mysterious 'something' is so many things in one (emotional and physical, single yet multiple, an inner sensation but perceptible on the face of nature) and remains evasive. It would seem to be associated, however, with the force of love ('fatigue amoureuse... l'étreinte des brises') and perhaps the suggestion of things joined in unity ('Parmi l'étreinte...Le chœur des petites voix'). Study the detailed possibilities of the structure of the poem: the movement from the impersonal 'C'est... C'est...', which divulges so little, to the more particular 'Cela... Cela', and then to the more definitive 'Cette âme...', which finally summarizes all the diverse impressions in one word but remains hardly less intangible; the way in which, as the description seems to become more particularized ('Cela gazouille et susurre'), this spirit is somehow more remote than ever, captured only in similes ('Cela ressemble... Tu dirais...') almost impossible to conceive; the gradual emergence of a first-personal voice as the poem passes from indefinite statements ('C'est... C'est...'), to an exclamation ('O le frêle...') which implies an emotional presence not too far away, and finally to the restless questionings and direct address by the poet himself ('La mienne, dis, et la tienne'); the gradual introduction of a second person ('Tu dirais... la tienne'), presumably the loved one; the unobtrusive change from ecstasy to lament (cf. the movement of *En sourdine*), from suggestions of early morning vitality to an expiring evening breath, from the fullness of 'chœur' to the muted remnant of 'antienne' (a short verse or anthem sung as a response or as a mere attachment to a longer psalm), from a general sense of fulfilment to the individual poet's doubt and need for reassurance. Does this make it a pessimistic poem on the theme of love?

Il pleure dans mon cœur...

Here Verlaine characteristically blends the mood of nature and his own poetic mood into one indistinguishable state (notice the effect of the impersonal form 'Il pleure...' in forging this common spirit). Ambiguously, the monotony of the rain seems both a source of melancholy and a relief for his heart-ache. One is aware again of the intense musical qualities of the verse (the rhyme-scheme which gives three common rhymes to each stanza, the richness of the internal rhyming, the repetitions which imply a nagging obsession, the liquid alliterations of the first stanza, the excess of monosyllables like so many verbal droplets). As in many of his poems, Verlaine fails to elucidate his state of feeling (cf. the questions which are left unanswered, the exclamations which express a simple and immediate emotional response but pursue things no further) and he remains a passive victim of this strange melancholia (cf. the form of 'Il pleure dans mon cœur' which implies that he is not responsible for his own tears, the word 'langueur' which describes a limp and pallid kind of affliction). Examine the development of the poem from a mainly descriptive and sentimental level to a deeper psychological one (cf. the gradual movement from external descriptive elements to inner drama in *Chanson d'automne* and *C'est l'extase...*). Which stanza represents the most acute and critical point in his feelings? Again, beneath the simplicity of the diction and the singing quality of the verse, one detects a subtle and complex state of mind (cf. *Soleils couchants*).

Les chères mains...

To appreciate fully the theme and emotional significance of this poem, one needs to know that it comes from the collection *Sagesse* (published in 1881), composed by Verlaine after the disaster of his relationship with Rimbaud, his subsequent imprisonment and his ardent return to the Catholic faith.

The hands are possibly those of his wife Mathilde and represent his nostalgia, after the turbulent illicit liaison with Rimbaud, for the purity and moral stability of his married life. But it does the poem a disservice to tie it to biographical detail. For they are a vision of hands, ethereal hands, a dream-image ('... m'ouvrent les rêves... Mains en songe, mains sur mon âme... ma vision chaste... Rêves bénis...'), suggestive of a variety of symbolic values. This is only one of many poems by Verlaine depicting an idealized feminine figure (one thinks of *Nevermore* where the woman's essence is summed up in the two details of white hands and a golden angelic voice, and of *Mon Rêve familier* with its dream-woman who offers perfect love, understanding and the solution of all his inner problems), or in which the poetic vision is situated indeterminately between reality and unreality. The difference in this case is the strong religious theme ('... païennes... âme... chaste... spirituelle... Remords... bénis... vénérées... pardonne'), which inclines one to look upon the hands as those of the Virgin or some other mysterious spiritual intercessor. Notice how Verlaine has run the first two stanzas together, so that the references to his aberrations seem contained between the two images of hands (seen firstly as a lost possession in the distant past, but then brought back to life as a miraculous influence in the present). Study the different stages in the development of the theme: the idea of an almost mythical access to a dream world (stanza 2); his incomprehension of the mystery, of this voice which has spoken quietly in the hubbub of scandal, and a kind of spiritual vertigo (stanza 3); doubt as to the reliability and reality of the vision, this being a sign of his humility and inability to believe his own good fortune (stanza 4); and finally the theme of remorse and repentance which stems from the previous suggestion of his own undeserving nature (stanza 5). What can we glean of the kind of life the poet is now putting behind him? What is the nature of the new ideal? Is the religious battle now won?

Le ciel est, par-dessus le toit...

Another poem from *Sagesse*, this was written in the Prison des Petits-Carmes where Verlaine was taken after shooting Rimbaud. One can imagine the poet looking from his cell at the infinite expanse of sky and the radiance of the day, and feeling that the secret of life lies, not in obscure artistic and erotic pursuits of the kind shared with the boy from Charleville, but immediately at hand, in the freshness and simplicity of everyday objects and perceptions. By what means does Verlaine convey a childlike candour and innocence? Does the verse-form (alternating lines of eight and four syllables) suit the subject? (One could usefully compare it with a poem written in less regular imparisyllabic lines, and look at the effects of symmetry achieved here, as well as the rhythm of a line like 'Mon Dieu, mon Dieu, la vie est là'.) Is the quality of the description slightly different from that found in many of Verlaine's poems? One notices, as before, a movement from impersonal description, through a note of greater restlessness, to an overt expression of the poet's own problem or torment: as if the subjective gradually encroaches against its own will upon a coveted objectivity. Examine the changes (of tense, syntax, rhythm, etc.) which accompany the new themes of alienation, wastage, remorse and time in the final stanza. Do you think the poem verges on banality? Do you find the religious theme more or less persuasively presented than in *Les chères mains*...?

Je ne sais pourquoi...

Like the preceding piece, this poem was written in prison in 1873. Verlaine's attention again turns to a symbol of the infinite, this time the sea instead of the sky; but the emphasis here is not on visual detail but on an inner imaginative flight, and the simplicity gives way to a more involved evocation of a complex state of mind. The verse-form, too, is remarkably different from that of *Le ciel est, par-dessus le toit*...: Verlaine intermingles a variety of *vers impairs* (five and thirteen syllable lines in one stanza, nine syllable lines in the other), creating an absence of rhythmical balance, an unsettled feeling, and the suggestion of movement to-and-fro. Notice how this gives formal support to the thematic content of the poem, which describes an anxious, fitful, precarious flight governed by the waves and blown about by the wind ('... une aile inquiète et folle... Elle suit la vague... au gré du vent se livre et flotte/Et plonge'). It is interesting to compare this with Baudelaire's use of different line-lengths in his sonnet *La Musique* to give an effect of upsurge and relapse, ebb and flow, and in general to suggest the rhythmical variations and changing intensities of music, the sea and the human spirit: Verlaine's treatment differs in that, instead of the Alexandrine, he deliberately chooses the thirteen syllable line, irregular and rhythmically 'out of true'; and instead of the carefully worked density of the sonnet, he adopts these loosely alternating stanzas with their greater vagueness and airiness.

Since the poet himself cannot fully fathom or explain his own mood and gives no indication of its origins, it would be incongruous if the reader could give a simple résumé of it: how many different aspects of feeling enter into it, and are they easily reconcilable? The image of the sea is ambiguous: is it a hostile or friendly force, and what might it represent in terms of his own mental reality? What relevance has the theme of love (what is it frightened of, what is it seeking to protect)? How effectively woven is the metaphor of the mind as a seagull? Study the balance between suggestions of direction and waywardness, order and disorder, the active and the passive, joy and pain. This is one of comparatively few poems where Verlaine uses the technique of extended metaphor, examples of which are more evident in the collection *Sagesse* than elsewhere.

L'échelonnement des haies...

This is a description of a Lincolnshire landscape on a Sunday morning. How well do Baudelaire's words 'Les parfums, les couleurs et les sons se répondent' apply to it? One could compare Verlaine's use of the verb 'Moutonne' in the first stanza with Hugo's image of 'La laine des moutons sinistres de la mer' in *Pasteurs et troupeaux* and the opening line of Baudelaire's *La Chevelure*, 'O toison, moutonnant jusque sur l'encolure': here Verlaine wants to convey the fleeciness of texture and 'frizziness' of outline of the hedgerows stretching out into the distance, their bubbly tops bathed in the morning fog, like a wave of sea-foam. In what ways does the poet make material objects lose their clarity of contour and seem unsubstantial? (Notice, as but one feature, that it is not 'haies' which is the subject of the verb 'moutonne' but 'échelonnement', and not 'poulains' which is the subject of 'vient s'ébattre' but 'agilité'.) Study, particularly, the play of *correspondances* which brings animal and vegetal life and the elements of sky and sea into unison: the coming together of tones of whiteness (clean fog, white fleece, sky like milk); the image of curls which links hedges ('Moutonne'), sheep ('leur laine blanche') and even the rolling waves of sound in the thick air ('roulée en volutes'); the way in which the earth (hedges which are a 'mer claire') is blended with sky ('... déferlait/L'onde... De cloches') and visual impression with aural impression (how do you explain the phrase 'cloches comme des flûtes'?). It is rare to find such a close-knit orchestration of image in Verlaine: like the use of the extended metaphor, it is more a feature of the period of composition of *Sagesse*. This is equally true of details used for symbolic suggestion: here one could see the colours white and green, the words 'brebis', 'cloches' and 'lait' as having religious connotations. What moral qualities emanate from this description? (The phrase 'Qui sent bon les jeunes baies' deserves a comment: it is a rare mixture of the two forms 'sentir bon', to smell good, and 'sentir les baies', to smell *of* berries, and means approximately 'which has a fine smell of young berries'.)

Sonnet boiteux

This 'limping sonnet' is a remarkable illustration of Verlaine's importance as a rhythmical innovator and originality as a verbal Impressionist painter. In choosing this thirteen syllable line he has given himself an awkward and ungainly medium, appropriate to his theme of a life out of harmony and a world in chaos: one can see this effect clearly in the first line, where the two parallel statements constitute one 'leg' of five syllables and one of eight so that the line seems off-balance, or in the penultimate where the split is nine and four, or in the description of London, where an unusual number of stresses at irregular intervals gives a jerky and agitated movement. Verlaine's love of the vague or confused impression is strongly in evidence here: he does not elucidate his state of mind and we never know what is sad nor what the misfortune or hopeless martyrdom is; it is only suggested in an unusual simile which implies a kind of 'split personality', with one part of himself watching his own life-blood spill away as if through a veil and impotent to intervene; internal impressions merge in an halluci-natory way with external ones (the imaginary flow of his blood mingling with the swimming flame of the gas-light and the garish red street-signs, and the painful caco-phony of his restless memories matched by the snatches of incomprehensible babble emerging from the city-fog); the description of London itself is slightly nightmarish (the wavering outlines, the rapidly changing kaleidoscope of colour, the awesome personification of the squat and shrivelled houses). Notice that, in this poem as else-where, there is the suggestion of a religious theme: London, as a 'ville de la Bible' upon which he calls down the fire of heaven, reminds one of Sodom and Gomorrah (and perhaps, too, in its confusion, of Babel); the poet's pain is seen as a martyrdom, a suffering stemming from a religious faith; and the imagined senate of little old women, although a lay power, would seem to sit in authority and judgment. Might this vision represent a penitence for his own sodomy? Or resentment against his own pricked conscience? How many different emotions enter into the poet's mood?

SUBJECTS FOR DISCUSSION

1. It has been said that Verlaine loves 'tout ce qui favorise un glissement vers la rêverie, la vision fantomatique, le songe' (J. RICHER). Is this so?
2. Does it seem adequate to describe Verlaine's poetry as 'the musical notation of vaguely sad impressions' (R. PERMAN)?
3. Study the distinctive features of Verlaine's art of description.
4. 'For all the subtle variations of his art, Verlaine plays only one emotional theme: the faintly melancholic song of lost love.' Discuss.
5. Verlaine has expressed his predilection for that point in poetry 'Où l'Indécis au Précis se joint'. What illustration do you find in his poems of this affection?
6. What expression is given to the following leitmotifs in Verlaine's work and how do they come together: reality and appearances, lucidity and confusion, self-awareness and self-abandonment?

Arthur Rimbaud

Les Effarés

For a guided commentary on this poem, see *The Appreciation of Modern French Poetry*, pp. 102–4.

Roman

A rewarding way in which to approach this poem is to compare it in detail with *Ma Bohème*. Although *Ma Bohème* is concerned with a lad's attitude to poetry and nature and *Roman* with his attitude to love and nature (two well-worked Romantic themes), both poems convey an energetic spirit of youth and an entertaining outlook on life, language and himself. One sees the same love of the open air, the joy of being apart from other human company (cf. 'J'allais sous le ciel...' and 'On va sous les tilleuls...'), the response to intense physical sensations (cf. '...rosée à mon front comme un vin de vigueur' and 'L'air est parfois si doux, qu'on ferme la paupière'), the communion with the pleasures of the balmy season (cf. 'Ces bons soirs de septembre' and 'les bons soirs de juin'), the drinking-in of the liquid life (dew or sap) of nature and the accompanying intoxication (cf. 'vin de vigueur' and 'La sève est du champagne'). There are other links: the image of nature as a supreme hostelry; the picturesque description of the sky and stars which rids them of abstraction and pretentious metaphysical dimensions and makes them a subject for the senses (cf. 'un doux frou-frou' with 'de doux frissons', and 'un tout petit chiffon/D'azur' with 'des haillons/D'argent' in *Le Dormeur du val*); the youthful dreams of love (cf. 'que d'amours splendides j'ai rêvées!' and 'Vous êtes amoureux'); the attraction of a story-book or legendary hero (cf. 'Petit-Poucet rêveur' and 'Robinsonne'). In style, one notices the use of colloquial exclamation (cf. 'Oh! là là!' with 'foin des bocks...' meaning 'a fig for your glasses of beer') which throws poetic decorum to the winds; the linguistic inventiveness (the coining of the verb 'Robinsonner', 'to go Robinson Crusoeing'); the racy expression in short direct sentences, punctuated by dashes. Above all, there is a similar spirit to that of *Ma Bohème*: a combination of realism and fantasy (what are the implications of the word 'Roman' here?), sensuality and dream, romantic enthusiasm and self-mockery (the image of himself as a lover, with his kiss quivering timidly and his snatches of sentimental song dying on his lips, is as mocking as that of himself as a poet plucking his accompaniment on the strings of his shoes), lyrical involvement and ironic detachment (note the verb 'Loué' indicating that his emotions have only been provisionally let out or put on hire until the end of the summer holidays and are not a permanent attachment, and the surprise twist which leaves this *roman* without its story-book ending). Notice how many times Rimbaud uses the adjective 'petit' in the middle sections, perhaps suggesting, for all its exuberance, the triviality of this episode of his life both in terms of characters and décor (with its little rag of sky and second-rate star pinned on it!).

Le Dormeur du val

In this sonnet, Rimbaud uses his talents as a landscape painter to bring out the horror of war, the incongruity of death in this lush and peaceful natural setting, and the scandal of the senseless waste of young life. Written in October 1870, this work no doubt has a stimulus in the events of the Franco-Prussian war. It is a poem built on contrasts and a carefully calculated false impression, an effect all the more dramatic in that Rimbaud interposes no commentary, no moral, no invective of his own: he simply describes nature and the soldier and leaves the details to speak for themselves.

Look at the elements which contribute to the mood of the opening description: the carefree vitality, the sparkling luminosity, the impression of a cosy haven (cf. the opening of Hugo's *Pasteurs et troupeaux*). Notice the Impressionist quality of the effects of light (brilliant reflections scattered in little shreds, sun's rays broken into a frothy or mottled effect, the intermingling of light and water) and the way in which Rimbaud gives them an extra surge of energy by means of *rejets*. The second stanza, introducing the figure of the young man, continues to impress a rich liquid quality ('... baignant dans le frais cresson bleu... où la lumière pleut') and reinforces the sense of peace and physical relaxation. Only the word 'Pâle' might strike an ominous note, but this could be a mere colour impression in the green and blue setting. However, the greater density of the tercets is dramatically used, firstly to sow a deepening suspicion, then to make the brutal revelation: note the image of nature as a mother; the pathos of the colloquialism 'il fait un somme'; the more abrupt syntax which makes one aware of a changed mood; the repetitions of the verb 'dort'; the irony of the final *rejet*; the monosyllabic brutality of the words 'deux trous rouges'; the vivid colour-contrasts of the first and last lines of the poem, green being nature's life-source, red that of man. The poignancy is increased if one compares the use of the words 'parfums' and 'frissonner' with that in *Roman*, a poem of the pleasures of youth.

Ma Bohème

For a guided commentary on this poem, see *The Appreciation of Modern French Poetry*, pp. 105–7.

Les Corbeaux

This is another poem which shows the poetic mind alone with nature. It shares with *Le Dormeur du val* the theme of death. Despite Verlaine's description of it as 'une chose patriotique bien' (the 'morts d'avant-hier' are, one supposes, the victims of the Franco-Prussian war), it is a mysterious and unnerving piece. The setting is bleak and derelict; the human habitations seem dejected or broken down ('abattus' could mean either of these things), the face of nature is devastated or touched by some strange malady ('fleuves jaunis' gives an unhealthy impression). There are religious references, but the traditional symbols ('angélus' suggesting prayers which are now useless and 'calvaires' a place of past suffering) are out of function, and in their place is an invocation of a somewhat sinister, retributive 'Seigneur' who is presumably lord of the crows, his saintly emissaries. The crows themselves, traditionally associated with death ('notre funèbre oiseau noir'), are described in martial terms ('Armée étrange... ralliez-vous') and seem to bring destruction in revenge for destruction (cf. 'hameaux abattus... Faites s'abattre', 'Les vents froids attaquent vos nids!' and 'Laissez les fauvettes...' which implies that they will leave nothing else intact); and yet they are also 'chers', 'délicieux', 'saints du ciel'. Note the delaying of the main verb in the first stanza to give it more impact; the lingering emphasis on 'délicieux'; the onomato- poeic hiatus of 'Armée étrange...'; the chanting repetitions of the second stanza. The poet's rôle is that of a kind of sorcerer's apprentice, putting all his will into this prayer or spell (a rôle which anticipates *Après le déluge* and the theme of the destructive and recreative imagination). It appears that the crows have a positive moral purpose, to act as a perennial reminder of those who have died for a cause. But the finale is heavily pessimistic (cf. the expression 'au fond du bois' with the 'au bas du bois' at the end of *Aube*: do they both suggest dejection?); and the delicate gesture of leaving the May warblers (suggestive of melodic grace, springtime and youth) is charged with pathos (cf. 'frêle comme un papillon de mai' in *Le Bateau ivre*). It can do nothing to unlock the fatal closure (reinforced by inversion) of the last line.

Voyelles

It serves little purpose to try to trace this poem back to its origins: one cannot pretend to fathom all the factors which might have played in its inspiration nor all the shades of transformation between the raw materials and the artistic product. Perhaps it does not matter whether its 'source' was a child's picture-alphabet with coloured letters. The important thing is that here is a poem of rare imaginative colour and vigour, which provokes the senses and challenges reason, conjures up possibilities and defies restriction. It is relevant to mention, however, that poetry of the time was alive to the question of analogies between the different senses: between scents and colours, sounds and colours, colours and feelings (cf. Baudelaire's *Correspondances* and Cros's *Hiéro-*

glyphe), this being part of that exploration of the higher principles of the imagination which characterizes Symbolism. One should add that Rimbaud, in suggesting the wealth of sensual and imaginative material which lies in potential behind what most people see as a set of empty symbols, is proposing a new view of the possibilities of language.

Study the dramatic opening (the undiluted juxtapositions, the unexplained switch in the order of vowels); the poet's taste for the secretive; the emphasis on a hidden life which can surge forth (cf. in Baudelaire's *La Chevelure*, 'Pour peupler ce soir l'alcôve obscure/Des souvenirs dormant dans cette chevelure'); the complexity of the appeal to the senses (the combination of sight, sound, scent and touch called up by the letter A); the intermingling of physical and moral impressions ('...puanteurs cruelles'); the contrasts ('noir' with 'éclatantes', the immobility of 'glaciers' with 'frissons'); the way in which each letter governs a quite distinctive mood or set of qualities (A, the aggressive, impure and distasteful; E, the pure, proud and regal; I, the dramatic, uninhibited and passionate; U, the peaceful, rhythmical and serene; O, the mysterious, absolute and universal). The structure is particularly revealing: the alternations between impurity and purity, violence and peace, sound and silence; the passage from Alpha to Omega, from the sensual to the spiritual, from the microscopic to the immeasurably vast; the use of the tercets for the 'higher dimension'; the way in which the poem is framed between two mysteries, one concerned with origins (what explains the upsurge of these *correspondances*?), the other with end purposes (who is referred to by 'Ses Yeux', some absolute divine power?). Note that, in the images governed by the letter U, there is hardly a 'u' sound: a reminder that it is not primarily the vowel *sounds* which give this poem its creative impetus, but their colour-associations. The sonnet is remarkable, too, for Rimbaud's startling, inventive vocabulary: 'bombinent' is a verb fashioned from the Latin 'bombus', the buzzing of bees, or from the scientific name 'Bombylius', a kind of fly; 'ombelles' is a technical botanical term to define an umbrella-like flowering growth of many stalks from the same point on a stem; 'virides' is a rare Latinate form of 'verts', associated here with both the vibrant green of the sea and the peaceful green of pastures; and 'strideurs' is an eccentric coining replacing the usual 'stridences'. In this respect, as in his daring metaphors and revolutionary vision, we see Rimbaud expanding the mould of traditional poetry, before bursting it absolutely.

Le Bateau ivre

This poem represents an intoxicated journey away from the call of the known world into the exotic reaches of the imagination or, as Rimbaud says elsewhere, into 'la plénitude du grand songe'. It is a lavish visionary work built on the metaphor of the poet–boat sailing beyond bounds, plunged into unsuspected currents and tides, colours and forms, sights and sensations. (Baudelaire uses the same basic metaphor in *La Musique*.)

The first phase extends as far as '...dispersant gouvernail et grappin'. It shows the adventurous backwater boat breaking from its restrictions, leaving behind the world of utilitarian pursuits (the cargo boats representing a humdrum and somewhat squalid social function, repetitive and unromantic), and absorbed into a new element. Note the flavour of the boy's adventure-story (with the Wild West and Redskin torture-stakes mingling fluently with the tow-paths of Northern Europe) and the emphasis on the special value of childlike perception (the child's spontaneous ability to live in fantasy and deafness to common reality, his intensity of sensation); the way in which the 'Fleuves' are mysteriously expressionless compared with the trivial human 'tapages' and in themselves impose no limitations; the onomatopoeic effects and agitated rhythm as he enters a tidal pull; the splendid image of 'unmoored Peninsulas', suddenly cut loose to join the element in whose atmosphere they are bathed and to whose voices they respond; the loss of the normal notion of time; the mocking backward glance at the grandiose commonplaces of traditional sea-poetry ('rouleurs éternels de victimes') and the timorous mentality of those who need the reassurance of the stupid winking eye of signal-lanterns ('falots'); the idea of a process of initiation and purification (illustrated first by a startling cross-reference of different sensations, then by the suggestive image of 'vins bleus' and 'vomissures' which could refer to the blue water and foam of the surface of the sea, or to the real wines and sickness which provoked this journey of intoxication and now seem to be put far behind him); the cohesion of the navigational imagery, passing from elements of external guidance ('haleurs', 'falots') to a loss of the ability to govern his own course ('gouvernail') or ever to be halted or hooked back to the world ('grappin' is a small anchor or grappling-hook).

The words 'Et dès lors. . .' introduce a new level of experience: how does Rimbaud convey this? Compare '. . . le Poème/De la Mer infusé d'astres' with the definition of *l'éternité* in Rimbaud's poem of that title: 'lactescent', a rare Latinism, suggests that the stars or the reflections of stars are eaten down into the sea, which turns a milky hue as their effect is spread. The capital letter of 'Poème' is noticeable: it indicates that this absolute sea, this Infinity, is a vast harmony in its own right, a universal Poem extending far beyond the meagre resources of ordinary human poetry. Just as the boat's hull was first penetrated, so all divisions give way (sky and sea, dawn and sunset, colour categories, the boundaries of different sense impressions), showing the world in its bewildering interpenetration: consider particularly a line like 'Fermentent les rousseurs amères de l'amour' where an emotional or spiritual force translates itself simultaneously in terms of colour, taste and tactile sensation. Note the variety of colours (conceived, in the invented word 'bleuités' and 'rousseurs', as independent living substances); the numerous effects of light (cf. descriptions of dawn in *Aube*) ranging from volatile, palpitating whiteness in the sky to purple-toned coagulations lighting up the sea's surface as it gestures like an actor in Greek tragedy; the dynamic quality of the vision (the force of the verbs, the state of constant movement and metamorphosis, the stress on rhythms and untamed energies such as the 'trombes', waterspouts, and the 'ressacs', the violent undertow); the non-rational nature of the experience ('délires', 'Hystériques' or the contemplative transport of the floating corpse); the way in which the 'je' only triggers off a wealth of impressions which then take flight of their own accord (cf. 'plus vastes que nos lyres' and the disappearance of the boat imagery). The poet's excitement and wonder that he has been admitted to a realm of vision of which men have only had the slightest glimpses and his earlier belief that 'La tempête a *béni* mes éveils maritimes' are not irrelevant to the reference to the 'Maries', the three Marys who, by some grace, passed miraculously through a superhuman sea-storm and landed at the point on the South coast of France which is now known as Saintes-Maries-de-la-Mer.

With the words 'J'ai heurté. . .' a new mood insinuates itself: what evidence do you see of this? Perhaps the poet is not privileged initiate or immune spectator in the magic land of his own visions; and just as the sea can be ecstatic or violent (cf. 'horreurs mystiques'), divine or bestial, one wonders what is the nature of the forces which lie beyond the lock-gates of the human mind. Study the images of imprisonment and rot, the suggestions of animality (which, in the case of the panthers, can threaten human identity), the changed colours, the acknowledged ambiguity of the venture ('par instants. . . Parfois'); the awareness of physical weakness and self-disgust ('bonaces', a lull or doldrums, and 'Echouages', banks on which boats can be stranded, both threaten immobilization, while the 'ventouses', strange suckers, reach towards him as in a science-fiction nightmare and remind him of his womanish impotence). The

'Léviathan' was a Biblical sea monster but has since been taken to mean a ship of huge size: in either sense, it serves here to cast a warning over the ambitious venture of this tiny backwater craft, which is trying a journey for which it is not equipped. Note how the desire to disengage from the experience and return momentarily to the innocent spirit of childhood follows immediately after images which could represent man's fall from grace and loss of purity. Is there a suggestion that the terms of the experience are now reversed (the different breed of birds with their graceless shrieking and filthy droppings, the return of the corpse in more sinister form, the reference to his 'liens frêles' contrasting with the earlier 'Plus léger qu'un bouchon')?

The penultimate section (from 'Or moi...' to 'Je regrette l'Europe') is a rhetorical movement summarizing in grandiose terms the extent of his achievement. 'Monitor' was an ironclad vessel invented in America in the early 1860s, and the Hanse towns were those which took part in a great commercial league between Northern European states: these points of comparison show how far beyond the mightiest sea-dreams his imagination has plunged. These images of his own person are the most profuse and extravagant of the poem: the poet's imagination has pierced the flaming wall of the sky, has come to know a food of the gods of unimaginable rarity (not the conventional ambrosia, but an ambiguous and partly repellent mixture of sunlight, mosses, gelatinous liquid mucus and sky-blue), has been escorted by sea-horses like a king of fairy-stories and caught in the roving spotlight of the most garish, innovatory sources of light, has run close to the most awesome forces (seasons being threshed out; great hollows forming in the universe; the sexual energy of the Behemoth, the Biblical name of a monstrous animal, probably the hippopotamus; the thick swirl of the Maelstrom or whirlpool), and has taken part in spinning the actual fabric of the changeless blue sky. And now this whirling kaleidoscope of vision can only be contrasted, as if in disbelief, with his present yearning for the stable and familiar: after the turbulence and the magnificent transcendence of mediocre human destiny, the need for rest. Note the sudden use of the present tense, and the contrast between the earlier 'sans regretter...' and 'Je regrette'.

Yet the boat's nostalgia for the reliable and the solid can be no more than a momentary urge against its own nature, and Europe and its civilization is no answer. The 'je' wavers between pride and the inability to forget ('J'ai vu...') and doubt and near-despair ('Est-ce en ces nuits...'). It is this question, implying that a secret of flight, magical transformation and strength has evaded him, and the following acknowledgement that all sources of light, symbols of idealism and quest, are bitter, which bring on the urge for self-destruction, an urge which veers back almost immediately to the perhaps contradictory one of nostalgia for childhood (cf. earlier references to the child's world). Note how suggestively the last quatrain returns to the original navigational imagery ('flammes' here being pennants, 'pontons' prison-ships, and 'enlever leur sillage' meaning 'to follow in the wake of'). The final four stanzas draw to the surface the deep lyrical themes of the poem: restlessness, inadaptation, impossible idealism, liberty and imprisonment. How do you interpret the poet's dilemma?

What remains in one's mind after reading this poem is the magnificent imagery: the tang of sea-water breaking in like the taste of an unripe apple as teeth burst its skin; dawn taking flight like a flock of doves; the sea pounding the rocks like a wild-eyed, frothy beast in its pen; the rainbow as a bunch of multi-coloured reins stretching down to underwater herds; a child alone by a pool in the evening light with a toy boat. But one should not overlook its vast lyrical range: what different emotions does it express? And how many moods and aspects of the sea does it evoke? Nor can one neglect the surprising variety and internal shading of its stages of narrative development. Make a detailed comparison and contrast between Rimbaud's poetic imagination as seen here, and that of Baudelaire in such poems as *La Chevelure* and *L'Invitation au voyage*.

Chanson de la plus haute tour

Taken from the *Derniers vers*, this piece, like *L'Eternité* which follows, represents a different vein in Rimbaud's poetry. The title gives the clue: Rimbaud is not noted for the smooth musicality of his verse, usually preferring shock-effects, flamboyant vocabulary and disrupted rhythms; and yet this has the simple melodic qualities and direct lyrical appeal of a *chanson* or ancient ballad. In what respects can one see here the influence of the contact with Verlaine? Describing this and similar works, Rimbaud expresses his affection at the time for 'refrains niais, rhythmes naïfs' and says 'Je disais adieu au monde dans d'espèces de romances'.

But the second part of the title, the reference to the highest tower, is far less patent. It might suggest imprisonment, contemplative aloofness or some legendary prize to be won by high deeds, all of which are relevant to the subject of the poem. Analyse the various themes and the way in which they support each other: a mis-spent youth and a wasted life (cf. Verlaine's '...qu'as-tu fait, toi que voilà/De ta jeunesse?'); a sense of imprisonment, all-embracing rather than particular (cf. themes of *Le Bateau ivre*); the longing for an advent associated with reciprocal love (cf. 'Mille veuvages'); the abandonment of a fruitless idealism and reconciliation to a second-best (what is meant by 'délicatesse' and 'J'ai tant fait patience'?); the desire for self-effacement and a solemn or dignified retreat from the world, far from the frustrations of a hopeless pursuit (cf. the reference above to 'saying farewell to the world'); the idea of being in sterile doldrums or a limbo which is drained of any powerful emotion, even painful ones such as 'Craintes et souffrances', which might give it a saving impetus (cf. Baudelaire's state of *ennui*); the suggestion of a malady and a degeneration possibly of a religious nature and in need of a religious solution (it is hard to know here whether 'la si pauvre âme' is a self-pitying description of himself, a contemptuous view of the limited and effeminate spiritual possibilities of a Verlaine who, at the time of *Sagesse*, returned piously to the Catholic fold, or simply a generalization on the nature of the human soul). Study the special use of the rhyming couplet at the end of the stanzas; the suggestion of the poet suspended between something finished in the past and something hoped for in the future; the changed form of the fourth stanza (a single extended image, verbless, proliferating in a rather undisciplined way) and its function as a symmetrical parallel to the third stanza and an introduction to the religious references of the fifth; the use of the final refrain as the only answer, and by implication a negative one, to what is the first question in the poem. The fourth stanza is perhaps the most difficult: at this point the poem appropriately stands on the spot, since these lines are simply a pictorial simile illustrating the state of mind described in the previous stanza. The grass-land, and all that it represents as potential fertility, has been allowed to run to seed: note that 'ivraies' is the Biblical word for 'tares' as opposed to good wheat, as well as having an etymological link with 'ivre' and therefore with the theme of 'soif malsaine' (cf. *Le Bateau ivre*); 'bourdon' means a great droning sound, but can also mean either a bumble-bee or a great bell, thus keeping suggestions of the natural world and the religious world side by side.

L'Eternité

A laconic and enigmatic poem, this is Rimbaud's attempt to define an intuition of eternity. Speaking in *Une Saison en Enfer* of its period of composition, he writes, 'Ce fut d'abord une étude. J'écrivais des silences, des nuits, je notais l'inexprimable'. One can see in this statement the seeds of an artistic dilemma: the need to transcribe in written form what was the fruit of a meditative silence, and to give expression to what was beyond words. How appropriate to such an aim do you find the verse-form at which Rimbaud has finally arrived (the brief stanzas in pentasyllabic lines, the very approximate rhymes which do not stitch things together too firmly, the dense sentences which resemble formulae)? Notice the way in which the theme of near-silence is discreetly stressed throughout the poem: what does this contribute to the atmosphere? How does Rimbaud suggest that this moment of supreme fulfilment, which releases the spirit and sets it apart from ordinary human ambitions and moral judgments ('suffrages' are votes or signs of approbation), is almost synonymous with a state of self-abolition or nullity? What is the value of leaving the preposition 'selon', 'according to', suspended without a noun? (Again in *Une Saison en Enfer* and just before quoting a version of this poem, Rimbaud reminisces, 'Enfin, ô bonheur, ô raison, j'écartai du ciel l'azur, qui est du noir, et je vécus, étincelle d'or de la lumière *nature*'.) Study the development of the imagery of fire and light (where does the dense metaphor 'Braises de satin' grow from?); the way in which opposite qualities tend to be fused and joined in a single state (sea and sky, water and fire, day and night); the strong impression which emerges of a simple but incontrovertible fatality; the particularly cryptic language of the penultimate stanza ('orietur' is a Latin word meaning 'There shall arise': cf. Malachi 4:2). What do you think is the effect of the repeated stanza closing the poem? Do you take this to be an optimistic or a pessimistic poem? Is there, for instance, a positive way of interpreting 'Là pas d'espérance' and 'Le supplice est sûr' (cf. being burned at the stake), in view of the fact that this stanza is followed by the melodic and utterly simple 'Elle est retrouvée'?

O saisons, ô châteaux...

Like *Chanson de la plus haute tour*, this is not a visionary poem (in the way that one could apply this term to *Voyelles* and *Le Bateau ivre*), but the lyrical expression of a mysterious emotional and spiritual mood. It shows the same distinctive combination: of a simple musical formula and obscure allusions; of direct exclamations charged with emotion and a baffling theme. As Rimbaud says in the final couplet: 'Que comprendre à ma parole?/Il fait qu'elle fuie et vole!'. Some magical force (or influential person) governs his expression which makes it elusive and incompatible with reasonable explanation. One thinks of Verlaine's lines:

> De la musique encore et toujours!
> Que ton vers soit la chose envolée
> Qu'on sent qui fuit d'une âme en allée
> Vers d'autres cieux à d'autres amours
> *(Art poétique)*.

Note the vast range of interpretation offered by the indefinite opening address, given a haunting emphasis by its repetition (e.g. seasons and castles may represent an idea of perennity or durability, contrasting with the airy transience of 'qu'elle fuie et vole,' to which the human soul cannot aspire; or they may represent the two great sources of the child's inspiration, nature and the realm of legend, which stand apart from one's own imperfections). Note, too, the emphasis on studious magical pursuits (cf. 'paix des rides/Que l'alchimie imprime aux grands fronts studieux' in *Voyelles*, and 'Science avec patience' in *L'Eternité*); the idea of the hunt for the key to happiness being an inescapable universal fate; the simple prayer that the absolute (some secret of ultimate

Happiness) might be resurrected with every new dawn (cf. the prayer of the 'lièvre' in *Après le déluge*, and the image of the cock-crow in *Aube*); the renunciation of over-ambitious hopes (cf. *Chanson de la plus haute tour*); and the acknowledgement that his life has been taken over by a mysterious force stronger than himself, leading to self-dispersion and wasted effort. This is a restless little poem, fitful and fragmented, caught between promise and resignation.

Après le déluge

Here Rimbaud takes the Biblical story of the Flood and turns it into his own picturesque legend, a pessimistic and increasingly despairing one. The poem shows the moment immediately after the imagined re-cleansing of the world. It begins with an element of children's story or fable, with a dramatized animal figure as main protagonist: there is a description of great freshness and delicacy (the liquid lushness of clover and the grace of the swaying bell-flowers contrast with the desiccated 'Prairie' of lost youth in *Chanson de la plus haute tour*), a religious prayer from this timid undomesticated creature (itself a kind of *effaré*), the image of a magical vision disappearing (cf. the rainbow with Rimbaud's definition of eternity as 'la mer allée/Avec le soleil', and with the reference in Genesis to God's bow being the covenant between Him and the earth), and a kind of screen drawn between this glimpse of light and promise and the onlooker (cf. the urchins in *Les Effarés* gazing longingly through a grating at 'ces lumières/Du ciel rouvert').

But from this moment on, life falls back crudely and inexorably into its habitual motions. Look at the time-emphasis ('Aussitôt que...regardaient déjà'); references to windows, light which has lost its sparkle or transparency, and liquids which are murky, cloudy or of dubious value ('mazagrans' are coffees, probably laced with spirits, steaming away in little bars); images of workaday, utilitarian or brutal activity (e.g. the setting up of 'étals', butchers' stalls, to be followed by the greater butchery and blood-letting of Bluebeard, as opposed to the more contemplative devotions of the 'lièvre' and the 'enfants en deuil', and to the joyful reaction of the child in the village-square who whirls about drenched in the 'éclatante giboulée', the radiant downpour which belongs to the same world of light and water as the 'arc-en-ciel'); the theme of human encroachment on the unsullied face of nature (or, in the case of the sea, on its elevated and statuesque surface as it rises high in tiers towards the heavens); the satire of a bourgeois civilization and culture, whose cheap symbols of refinement and grandeur are incongruous blots on a primeval purity; and the religious allusions implying a Christian theology which is a veil between perception and original purity ('le sceau de Dieu' is a direct ironical reference to the rainbow as 'God's covenant') and whose forms of worship are a proliferating, mechanical ritual.

The words 'Depuis lors...' strike a conclusive note and introduce the closing 'para-graph' of this movement: there is a picture of nature turned savage or degenerate (the Moon is often thought of as sterile and pallid; eclogues, usually representative of a poetic pastoral dream, are here grotesquely personified and imprisoned in a peasant clumsiness); an irony in the nymph's name (cf. *eucharistie*, the sacrament which is supposed to contain in material form the spirit of God and offer the promise of spiritual transformation); a finality, even a fatality, about the naming of spring. Note that a reference to the first person ('*me* dit') now occurs.

Study the distinct changes in theme, syntax, rhythm and mood which take place as the poet tries to conjure up a return of the flood; the swelling force of the imperatives, the accumulating pressure of nouns and verbs, and the change from vision to lyricism. Notice that, from the beginning, it has been only '*l'idée* du Déluge' which has subsided:

perhaps this is a comment on the inadequacies of creative idealism and the imagination. Where does the Flood now need to be reconjured from? Compare the mysterious figure of 'la Sorcière' with the reference to 'la magique étude' of *O saisons, ô châteaux...* How would you describe the conclusion (with its switch to the pronoun 'nous')?

Aube

This prose-poem, like *Après le déluge*, comes from Rimbaud's *Illuminations*, a collective title which can be seen in two ways: either as illuminated engravings ('coloured plates' as Verlaine has called them), or as transcriptions of brief moments of illumination or visionary inspiration. *Aube* gives evidence of both qualities: a luminosity and imagery which stands out in bright visual relief, and the atmosphere of a privileged experience in which the child–poet becomes almost the equal of a divinity.

Study the structural development of the poem: the strikingly simple, yet almost unimaginable, opening claim (cf. 'Je sais les cieux...je sais le soir' in *Le Bateau ivre*); the dramatic progression of his account from pictures of surrounding immobility (how suggestive is the metaphor 'Les camps d'ombres'?), to the idea of an awakening vitality (cf. 'les pierreries', possibly dewdrops on the grass, with those of *Après le déluge*, and 'les ailes' with the image of 'L'Aube exaltée ainsi qu'un peuple de colombes' and the ultimate dream of 'Million d'oiseaux d'or' in *Le Bateau ivre*), to a first exploit or heroic achievement in which Nature communicates and tells some of its meaning (cf. the intimate relationship with an aspect of Nature in *Ma Bohème*: 'Mes étoiles au ciel...'), to the indubitable recognition of a divine presence as, at this moment of 'illumination', brilliant light strikes the 'head' of the waterfall and luminous water intertwines with the profusion of the vegetal realm (why the use of the verb 'ris', the German form of 'wasserfall', and the word 's'échevela'?), to a quest for actual possession and total knowledge (why should he *denounce* her to the cock? cf. this reference to 'coq' with 'O vive lui, chaque fois/Que chante son coq gaulois' in *O saisons, ô châteaux...*), to a final physical union in which he enters, even if only partially and for a moment, into the harmony of the world. How important to this pattern of development is the notion of time? Are there any noticeable changes of pace and mood (what variations in sentence-structure, presentation, or use of tenses accompany these)? Note how the narration of the child's exploits is framed between two brief, unelaborate statements, which stand isolated: what effect does this have? How do you explain the penultimate switch from 'je' to 'l'enfant'? By what means does Rimbaud conjure up a legendary atmosphere? (One remembers the Classical legend of Apollo, the sun-god, pursuing the nymph Daphne who was finally turned into a laurel bush before he could ravish her.) Notice Rimbaud's 'animated' vision; the strain of acquisitive sensuality which mingles with the fresh, ingenuous 'fairy-tale' atmosphere; and the impression that the young adventurer is in a realm apart from the preoccupations of the world at large. Study also the tension which exists between the idea of magical potency, conquest and intimate communication with Nature, and the theme which finally emerges of inadequate possession and Nature's evasiveness. Compare the progression of mood in this poem with that in *Le Bateau ivre*. Trace the theme of love, in all its different expressions, through the selection of poems by Rimbaud.

SUBJECTS FOR DISCUSSION

1. 'Rimbaud, poet of intensified sensations': illustrate what might have been meant by this comment.
2. What part is played in Rimbaud's poetry by what one might call 'a religious sensitivity'?

3. It has been said that, in *Le Bateau ivre*, 'Rimbaud exprime, avec puissance et solennité, le caractère aventureux de l'imagination adolescente' (P. SEGHERS). Develop this remark with reference to the selection as a whole.
4. How dramatically does Rimbaud treat the themes of revolt, solitude and liberty in his poems?
5. Study the importance of childhood in Rimbaud's work: its values, its vision, its emotions.
6. Rimbaud's imagination has been described as 'coloured, dynamic, theatrical'. Study the appropriateness of this description. What other adjectives would you add to complete the picture?

Jules Laforgue

Complainte à Notre-Dame des Soirs

This poem is a lament to the female divinity of the Moon, Our Lady of the Evenings (sometimes called 'la reine des ombres' or 'Vénus' in earlier Romantic poetry, but associated here by Laforgue, for the purposes of religious protest and satire, with the Virgin Mary). Behind Laforgue's 'lunar' inspiration, one detects the influence of such Baudelairean poems as *Tristesses de la lune* (where the pale-sheened, self-caressing celestial body occasionally lets a tear fall down to this earth, which the poet furtively captures) or *Le Revenant* (where he promises to give back 'Des baisers froids comme la lune' to his indifferent mistress), and, perhaps more particularly in this context, *Avec ses vêtements*..., the last lines of which read: 'Resplendit à jamais, comme un astre inutile,/La froide majesté de la femme stérile'.

To what extent does this *complainte* reflect a religious crisis ('ange malade', 'Ciels vrais', 's'y crucifige', 'la Mecque' etc.)? Aspects of the fourth stanza especially could be compared with Rimbaud's *Chanson de la plus haute tour*, which speaks of '...la si pauvre âme/Qui n'a que l'image/De la Notre-Dame!/Est-ce que l'on prie/La Vierge Marie?'. Is Laforgue's treatment different? In what way is it a deflation of some of the most hallowed Romantic myths, a mocking antidote to poetic idealism? Make a detailed comparison with Baudelaire's *Harmonie du soir* (the use of the rhymes 'encensoirs' and 'Reposoirs', the opening description of Nature's perfumes, the image of the sun congealing in its own blood, etc.): would it be fair to call this poem 'dissonance du soir' and is it mainly a sarcastic parody? One should also look at Baudelaire's *Correspondances* (cf. 'La Nature est un temple...' with the scientific idea here of Nature as a sap-factory) and the ending of *L'Invitation au voyage* (cf. the description of boats coming to rest in a rich sunset light with the curt 'couchants *défunts*' and somewhat babyish 'Dorlotent' found here), as well as Verlaine's *Soleils couchants* ('Berce de doux chants/Mon cœur qui s'oublie/Aux soleils couchants'). Two of Laforgue's favourite images feature prominently here: the death of the sun, and the evasive journeyings of the moon, an obsessive but sterile planet. The picture of the sun drawing its quadriga (or four-horse chariot), though taken from Classical mythology, is anti-heroic in that this chariot is seen to bleed in what seems like a cosmic disaster and the sun is dying in a grotesque rearing posture. The moon, traditionally thought to be a celestial sign, is used to mock the idea of correspondence or communion between heaven and earth (in the case of 'Lune aux échos dont communient les puits' the moon's echo or reflection is seen as a holy wafer in the watery mouth of a well, while later the moon invites the poet to capture it in the 'ciel des eaux', a kind of reverse image of heaven in which he would drown!). Study the stylistic effects: the highly original word-coining ('crucifige' combining 'crucifier' and 'figer', 'sexciproques' being an ironic comment on the imagined reciprocity of sexual grape-gathering), the sprinkling of scientific vocabulary mixing with the religious ('lymphatiques', 'axiomes'), the use of colloquialisms or a familiar tone especially in the addresses to Our Lady ('Have I told you straight what I think of you?' etc.), the positioning of the most explosive words ('peuh!', 'fade', 'dissèquent', etc.), the staccato exclamatory style of the second stanza which gives a sense of confusion, anguish and futility, the exploiting of the two different line-lengths.

Is the theme of love the key to this poem? Compare the vigorous descriptions in the third stanza of other men sucking pathetically at the folds of women's dresses (or creases of their bodies), willing to mutilate themselves for a promise of affection, and returning time and time again to sterile breasts with Baudelaire's picture of '... la multitude vile/Sous le fouet du Plaisir' in *Recueillement* or the gross sexual enslavement of man in the well-known *Au Lecteur*, where we see '... un débauché pauvre qui baise et mange/Le sein martyrisé d'une antique catin'. Note the recurrent detail of the look: 'Yeux des portraits...Pour un regard...De *vrais* yeux...' How is the love theme linked with that of the quest for truth (little principles of wisdom plucked uselessly at the very moment of death; things running away from him or tantalizing him 'au tournant d'une vérité'), with references to religious frustrations (far too many stations or stopping-places along the endless processional route of his life; studies of religious ritual which have ruined his youth and dried up his appetites; the prospect of an ultimate arrival which will dissolve like a mirage, of a meeting with supernatural lips which will only dissect him and disperse him forever into the great nothingness) and with the sense of the absurd? Is the predominant spirit of this poem anguished or flippant?

Complainte de la lune en province

For a guided commentary on this poem, see *The Appreciation of Modern French Poetry*, pp. 109–11.

Complainte du Roi de Thulé

Many poems have been written dramatizing the isolated regal figure, a symbol of the poet and his dilemmas. One thinks of Baudelaire's 'Je suis comme le roi d'un pays pluvieux', where the king can find no earthly satisfaction, Mallarmé's *Hérodiade*, where the princess is obsessed with purity, and Rimbaud's *Conte*, where a fairy-tale prince virtually leaves this world to pursue a relationship with a genie. Here, the King of Thulé's splenetic sadness resembles that of Baudelaire, his immaculate idealism that of Mallarmé (situated 'aux purs glaciers de l'esthétique'), and his superhuman ambition that of Rimbaud ('moi qui me suis dit mage ou ange'). There are also models for the King of Thulé himself: Nerval has written a *Roi de Thulé*, inspired by his translation of the ballad sung by Marguerite in Goethe's *Faust*.

What is your interpretation of the central enterprise: in what way might the veil, embroidered at length in the quiet and purity of the night and finally hem-stitched ('ourlé') before being taken towards the horizon (the island of Thule in the North Atlantic was once thought to mark the limits of the world), be representative of poetry? How do you explain the protagonist's tormented solicitude with regard to the sun (cf. 'Soleil-crevant' and its 'sang martyr' with 'couchants défunts' and 's'y crucifige' in the previous poem)? Is it ultimately a negative and self-destructive project, and what has it to do with the theme of love? Note that, just as in *Complainte à Notre-Dame des*

Soirs there was a parodic or negative *correspondance* between heaven and earth in the form of the moon's reflection in wells, here there is a terrible negative parallel between the sun, dying in flame and blood, and human life and love to which the sun applies its torch ('holocaustes vivipares' refers to a life-bearing process which is nothing but a series of sacrificial offerings to fire). Again religious references are prominent: 'Alcôve', usually applied to an intimate setting for love (cf. Baudelaire's *La Chevelure*), is used ironically here to refer to that ultimate mystical Boudoir at the door of which the sun makes its nightly martyr's offerings in the hope of being saved from darkness; and the 'Saint-Suaire' is the poet's version of the holy shroud in which Christ's body was wrapped, destined in this case to envelop the 'sacred heart' of the sun and put an end to the life of blood and pain. Compare this kind of 'descente aux enfers' undertaken by the King with the following words from Baudelaire's *Chant d'automne*: 'Et, comme le soleil dans son enfer polaire,/Mon cœur ne sera plus qu'un bloc rouge et glacé'. How rich a pattern of suggestion has Laforgue derived from the contrasting colours white and red (especially the 'métempsychose', or transmigration of the soul into another body, of the lilies into roses)? By what means has he combined simplicity and deep symbolic significance, both in the portrait of the king and in his own poetic style? Study the use of different line-lengths and stanza-forms (e.g. to isolate and emphasize certain words, to differentiate narrative from monologue, to heighten the characterization of the king and his idiosyncrasies of language and conception). Note the two deviations from the pattern of tenses ('... le soleil qui s'agonise' and 'Est descendu'): do these have any special effect? Do you find odd the mixture of abstract symbolism and popular ballad, solemnity and colloquialism, the portentous and the casual (e.g. the reference to his own song as 'cette scie', a hackneyed and boring refrain)? Why the final address to the 'braves amants' (in view of the fact that he is 'loin des jupes et des choses', removed from sexual snares and all the trivialities of physical love, and 'raillé des doux corsages', mocked by women in attractive bodices)? What similarities do you see between the king's journey and that of *Le Bateau ivre*? Compare the spell of the ice-realm as described in this poem with that in Mallarmé's *Le vierge, le vivace et le bel aujourd'hui...* and Michaux's *Icebergs*.

Complainte du soir des comices agricoles

Here we see Laforgue as the pungent and spirited satirist. His subject is the local agricultural show, the epitome of provincialism on display, at that moment when the festivities are coming to an end and one can best savour the mediocre pretention and hollowness of it all (cf. the setting of small-town sleepiness in *Complainte de la lune en province*, and the ironical reference to 'Soleils plénipotentiaires...Des spectacles agricoles' in *L'Hiver qui vient*). He also shows himself an expert master of form and ironic effect, mixing the stately Alexandrine with a limping three-syllable line which gives it an importunate jerk, and alternating the off-balance three-line stanza with a firm-footed refrain which acts as a common-sensical Chorus and has quite a different tone. Notice his use of incongruous or deflating juxtaposition: not only the mock gusto and bonhomie of the refrain which clashes with the rather wretched spectacle which it punctuates, but also the quick passage from the elevated to the plebeian (e.g. from 'là-haut' to 'se recrotter', from 'l'Idéal' to 'sillons', from royal hunting horns to snuffling fireworks, from tear-jerking violin strains to the piping, squeaking note of the flageolet). Study the various ways in which Laforgue's humour expresses itself: e.g. in linguistic inventiveness ('reniflent s'étouffer' as a variant on the standard form 'vont s'étouffer'); in the touches of literary parody (think of Baudelaire's 'Le violon frémit comme un cœur qu'on afflige' and Verlaine's 'Les sanglots longs/Des violons...', the reverence in which the idea of a return to one's authentic spiritual homeland and the word 'Idéal' are held by Baudelaire and Mallarmé, the cult of a kind of musical mysticism in Symbolist poetry to which the present 'piston', or cornet, does not make a very graceful contribution); in the satirical snapshot of the courting couple (her scruples of conscience and discomfiture so economically summed up in her worried fingering of the 'médaillon', and the unofficial union and loss of virginity so briskly and indirectly reported); in the adoption of a forced colloquial or music-hall tone (seen in 'Qu'on s'en donne une fière bosse', 'Let's have a real old beano!', and in the dropping of the mute 'e' in 'mâl's et femelles'); in the art of disguise, ironically saying one thing while meaning another. Follow the structural development of the poem: the widening perspective from 'gens de la noce' to 'gens de la Terre', the movement from satirical description to philosophical commentary, the final emotional surge on the part of the commentator. Is there evidence here of a disillusioned and fatalistic attitude to life, and a patronizing, derogatory view of humanity? (For the purposes of wider reading and to find a probable influential source, one should turn to the famous anti-Romantic description of the *comices agricoles* in Flaubert's novel *Madame Bovary*.)

Pierrots I

This poem is the first of a series of portraits of the clown Pierrot, a figure which, like the elegant man-about-town with a skeleton's skull found in so many of his drawings, haunted Laforgue's imagination. (Series of studies of this kind are more common in painting than in poetry – one thinks of Degas's ballet dancers or the acrobats and harlequins of Picasso's 'Pink period' in the early 1900s – but the reference to the Mona Lisa, 'la Joconde', suggests that Laforgue, in this his 'White period', was aware of the analogy and of giving a modern twist to the art of portraiture.) It is a significant piece, partly as an illustration of the author's quirkish but brilliant descriptive talents, and perhaps more especially as a documentary image of the so-called Decadent poet of the 1880s, steeped in an effete *fin de siècle* atmosphere, an atmosphere fed by Baudelaire's *Les Fleurs du mal* and producing weird flowers of a deviant, hybrid strain.

Make a detailed portrait of the clown-figure: how well does Laforgue make the stiff inventory of physical features conjure up a complex temperament; in what way is the clown a meeting-point of baffling contrasts and what is his attitude to life; where would you situate him between comedy and despair; is there anything in common between this anaemic nature (a study in whites) and the 'Roi de Thulé', devoted to the whiteness of the lily and a glacial purity? The fact that Pierrot gains sustenance from 'l'azur', from the ethereal realm, deserves further comment:. Baudelaire has already depicted the duality of the earth-bound poet, a creature of spiritual flight and comic degradation, in the symbol of the captured albatross, describing it as 'Ce voyageur ailé, comme il est gauche et veule!/Lui, naguère beau, qu'il est comique et laid!' and referring to '...ces rois de l'azur, maladroits et honteux'; while the last line of one of Mallarmé's well-known poems reads, '*Je suis hanté. L'Azur! l'Azur! l'Azur! l'Azur!*'. Laforgue's clown, the Decadent poet, is no longer 'hanté' or 'honteux', but nibbles in finicking fashion on 'l'azur', turning empyrean needs into a posture, a mockery, an artistic eccentricity (perhaps as the antidote to despair, the only deviant outlet for the impossible). In this respect, one should stress the importance of 'la dépravation du sens de l'infini' in Baudelaire's work and the fact that *Les Fleurs du mal* contains, in his own words, 'toute ma religion (travestie)': how relevant are these comments, especially to the final stanza? How would you explain the concluding maxim, 'mi-carême' meaning the middle of Lent, the period of fasting and deprivation (cf. 'Tout est pour le mieux dans le meilleur des mondes possibles' which is a legendary phrase from Voltaire's *Candide*, one of the most acute satirical exposures of naïve romantic idealism)?

Study Laforgue's pictorial ability: the way he freezes features into emphatic shapes (a hydrocephalic stick of asparagus, a bewitching geranium-shaped mouth, a conical hat planted on the kerchief which surrounds the head) and colours into substances (the white of the face in the form of cold-cream, the white of the clown's hat resembling flour, the white of the costume as that of rice though somewhat duller). Note also the use of vegetal images (asparagus, geranium, clover, dandelion, green vegetables, all implying a delicate hybrid upward growth which is fatally rooted to the earth). The poet's sense of dramatic presentation is very evident: it is seen in such contrasts as the Egyptian ring (the 'chaton de bague' is the stone-setting of a ring) set against the dandelion of the wastelands (cf. T. S. Eliot's title), or in different expressions of the mouth ranging from a bung-hole without a stopper to a Mona Lisa smile; in the revealing rhyme-pairings which link the vulgar word 'bonde' with the prestigious figure of 'la Joconde' and the suggestiveness of 'l'azur' with the ridiculousness of 'œufs durs'; in the final bringing to life of the figure for the brief climactic statement which breaks the purely descriptive sequence and surprises the reader. Above all, it is the rarity of the phrase-making which is the most striking feature of the style: the playful Latinism of 'fraise empesée *idem*', a ruff starched the same as his neck; the daring modernistic rhyme on 'cold-cream' to describe the pallid hue of his beardless effeminate face; the semi-scientific 'hydrocéphale asperge' depicting an unhealthy overgrown brain which has grown too heavy for the body; the paradox of 'Glaciale-ment désopilé', glacially hilarious, with its contradictory ideas of cool impassivity and riotous laughter; the strange coining of 'transcendental en-allé', based on the verb 's'en aller', referring comically to the out-of-this-world 'gone-ness' of the Mona Lisa's futile smile.

Compare this poem with Michaux's *Clown*, which offers an image of the clown–poet with a very different spirit.

Locutions de Pierrots XII

As well as drawing portraits of Pierrots in their external appearance, Laforgue has done a series of studies of their pithy verbal expressions. Some of these could be des-cribed, to use a phrase from *Complainte à Notre-Dame des Soirs*, as 'Axiomes *in articulo mortis* déduits': brief truths or words of clownish good sense uttered in the proximity of death.

Note the laconic style of the first stanza, emotive yet inexplicit. What relation exists between the book and his yearnings, meaningfully linked by the arrangement of the first line: are the words '...nos phraséologies' contemptuous (cf. 'mots à vertiges!' in *Complainte à Notre-Dame des Soirs*) and what is gained by keeping this phrase as the conclusion to the stanza? Compare this desire to escape from sensual vulgarity ('goujates' means crude and boorish), compromise ('saluts' here would refer to bowing) and utilitarianism with Baudelaire's yearning to be 'n'importe où hors du monde', Mallarmé's 'Fuir! là-bas fuir!', and Laforgue's own King of Thule whose spirituality moves '...loin des jupes et des choses'. In the second stanza the words 'Encore un...' and 'chronique' maintain the tone of weariness and *déjà vu*. How is the sense of an impasse or vicious circle reinforced? (Note that not only is this a 'locution de Pierrot' but that what he procreates are also 'pierrots', reflective images of himself, so that he is a kind of sterile literary Narcissus.) How do you interpret the diagnosis of 'orphe-linisme'? The summary of the dead Pierrot's nature reveals much about both Laforgue and the style of his poems: there is a dose of 'cœur' (a highly vulnerable emotional sensitivity), a 'dandysme' (posturing, an elegant aloofness and cynical indifference), an outlook on life which is 'lunaire' (other-worldly, spectral and even sterile), and the whole contained in an eccentric if not absurd body (in Laforgue's own case eroded by tuberculosis, in the case of his poetry marked by contortions of verse-form and vocabulary). The final stanza widens the theme to include the death or twilight of the gods (one source of the 'crepuscular spirit' in late nineteenth-century poetry), bringing together the ideas of a literary and a religious impasse (cf. 'Vos Rites, jalonnés de sales bibliothèques... m'ont tari de chers goûts' in *Complainte à Notre-Dame des Soirs*): 'hures' are the severed useless heads of fish or wild-boar and suggest, by association, gods chopped off from the body of the world which is left to bleed and be digested into nothingness. What is the effect of the more brisk and colloquial tone in the penultimate lines? Has the poet achieved an appropriate ending with his words 'Inclusive Sinécure', a sinecure being a job or position where one receives a big reward for doing next to nothing and literally a state without cares, 'Inclusive' because it encloses everything within it and nothing escapes? (Notice that, in this dismissive 'signing-off', he is fulfilling the implications of the initial 'Encore un livre...', as if now disinterested in his own product.) Do you find evidence in other works by Laforgue of an opting out of life or some other futile cycle ('déguerpir' means 'to clear off')?

Locutions de Pierrots XVI

Like all the other poems in this sequence of *locutions*, this takes the form of three brief stanzas, hardly longer than an epitaph, written in a controlled, spare style. The speaker here might be seen as a distant descendant of the characters in Verlaine's *Fêtes galantes*: superior idle people in elegant, moonlit parks, indulging their fantasies and unconfessed dreams in play and pretence. But he is intellectually more complex and more lucid, and his needs are of a metaphysical kind.

In what way is it appropriate to speak here of a tragi-comic incongruity or discrepancy between the means and the end? Notice how Laforgue brings his stanzas to an understated, enigmatic conclusion: what does he mean by '...devenir un légendaire' (to be taken out of time into myth, out of reality into superreality?) and by '... j'exhale/ Des conseils doux de Crucifix' (that all that issues forth, instead of a superior Pythian wisdom, are a few limp and harmless religious clichés? cf. Rimbaud's disgust at his own weakness to Christian influence, expressed in his words 'Je suis esclave de mon baptême')? What is the significance of the image of the circle, either in the form of rings in the pools or smoke-rings blown in the air, and what has it to do with the project to become 'un légendaire'? (One might compare 'Qui fait des ronds dans les bassins' with the *correspondance* between moon and water suggested in the phrase 'Lune aux échos dont communient les puits' in *Complainte à Notre-Dame des Soirs*, and 'J'arrondis ma bouche et j'exhale' with the first stanza of Mallarmé's poem *Toute l'âme résumée...*) What similarities do you find from the point of view of theme, emphasis, style and tone, between the final stanza and that of the previous *locution*, 'Encore un livre...'? The reference to 'Lunes d'antan' is a parodic variant on the refrain 'Mais où sont les *neiges* d'antan?' of a ballad by Villon: here it represents a lost faith in those fulsome Moons that one could celebrate as demi-divinities and sing about ingenuously in poetry, these having died with yesteryear. All that is left is only Laforgue's spectral and deathly version, tinged with scepticism and cosmic disillusion. Note that the phrase 'un viveur lunaire', with its nice paradox which catches the attention from the first line, echoes the 'dandysme lunaire' prominently displayed in the previous poem; while the 'mandarin *pâle*' makes one think back to the immaculate 'Roi de Thulé' in love with lilies and 'd'amour pur transi', as well as to the farinaceous hue of the Pierrots (who, in fact, fed on 'mandarines', the effeminate form, as it were, of 'mandarins').

L'Hiver qui vient

For a guided commentary on this poem, see *The Appreciation of Modern French Poetry*, pp. 113–17.

SUBJECTS FOR DISCUSSION

1. 'Laforgue mêle subtilement l'élégance et la vulgarité' (P. REBOUL). Discuss and illustrate.
2. How appropriate do you find the following description of Laforgue's work: 'ces poèmes clownesques, durs et fins comme des aiguilles' (P. REBOUL)?
3. In what way would it be true to say that Laforgue's poetry is the expression of a contradictory spirit? How is this felt in the tensions of his style?
4. 'Avec un humour apitoyé, trop réussi pour ne pas faire mal, il a exprimé le désespoir métaphysique de la conscience humaine' (P. REBOUL): what evidence do you find of a despairing view of life in Laforgue, and what part does humour play in its expression?
5. What is the suggested significance of the following obsessive images in Laforgue's poetry: the moon, the clown-figure, the death of the sun, the seasons?
6. Does it seem to you that, after Baudelaire, Mallarmé, Verlaine and Rimbaud, Laforgue definitely closes a chapter in the history of nineteenth-century French poetry?

Paul Valéry

L'Abeille

One of the most frequent questions which arise out of Valéry's poetry concerns the absence or presence of symbolic interpretations. One critic will tell you that *L'Abeille* depicts the poet's benumbed soul seeking a moment of spiritual inspiration, another that it shows the poet fascinated by the flitting dart of poetry, another that it is simply a sexual poem in which the woman's desire demands renewed or superior satisfaction. To make a choice is an impoverishment of the poem's evocative power; and, in any case, arguments over meaning must not be allowed to push into the background the success of *L'Abeille* as an exploitation of other properties of language.

What does the syntactical rhythm of the first stanza help to evoke? The contrast between the two protagonists is clearly established: the aggressive, lethal sharpness of the bee's sting ('fine...mortelle...pointe') and the delicate, coquettish vulnerability of the feminine 'je' ('tendre... songe...dentelle'). What is gained by the fact that the speaker refers to herself here only in figurative language? What does the use of the word 'songe' suggest? What emotions are present in the woman in the first two stanzas, and what seems to be her attitude to herself? How is the analogy between fruit and the woman's body developed? Do you see a visual similarity between 'corbeille' and the rib-cage, for instance? The indirect sexual provocation of the first quatrain becomes a direct exhortation in the second, reflecting the growing swell of a desire which yearns to know more than this surface lethargy or deadness of feeling. Compare 'un peu de moi-même vermeille' with the red juice of self-discovery bursting from under the surface in *Les Grenades*. Study the difference in tone between the octet and the sestet; the effect of the switch from feminine rhymes (all visually similar) to masculine rhymes (all subtly linked: '*tourment...terminé...dormant...d'or*'); and the elements which give a rapid, affirmative rhythm to the first tercet. The final stanza moves significantly and discreetly from the body to the mind through the use of the singular 'mon sens' and the intellectual associations of 'illuminé' and 'alerte': can these be seen as indications of a tacit symbolism (which would transform the bee-sting into a moment either of inspiration or of intense spiritual awareness)? Note how Valéry gives the poem a well-rounded unity (as well as a conclusiveness) by setting up close sound-echoes between line 13 and the first line; by introducing a kind of final refrain intensified by the passage from 'sommeille' to 's'endort'; and by stressing the paradox that this salvation from death is accomplished by something which is 'si mortelle'. The near-repetition of the resonant 'Sur qui l'Amour meurt ou sommeille' has been described as an element of preciosity; to what extent could the whole poem be called precious? Compare the unclear merging of the erotic and the intellectual in this poem with similar ambiguities in *Les Pas* and *Le Sylphe*.

Les Pas

A graceful love poem or a clever piece of symbolism which evokes the poet's attitude towards his inspiration? The level of interpretation may be left to the reader; but, unlike some clearly symbolic poems, *Les Pas* is rich on its simplest level which portrays the lover anticipating the presence of his willing mistress.

The close relationship between the poet and the footsteps is made at once by the image of the first line which suggests an atmosphere of innocence and hushed intimacy. What rhythmical effects does Valéry seek in line 2? Study the gathering adulation of the poet for the approaching figure; the teasing balance between approach and distance, between physical images and indefinite abstraction, between excitement at imminent physical possession and a feeling of quasi-religious devotion, between what seems to have external reality and yet might be a purely inner drama; and, in the phonetic weave of stanzas 1 and 2, the measured use of plosives (which may or may not be expressive). How would you explain the dilatory syntax of the 'si...' clause? What insight does the unusual 'l'habitant de mes pensées' give into Valéry's notion of the self? The growing anticipation of the kiss that will relieve the poet's hunger so infuses this third stanza that the imperative 'Ne hâte pas cet acte tendre' comes as a surprise and adds complexity to the poet's mood. To what does the syntactically ambiguous 'Douceur d'être et de n'être pas,' refer: the kiss which is prepared but not yet given, the poet's ecstasy in which he trembles between awareness of self and loss of self, or the footsteps which by definition consist of alternating silence and sound, absence and presence? What is the effect of the sudden change from present to past tenses, and from 'tu' to 'vous' (underlined by the conspicuous 'echo' of 'Tes pas' in the final 'vos pas')? The suggestion in the last three lines is perhaps that the mistress is now there in front of the poet and that his heart, once perfectly in phase with the footsteps, is now (as they are) still, stopped by the breath-taking apparition of the 'ombre divine'. But Valéry has made his last line the most ambiguous: how might it link back with the first line and the idea of an apparition self-created?

Valéry himself said of *Les Pas* that it was a 'petit poème purement sentimental auquel on prête un sens intellectuel, un symbole de "l'inspiration"'. How valid is a symbolic interpretation in your opinion? Compare and contrast this poem with Verlaine's *Les chères mains qui furent miennes...* (also concerned with a partial physical apparition and a devotional dream-atmosphere).

La Ceinture

For a guided commentary on this poem, see *The Appreciation of Modern French Poetry*, pp. 118–20.

Le Sylphe

The meaning of this wispish sonnet, written in playful five-syllable lines is teasingly elusive: is the sylph the poet himself? is he inspiration, breathing power into poetry? or is he rather a poetic spirit which emanates from poetry? Those looking for an intellectual reading may be either reassured or provoked by the sylph's mischievous remark, 'Aux meilleurs esprits/Que d'erreurs promises!' Perhaps, in the light of this, we should just accept the poem as a game in which the 'je' plays hide-and-seek with his reader.

What features in the first stanza establish the 'je' as a puckish, ethereal figure? How does the form enhance the content (consider the lack of punctuation, the rhythm and internal sound-echoes)? As if with the cast of a wand, the sylph can finish off tasks; in the same way, one might argue, a flash of inspiration (the result of chance or a stroke of genius?) can supply the poet with the word or image he has been waiting for. What are the two meanings of the word 'génie'? In the tercets, notice how the 'je' has vanished into thin air, leaving behind him his taunting adjectives which proclaim his intangibility; how the refrain is varied (although the rhythm and some of the sounds are kept) in a stanza which encourages and at the same time mocks attempts to construct symbolic interpretations of the poem (cf. the final couplet, though it has a very different mood, of Rimbaud's *O saisons, ô châteaux...*); how the conclusion (as in *Les Grenades* and *Les Pas*) is the most provocative part of the poem. The suggestive eroticism of the glimpsed breast closes the sonnet, impishly prodding desire, yet giving no hope of satisfaction. Note how, as in *L'Abeille*, Valéry has brought together the images of an airy mobile creature and of the breast, momentarily glimpsed or exposed from beneath its protective coverings.

Finally, study the rhyming (the arrangement, the dominance of masculine rhymes and rhymes containing 'voyelles aiguës', [y, i]).

L'Insinuant

This poem uses the same pentasyllabic metre as *Le Sylphe* which it follows in the definitive edition of *Charmes* and has as its voice an evasive spirit possessing the same self-confidence and the same deceptiveness (cf. 'erreurs promises' and 'Secrets du menteur') as the sylph. But here the skipping impudence is replaced by a sinuous charm which winds its way around the reader. Once again there are various levels of interpretation: the 'insinuant' may be the Serpent seducing Eve (Valéry was later to write on this subject in *Ebauche d'un serpent*); or a Don Juan caressing his mistress; or, more symbolically, the poet bewitching his readers.

In the first stanza the speaker seems to be self-admiring, unhurried and sure of his skill. What do the 'Courbes' suggest: the hypnotic undulations of a snake, the amorous caresses of a lover or the sway of poetic rhythm? Is the ambiguity a merit or defect? The second stanza is more assertive with the dominant 'je' confessing freely to the woman that the 'mazy motion', however bewildering, is carefully directed and has a purpose behind it. Study the wily paradox of lines 7–8; the effect of the *points de suspension*; the change of tone as the totally composed seducer makes an aside to comment on the effect of his libertine attitude; the contrast between the confusion of 'désoriente' and the decisiveness of 'Je sais où je vais'. The poem coils back to its beginning with a repetition ('O Courbes...') which is calculated to charm the woman, to penetrate subtly into her consciousness by offering her a familiar landmark just when she is lost. Compare the ending of the poem with that of *Les Pas*; if one accepts that both poems might have symbolic readings, what are the basic differences between them on this level? What neat effect does Valéry gain from disturbing the balance of rhymes in the last stanza, leaving 'menteur' without a partner? What variations of tone would you use if you were reciting this poem?

Les Grenades

This still-life from *Charmes* casts its spell immediately with the rather grotesque transformation of the pomegranates into symbols of the human brain in which intellectual musings (including the poetic) are nurtured, ripened and finally brought to fruition, exploding seeds of ideas like shrapnel. What is the tone of the first stanza? How is the verse-form used to strengthen the analogy between 'grenades' and 'fronts'? Notice the opulent rhyming of lines 1 and 4, and the rich visual pattern of 'entr'*ouver*tes . . .*souve*rains. . .dé*couver*tes', both of which help to give these opening lines a unity and a quality of self-enclosure. A new movement begins, its grammatical tension to be broken only in the final stanza with the main verb 'Fait rêver'. Study the development of each of the two central stanzas; the parallel expressiveness of the detonating verbs 'Craquer' and 'Crève'; the introduction of mineral images; the teeming sound-patterns which, in some cases, echo the sense (compare, for instance, the husky, anagrammatic 'Et que si l'or sec de l'écorce' and the aggressive 'Crève' with the luscious alliteration of 'gemmes rouges de jus'). In the sensuous relishing of the mellow fruit (lines 5–11), is the initial analogy forgotten, or enriched by accumulated suggestions? The final stanza re-introduces it but now with a much more personal application: the sight of the bursting pomegranates makes the poet think of a past, fleeting state of spiritual intensity ('une âme que j'eus') which was the fruit of some hidden process of maturation and some formerly undivulged structural pattern ('secrète architecture') in his inner self. The paradox is that this past soul, now detached from the poet and proved to be at a kind of 'dead' distance, can still be made to dream, so that it is both presence and absence (cf. *Les Pas*). Coming after two 'si. . .' clauses which express outward, dynamic force and ultimate dispersion, in what way could these last three lines be seen to offer a sort of compensatory conclusion? Or does the conclusion propose a pessimistic contrast between the fruits' fertility and the poet's sterile introspection? Or do you see any other interpretation? Valéry has been deliberately inexplicit and has carefully ripened the suggestiveness of his poem which grows out of the narrow, intellectual grain of the first verse into the sensuous pulpiness of the central stanzas and then finally bursts into the unclear, thought-provoking image of a past soul, dreaming of its 'secrète architecture'.

How far would you accept the view that *Les Grenades* contains an analogy of the act of poetic creation (cf. Mallarmé's *Toute l'âme résumée. . .*)? Consider, for instance, Valéry's own assertion that 'Le beau vers se trouve à l'extrémité d'un développement de la pensée dont il est le véritable fruit'. Compare these images of a burst or penetrated skin and a luminous stimulus with those in *L'Abeille*.

Le Cimetière marin

For a guided commentary on this poem, see *The Appreciation of Modern French Poetry*, pp. 124–31.

La Caresse

The theme of this poem is the power of love to soothe pain; it is one of the least ambiguous of Valéry's poems. The poet's feverish hands are cooled by those of his beloved: notice the movement from the initial plea (emphasized by the construction: 'Mes chaudes mains' followed by its pronoun 'les' and stressed by the urgent *enjambement*) to the relief, once his plea has been answered (indicated by the *points de suspension* and the relaxed general observation which comes after them). The remaining two stanzas smooth into each other with very little punctuation to halt the undulating, airy rhythm of the *impair* line. Study the way in which the hard, the glittering, the mineral lose their rigidity; the way in which Valéry accumulates images of movement, suppleness and relaxation; and the way in which he uses waves of sound-patterns which give fluidity to his verse (particularly the [f]'s in lines 5–8 and the permutations of [e, t, a, l, ã] in lines 9–12). The poem ends with the poet's pain (physical or mental?) diluted by the caress into the less piercing emotion of melancholy.

Compare this piece with Verlaine's *Les chères mains qui furent miennes*...

SUBJECTS FOR DISCUSSION

1. The poems in this selection all come from Valéry's collection *Charmes*. Does this seem an appropriate title for them?
2. In reply to those who see Valéry primarily as a philosopher–poet, M. Raymond writes, 'Etranger à tout didactisme, jamais le vers ne se laisse dépouiller de sa pulpe, ne se laisse *traduire*'. Does Valéry, in your opinion, succeed in avoiding the dangers of the philosophical and the abstract?
3. 'La richesse d'une œuvre est le nombre des sens ou des valeurs qu'elle peut recevoir tout en demeurant elle-même' (VALÉRY). Discuss.
4. J. R. Lawler, referring to *Charmes*, speaks of 'le voluptueux dessein métaphorique de chaque pièce'. How well does Valéry exploit the extended metaphor? How would you justify the adjective 'voluptueux'?
5. Consider Valéry's poems in the light of his own definition of poetry as 'cette hésitation prolongée entre le son et le sens'.
6. In view of the fact that he looked upon poetry partly as a game, a play of technique and the intellect, to what extent would you call Valéry a lyrical poet?

Guillaume Apollinaire

Le Pont Mirabeau

This is one of Apollinaire's most hauntingly musical poems, reminiscent of Verlaine in its use of the melodic refrain, intense rhyme-scheme and interplay of repetitive sound. Its effect is all the more direct in that its themes are the most universal (loss of love, passage of time, frustrated hopes, pain of memory), and there is nothing *recherché* in its vocabulary or expression. But, as is often the case with Verlaine, one finds a complex, shifting mental state beneath the deceptively soothing musical monotony. The first stanza indicates a restless mood, with the poet's mind slipping in four brief movements from descriptive impression to a deeper figurative impression, and then from plaintive question (implying an inability to rule his own thoughts and memories) to a reminiscence of a former pattern of events (the significance of which is not too certain: is he trying to assure himself that the alternating cycle of happy and unhappy periods is bound to run true to form again?). After the refrain, the following stanza takes a new direction. It brings a wishful urge to defy the natural course of things (and the truth of the lovers' relationship as fatally acknowledged in the first lines of the poem) by identifying himself and his loved one with the stable and the perennial. The image of holding hands to form a bridge is quite childlike in conception: in what way does the fourth line of this verse make it more unusual and ambiguous? The more forceful syntax and expression of the third stanza tightens the sense of inevitability and carries an acute note of emotional weariness. Here the statement that hope is not a consoling and positive force as is often thought but a violent and destructive one (cf. Baudelaire's *Quand le ciel bas et lourd. . .*) has an element of the unexpected. The last stanza, confirming that nothing can be halted or called back, sinks finally into a mood of resignation or philosophical acceptance of fate (what part does the recurrence of the poem's first line play in this?). Note the movements of ebb and flow: from 'Vienne la nuit' to 'Restons. . .', from pain that love slips away so swiftly to 'Comme la vie est lente', from a disinclination to remember to fond reminiscence.

Compare Apollinaire's handling of the refrain alternating with stanzas of irregular metre with that of Baudelaire in *L'Invitation au voyage*. Show how this refrain is not simply repetitive but continually changes its emphasis and value according to what has preceded it. If the poet had joined the second lines (whose last word never has a matching terminal rhyme) and the third lines of his stanzas, he would have produced a more regular verse of three rhyming decasyllables: why do you think he chooses this division into two smaller lines? What effect is drawn from the use of tenses? How well has Apollinaire blended the three leitmotifs of the river, love and time? What contribution does the absence of punctuation make to the success of the poem?

Marie

Published in 1912, this poem reflects the rift which occurred in that year between Apollinaire and Marie Laurencin, a woman painter with whom he had had a particularly close relationship. But it is pointless to look for further biographical detail. Few poets have disguised their lyrical sources more than Apollinaire (either by a mask of irony, apparently illogical juxtapositions, or a confusion of times and places). *Marie* itself has the simple, ingenuous quality of a folk-song, but its brisk, slightly inconsequential style ensures that the lyrical thread is not always prominent and, despite its direct plaintive appeal, not always easy to fathom.

Examine the way in which the themes of time (youth and age, the seasons, the changing colour of hair), departure (a missing person, music drifting away, sheep moving off into the distance, leaves and hairs falling), instability (soldiers on the move, a heart fitful and changing, the poet as an impermanent passer-by) and uncertainty (the questioning and self-questioning form, the image of masks or temporary guises, the suggestion of broken promises, the desire to be sure of the constancy of both his own and another person's identity) are introduced and expanded. Study the varied nuances of the theme of love: what is the value of the one Alexandrine thrown in to break the octosyllabic pattern; do the words 'Quand donc reviendrez-vous Marie' and 'mais vous aimer à peine' indicate a conflict of feeling; are the final lines of the third stanza a confession of the impermanence of his own emotional attachments and is this to be linked to the reference to 'aveux'; how relevant is the discreet transition from the 'vous' to the 'tu' address, and does it have any bearing on the transition from 'mon mal', described as 'délicieux', to 'ma peine', which is said to pour out unstemmed? Note the overall structural development: the way in which the last stanza joins again with the first by the repetition of the 'Quand donc. . .' form (at first suggesting a possible renewal and then a hoped-for finale), and by the fact that these stanzas alone bring together all three tenses, past, present and future; and the progression from a rustic folk atmosphere ('la maclotte' is a regional dance of the Ardennes district of Belgium, where Apollinaire spent several months in the summer of 1899) to a modern city setting, from collective festive gaiety to hints of a solitary introverted wandering. Are there reminiscences here of *Le Pont Mirabeau*? Which do you find the more moving poem?

La Tzigane

For a guided commentary on this poem, see *The Appreciation of Modern French Poetry*, pp. 132–4.

L'Emigrant de Landor Road

The title is explained by two trips made by Apollinaire to Landor Road, London in 1903 and 1904, which was the home of Annie Playden, an English girl-with whom he had fallen in love in Germany a year or two earlier while he was tutor and she was governess in the same aristocratic household. The London visits were not a success, Annie, it appears, evading his offers of marriage by saying that she was departing for America (a rôle which, perhaps as a kind of morale-booster, the poet pretends to adopt for himself in the third stanza where he talks of grand dreams of the 'prairies lyriques').

The scene for the first six stanzas is a high class English tailor's shop (presumably at some time *after* a demoralizing experience, although this is never actually referred to, for the client speaks of his resolve never to return to these shores and is described with a touch of humorous exaggeration in the title as an emigrant). Note the emphasis on symbols of English nobility and glory ('fournisseur du roi', 'un lord', 'un soldat des Indes' and 'crachats', which are stars of an order), as if the poet had a subconscious need to identify himself with these. Look closely at the theme of appearances (e.g. the contrast between the first and second stanzas which isolates the false, glossy world of the shop from the aimless and loveless human reality milling on the pavements outside; and, in the third and fourth stanzas, the small details such as 'ombre *aveugle*' and 'dormir *enfin*' which make one suspect a more vulnerable personality with a painful history lurking beneath the bold talk and impressive front). By what means is the illusion that a new suit of clothes can make a new man deflated? Apollinaire's humorous vision in this section is particularly remarkable: the touch of fantasy which turns the tailor into a cross between Beau Brummell and Bluebeard; the incongruous image of the civilized European lying on some desert isle in his best King's Row togs; the personification which brings the dummies to life, in a kind of dream-sequence, to give him their clothes and perhaps exchange rôles with him. The little stanza in a faster tempo adds a further personification, that of time, probably the most influential force in Apollinaire's poetry: how do these four lines (harking back to the second stanza in that they switch back to what is moving past outside the window) reinforce the idea of the falsity of the world of the shop and the protagonist's attempted escapism, and give depth to the poem?

The theme of time is expanded (and given a different perspective) in the following stanza, which acts as a kind of interlude or momentary suspension of the action (the detail of 'la femme du diable' stems from an old saying 'Le diable bat sa femme et marie sa fille', referring to weather which is rainy and sunny at the same time, but the poet has made a significant change of rôles). Then, time having moved on and done its fatal work, the last six stanzas switch the drama to a new location: the tailor's shop has gone; in its place the port. Is there a discernible change of mood from now on? Compare 'Et s'assit' with 'se traînaient par terre' earlier. Note the new emphasis on 'la foule' (of which the protagonist is now part), and on wishful gestures of human communication and unity (cf. 'Les mains dans les mains restons face à face' in *Le Pont Mirabeau*). How well does the poet bring out the pathos of the emigrants' situation, and dramatize his hero's isolation and emotional need? Study the indirect and suggestive way in which Apollinaire has developed the themes of love and death throughout the poem, culminating in the reference to the 'doge' (the Doge of Venice used to perform a symbolic wedding ceremony each year between the city and the sea by throwing a ring into the lagoon), the play on words of 'sirène', and the final haunting words 'derniers serments'. Study also the theme of memory: does it come into prominence at an appropriate point? how colourfully is it presented? how does it lead, through the image of 'poux' which bite away tormentingly at his head (cf. the opening picture of tailor's dummies with their heads cut off) into the final desire for a black oblivion in which the corpses of his past days will be ravaged by the waiting sharks? Notice that, in the final stanza, a first-personal voice again (cf. stanza 3) bursts through the third-personal narration: what does this contribute to the effect of the finale?

From a stylistic point of view, study Apollinaire's technique of unadvertised switches (from inside the shop to outside, from narrative to 'live' conversation, from one scene to another), and the way in which he has exploited line variations. How good an illustration is this poem of what one critic has called 'le rire en pleurs', a blend of the ironic humorist and the sentimentalist?

Rosemonde

For a guided commentary on this poem, see *The Appreciation of Modern French Poetry*, pp. 135–6.

Les Sapins

This is an early poem, written during Apollinaire's stay in the Rhineland in 1901–2. It is a descriptive piece, a light and fanciful study of fir-trees in all their moods and guises. Apollinaire's approach, though highly imaginative and metaphorical, is refreshingly picturesque and uncomplicated. It contrasts with the Romantic treatment of nature as a reflective setting for the drama of the poet's emotions and aspirations (here no link is made with the poet's personal preoccupations), and with the deeper metaphysical resonances implicit in Baudelaire's 'La Nature est un temple où de vivants piliers/Laissent parfois sortir de confuses paroles' (here, although there are references to the occult and the religious, these are captured in quaint and entertaining visual images which militate against over-seriousness or symbolic speculation).

How important is the theme of change? Is there evidence here of Apollinaire's common preoccupation with time? How well does he combine the mysterious and the homely? Could one look on the description of the firs as a comment on human life? It is not quite sure which seven arts he has in mind, but he depicts them as astrologers, philosophers, musicians, magicians, dancers, holy men, doctors, etc. in a seemingly endless series of personifications. Note, stylistically, the use of simple repetitions ('longues...longues', 'grands...grands', 'vieux...vieux'); the coining of words like 'ensongés' (as one might say 'bedreamed') and 'Incantent' ('to spellbind'); the playing with words ('abattus...les bateaux', 'changés/En étoiles et enneigés'); the rhythmical effects of lines such as 'Aux longues branches langoureuses' and the final line of the poem; the use of the shorter third line, which tends to break each stanza into two movements. In all, it is a poem of great charm and enchantment, a brilliant display of ever-changing appearances, of light, sound, outline and motion.

Les Femmes

This is another piece from the section in *Alcools* entitled *Rhénanes*, Rhenish poems or Rhineland sketches. It is a poem with a good deal of local colour, showing Apollinaire's taste (in contrast with that of the Symbolists for the mysterious, the quintessential and the rarefied) for humble settings, everyday people, 'unpoetic' details and quite mundane snippets of conversation. But despite the commonplace nature of the subject-matter, it is an experimental poem in form, a precursor of the modernistic *poèmes–conversations* of *Calligrammes*, in which casual and unpredictable *collages* are effected containing bits and pieces of live speech. Note the extremely free, supple organization of the verse (although all the lines are respectable Alexandrines): might one view Apollinaire's art here as one of stitching (cf. '...les femmes cousent')? Assess the balance he achieves between the particular (common proper names, plain foods like 'marmelade' and 'saindoux', lard etc.) and the universal (names like Herr Traum, Mr Dream, and Frau Sorge, Mrs Care, general truths such as 'L'amour rend triste', etc.); the trivial (the postman stopping for a chat, the stockings which have been badly darned, etc.) and the serious (the trembling barn-owl, the dying sacristan, the suggestion of the wind speaking Latin phrases, etc.). How, particularly, does the poet employ description of the natural setting (is there any similarity in this respect to the descriptive technique of *Les Sapins*)? What is the effect of the many religious references (cypress trees looking like the Pope, vineyards with their twisted plants looking like charnel-houses and shrouds under the snow, the women crossing themselves, etc.)? Do you find this poem an authentic and moving 'slice of life' or a somewhat forced and empty piece of eavesdropping? Is there any indication of the poet's own attitude to his subject-matter: is he more the satirist or the benign, sympathetic onlooker? Can one glean different personalities in this criss-cross of voices? The main themes here, as in *Le Pont Mirabeau* and *L'Emigrant de Landor Road*, are love and death, but Apollinaire's presentation in this instance is quite different and unique.

1909

So many of Apollinaire's poems have a woman as their central figure, sometimes named as in *Rosemonde* and *Marie*, sometimes anonymous and vaguely symbolic. She is almost invariably associated with the theme of time. In this case, as the title *1909* suggests, it is time seen in a historical as well as a personal perspective.

   This is a piece of very unpredictable free verse, the poetry of which springs not from the intrinsic melodic qualities or expert prosody of each line, but from the unusual interplay of parts. The opening, in fact, is strikingly flat and unpoetic, like a fragment of commentary on a fashion parade ('ottoman' is a silk fabric, originally from Turkey, and 'violine' a dark violet shade), and has neither rhyme nor rhythmical pattern. But this dispassionate listing of externals makes all the more dramatic the burst of spirit, colour, humour and unusual vision (like a dashing portrait by a Fauvist painter) of the following section. Notice how, from this point on, Apollinaire applies a tech-nique of alternation, switching from longer descriptions of the high-society woman's physical finery to terse emotive interjections, thus sketching a contrast between her extravagant self-advertisement and the poet's self-effacement, her aristocratic insou-ciance and his uncertainties and diffidence as a lover. (Does the phrase 'N'entendra-t-on jamais sonner minuit' have the same value here as 'Vienne la nuit' in *Le Pont Mirabeau* and 'Quand donc finira la semaine' in *Marie*?) The crucial contrast does not emerge until the final section. How relevant to this finale is the knowledge that Mme Récamier was a salon beauty of the late eighteenth and early nineteenth century, celebrated in a portrait by the famous neo-Classical painter David? In what sense can one speak of a conflict between two ages, two sets of values and two ideals of beauty (remembering that Apollinaire in his well-known *profession de foi*, *La jolie rousse*, has seen himself tossed between tradition and invention, order and adventure, and has said 'Je déteste les artistes qui ne sont pas de leur époque')? In what way does this final section make one reconsider the apparently frivolous association of the woman's face with the tricolour (made France's flag in 1798, after the Revolution)? Does the idea of fear assume an added level of meaning at the end? To what effect does the poet make the last section more emphatic in rhythm and vocabulary?

Liens

Liens, written in 1913, was used as the dedicatory poem of the collection *Calligrammes*, as if to sum up its spirit of modernism and innovation. It is a poem which conveys the energy of the new technological or machine age (already hinted at in the ending of the previous poem, *1909*), and a new revolutionary fervour (note that, with the celebratory ringing of bells spreading out across Europe, one has the vision of 'Siècles pendus'). It stresses the vast network of communications, the forging of world-wide links and the prospects for unity and human fraternity (the reference to Towers of Babel turned into bridges implies the transformation of incomprehension and confusion into contact and concord). Study the structural progression of the poem (the way in which Apollinaire's procedure is one of *liens*, links made by *jeu de mots* or similarity of sound and leaps of association); and the variety of images that he welds together under this one-word heading: images of land ('Rails'), sea ('Câbles sous-marins') and air ('Violente pluie qui peigne les fumées', a remarkable image showing smoke being combed out into strands like wool in a carding-machine, or 'Araignées-Pontifes', spiders sitting like all-important dignitaries at the centre of their airy web); links of a material and an immaterial, concrete and figurative kind (cries, hands, rays of light, love-ties, etc.). Is there some ambiguity in his treatment of the main theme (look at the use of words suggesting freedom and imprisonment, promise and threat, the mechanical and the sentimental)? Notice that the last seven lines (like those of *1909*) suddenly twist the poem into a more personal and problematical perspective; how do you explain the paradoxical address to the senses (why should they be celebrated as the chief *raison d'être* of the poem? why are they referred to as 'chéris'? in what way are they relevant to the theme of time?)? How does the final line change the balance of things? Make a detailed contrast between the poetic style of this poem and that of *Le Pont Mirabeau* or *Marie*. Does the style here suit the subject-matter?

Fête

The principal themes of this poem, written from the trenches in 1915, are the age-old ones of love, death and war. But whether one looks upon it primarily as war poetry or love poetry, the amalgam achieved by Apollinaire is something fresh and original. The instruments of war become subject to his poetic fantasy and erotic longings, the result being an extremely agile, virtually simultaneous blending of images: two rockets exploding colourfully into the air, the bursting bloom of roses, and the thrusting tips of a woman's bared breasts fuse in the same vision; the velvety curve of a rose-petal evokes the soft curve of a woman's hip; the smooth parabola of shells in the sky becomes an airy but sensual caress.

Note how Apollinaire has brought together contrasting elements (the martial and the decorative, the virile and the graceful, the idealized and the frankly sensual, the modern and the traditional, the playful and the serious). The duality of the poet's position is neatly summed up in the image of him dreaming of breasts and his posthumous reputation as a lover rather than the threat of a real-life situation, or emptily contemplating his revolver with its safety-catch on while his mind floats off into an enchanted garden of literature (Saadi, a Persian poet of the twelfth and thirteenth century, was the author of a famous work *Le Jardin des Roses*). Apollinaire has been criticized for an apparently flippant and entertaining view of war in the poems of *Calligrammes* (an 'oh, what a lovely war' attitude or a tendency to see 'la guerre en dentelles'). Do you see any justification for such a criticism of *Fête*? It has also been said that he is at his best as an elegiac poet: is the expression of sentiment here constricted by the surprise images and elliptical style? How many shades of feeling go to make the poet's mood (does the simple melodic octosyllabic verse-form contribute to the tone)? What evidence is there here of Apollinaire's concern (so dominant in *Calligrammes*) for the typographical lay-out of his poems?

SUBJECTS FOR DISCUSSION

1. It has been said that in Apollinaire's poetry, 'le sentiment dominant est celui de la fuite des choses, des êtres, du temps' (Ph. RENAUD). Does this seem to be so? Does any other poetic emotion compete for pride of place?
2. Apollinaire looked upon the element of surprise as a crucial factor in poetry. Give a detailed illustration of this aspect of his artistic taste.
3. The poem *L'Emigrant de Landor Road* has been described as 'un mélange unique de fantaisie, d'humour, de cocasserie et de tristesse soudaine, mais passagère. Il y a là une fraîcheur, un entrain, une gaminerie presque, qui font de ce récit un adieu désinvolte aux peines de l'amour' (Ph. RENAUD). Consider the various terms of this quotation not only as a description of the one poem but of the selection as a whole.
4. Apollinaire is a love-poet, and yet he fights shy of the subjective style and self-disclosure. How does this give a distinctive quality to his treatment of the theme of love?
5. Study Apollinaire's use of humour in his poetry: what forms does it take, and what functions does it serve?
6. Critics have suggested that Apollinaire is a poet strongly attracted by the mysterious, but with a predominant taste for plain, uncomplicated realities. Do you see evidence of both these characteristics in his poems?

Jules Supervielle

Prophétie

Like many of Hugo's poems, those of Supervielle have a cosmic vision, inquiring into human purposes and the Earth's place in the universal pattern of things. A measure of prophecy is also common to both poets, but one finds in Supervielle's case, instead of a tone of high seriousness or a rolling tide of sombre and resonant phrases, picturesque images, a strange matter-of-factness and a jaunty, humorous and slightly magical imagination.

Prophétie launches immediately into several of Supervielle's most obsessive themes: the movement or loss of the Earth, which takes the terrestrial security from under one's feet; the invasion of space and the plunge into a kind of vertigo or primeval chaos; the metamorphosis of the familiar into the unfamiliar and the substantial into the unsubstantial; the passage from body into spirit, from life into life after death (the epigraph to the collection *Gravitations* reads, 'Lorsque nous serons morts nous parlerons de vie'). What use does the poet make of illogicality and paradox (e.g. in the humorous description of the 1905 brougham)? How effective is his interplay of the particular or clearly delineated and the uncircumscribable (e.g. in the pairing of phrases like 'humaine mappemonde', a map showing the two hemispheres of the world, and 'tristesse sans plafond'); of disquieting, even awesome implications and what one critic has called 'welcoming words'? Notice how, though describing space and absence, he avoids abstraction; and, though describing a universal catastrophe, avoids the macabre and the melodramatic. Study the dramatic organization of the ending (the reinforcement of negatives, the subtle gradation of '...ne pourra situer,/Ni préférer, ni même entendre', the parenthetical 'lui', the isolation of the direct speech). Does the wayward rhyming, in your opinion, suit the poem? Would it be right to speak of the naïvety and innocence of Supervielle's style? What bearing might this poem have on the collective title *Gravitations*?

Montévidéo

For a guided commentary on this poem, see *The Appreciation of Modern French Poetry*, pp. 138–40.

Haute mer

For a guided commentary on this poem, see *The Appreciation of Modern French Poetry*, pp. 141–2.

Sous le large

In his poetry Supervielle has made himself the sympathetic patron of animals. He writes, 'J'aime les animaux. Je voudrais pénétrer en eux, les imaginer, les sentir vivre'. At times he seems to be their divinity, illuminating the obscurity which they cannot oversee, giving voice to what is imprisoned in their mute faces. At the same time, by casting back reflections from beyond another frontier, they help him to situate himself.

   Explore the possibilities of this childishly simple narrative piece as a sombre parable: note the idea that 'if God did not exist we would have to invent him'; the suggestion that spiritual or affective needs go hand in hand with physical deficiencies; the importance of the themes of communication, time and eternity (cf. in *Prophétie* the passage beyond chronological measures from 'Un jour' to 'Confondant la nuit et le jour'); the attempted exchange between different realms; the ironic implications that the 'accident' at sea would be seen as something else by the fish, and that these are anyway 'poissons de la nuit'. Examine the perfectly divided two-part structure of the poem: why is this in itself appropriate; how has Supervielle achieved an upward expanding movement in the first two stanzas and a downward narrowing one in the last two; in what way does each part reach its own climax, heightening a feeling of inevitability and, finally, of pathos? Study the following features of style, relating them to the thematic development as a whole: in the first stanza, the contrast between the contorted monosyllables of the second line and the fluent and melodious tone of the line which follows; in the second stanza, the subtle suggestion of the word *mandibule* in the phrase '...mandent une bulle', the playful ambiguity of the word 'bulle' which can mean a bubble or a religious decree (e.g. a papal bull), the moment's suspense achieved by the inversion and the attention drawn to the evocative verb 'circule', and the effect of the dense and ominous final phrase, with its rare adjective placed before the noun; in the third stanza, the almost startling concreteness of 'navire' and suddenness of action, the violence in the language, the internal rhyme on 'coule...Houle' which helps to give an unexpected turbulence, the onomatopoeic effect of '*ch*eminée...dé*ch*irée... *ch*audière'; then in the fourth stanza, the more subdued alliterative dominant ('fond...

enfumée...Frappe...fermé'), the accentuation of the idea of enclosure and separation, and the closing of the circle. Note the use of paradox here, as in *Prophétie*, and the light-dark motif, so central to *Visite de la nuit*.

Le Sillage

In this poem one sees a characteristic linking Supervielle with the Surrealist mood in twentieth-century poetry: a taste for the magical and sometimes eerie atmosphere in which reality is subject to unexplained illuminations and eclipses. It is a poem which lends itself to comparison with others in the selection. As in *Prophétie*, the material body of an object has been caused to vanish, leaving something less substantial as its representative or proxy, and an abstract emotion (cf. 'Une tristesse sans plafond' in the earlier poem) wanders like a lost spirit in a world without bearings (towards the end it is a semblance of 'douleur' which is signalling to the onlookers). As in *Haute mer*, it is a question of 'le sillage', a trail or sign left behind something which has gone (an image frequently associated with the theme of death in Supervielle: the dead are still intangible presences in the world, causing reverberations and leaving messages). The use of the word 'noyés' reminds one of 'le noyé' in *Haute mer* and the sadness of his search which yields nothing. But this is a boating accident with a difference, these being 'des noyés par amour', lovers reconciled with each other (no longer solitary, self-bound individuals) and reunited with the magic country of their youth (note the mythical quality and the reminiscence of the never-never land of children's stories in the description of the stags). It is also a reconciliation between the different realms or elements of terrestrial life: the sea, on which this ultimate adventure has taken place, becomes one with the earth, for the 'noyés' have stepped through each other's eyes like a magic portal into a fabulous forest glade (cf. *Montévidéo*, 'C'était moi qui naissais *jusqu'au fond sourd des bois* (...) *Et jusque sous la mer* où l'algue se retrousse'); and these in their turn leave their token in the air, a fragment of sail at one with the wind and with itself (cf. *Montévidéo*, 'Un peu de mon âme (...) se mêlant/A un bout de papier volant'). Note the importance of the look (cf. its importance for Eluard in such poems as *L'Amoureuse* and *La courbe de tes yeux...*); the suggestiveness of 'clairière' as an image of human relationships; the easy transfusion which exists between inner and outer worlds; the way in which the tenses accentuate the gulf between the experience of the lovers and the commentators. An alternative version of the second line of the poem reads, 'Parce que le bonheur avait passé par là'. Which version do you think harmonizes better with the rest of the poem?

Le Nuage

In a poetry so concerned with former times (sign-posted by titles such as *Le Matin du monde*, *Naissance* and *Age des cavernes*) it comes as no surprise to meet a first line beginning 'Il fut un temps...' Here, in a kind of lament, Supervielle refers to a rift between two ages of his own history, and to the collapse of the reliability of time itself. The rift is essentially that between childhood in which things are seen and felt in their intense reality, and adulthood, in which oversophisticated musings and dubious concerns can blunt true perception. The dilemma is posed initially in the simple dramatic opposition of 'ombres' and 'lumière'. But the words themselves never become too specific or fall into the clear language of self-analysis: 'ombres' could mean shade as opposed to light, spirits of the dead or any kind of collection of obscure forces, and its meaning is made more complex by association with such phrases as '...ne rêvaient pas' and 'l'eau du songe' or 'le temps se désagrège'; while 'lumière' could refer to clarity of vision, absence of fear, emotional warmth or innocence. What quality or mode of life is implied in the word 'fables'? What does the use of the possessive adjectives, '*leur* place véritable' and '*sa* lumière' suggest (cf. the sense of something out of place in *Le Sillage*, 'Une menace errait, comme cherchant la place' and, more generally in Supervielle's poems, the loss of contact with a reliable centre of gravity)? How do you interpret the theme of dream, to which Supervielle gives special point by reserving for it two of his most striking images, 'mes mains ne rêvaient pas' and 'Elle ne prend pas l'eau du songe'? What does he mean by 'mes mains ne rêvaient pas' and by '*la faute* des dix doigts' (suggesting, if not a fall from grace, then some error which has left them vaguely 'out of order', as opposed to his youthful eyes which achieved immediate communion by means of a mere look)? Note how he gives a more conclusive quality to the third stanza, at this pivotal point in the poem, before moving into the address to the allegorical figure. What do you think the 'Capitaine' represents? It is a subtle feature of the poem that the conjuring up of this mythical figure and the image of the boat are consistent, not only with the time of 'fables' which is looked back upon with nostalgia, but also with the need for an antidote to the ailment of 'cloudiness' which is besetting him. Notice the importance of the theme of things holding true to their own definition and maintaining their solidity when all else threatens to become unsubstantial (cf. the ending of *Prophétie*, 'C'est un chardonneret'): perhaps there is a comparison to be made, too, between the girls in *Prophétie* 'Restées à l'état de vapeur' and the phrase 'Tout m'est nuage'. How does the ending acquire an added touch of poignancy?

Visite de la nuit

This poem describes the stages of a difficult encounter with one of the many 'amis inconnus' who haunt the volume of that title: spirits simultaneously familiar and foreign, giving signs of their existence, seeking a relationship. In this case the spirit is night momentarily given human form, like the Classical gods in their amorous escapades, for this special visitation.

In what sense is there an otherworldliness in the setting and the poet's rôle? A critic has described Supervielle as 'le poète des métempsychoses', the poet of transmigrations of the soul: notice how the protagonist aspires to step outside his corporal limits in anticipation of this meeting, while night, the infinite in finite guise, is ill at ease in her new form and would happily revert to her natural gravitation. Can this situation be linked in any way to the image of the lovers and their long-awaited 'clairière' in *Le Sillage*? How would you interpret the fact that night has slipped out of her own context and sequence of time and appeared as a kind of foreign body in the broad daylight (cf. the attempted reconciliation of dark and light in *Sous le large*)? The process of communication is like a delicate act of love between creatures from different planets, speaking a language, or a silence, which the other cannot fathom (one can imagine it projected in shadow-theatre). Their lack of correspondence may be compared with the fate of 'le noyé' in *Haute mer* who listens in vain for a magical sound which would link him with another world. What makes the anti-climax of the eighth couplet particularly moving? In the final couplets night rejoins her authentic element and is converted back into her own true nature: not a small outlined form walking the street in potential self-offering, but something whirling giddily and inaccessibly in infinite space. (Note that, despite the deceptively approachable and vulnerable human form, the night's ultimate 'vertige' was always foreshadowed in the words 'Toute errante en soi', and her thousands of unseeing eyes in the words 'Elle regardait mais voyait ailleurs': cf. the use of the word 'aveugle' in *Prophétie* and *Haute mer*.) In what ways is the last line of the poem reminiscent of the finale of *Le Nuage*?

Do you see any similarity between this little legend and the story of Orpheus in the underworld? Make a detailed comparison and contrast between *Visite de la nuit*, Baudelaire's *Recueillement* and Michaux's *Dans la nuit*, all poems concerned with a most intimate relationship between the poet and the night.

Tristesse de Dieu

The collection *La Fable du Monde* represents the most ambitious expression of -Super-vielle's cosmic inspiration. It is natural that a poetry so concerned with the origins and purposes of creation, death and life after death, and man's destiny in the universe should ultimately include an attempt to portray and fathom the figure of God, though one should remember that Supervielle has said that 'Mes rapports avec Dieu ne sont pas toujours excellents', and that in the poem immediately preceding this one in the collection, *Prière à l'inconnu*, he has written, 'Mon Dieu, je ne crois pas en toi, je voudrais te parler tout de même'. Part of the richness of this monologue stems from the fact that, in defining himself, God is also inevitably defining man; and one is invited to savour, as elsewhere in the poet's work, both the separation and the reflective interplay between two planes.

Does it seem to you that Supervielle has created a particularly unusual image of God? Which features does he accentuate and what use has he made of contradictions in this portrait? Is there any swapping of rôles? Explore the various paradoxes, e.g. that it is in his distance and imperfection as a creator that God is human (so that his separation and impotence become an indirect proof of his sympathy); that, from his inevitable mutism or incommunicability, he is succeeding here in speaking the most patent language; and that, while accepting the implications of the metaphor of the potter and the pot, he is employing the most intimate terms of address and endearment. Note that, like the narrator of *Le Nuage*, God has known a turning-point in time when possession has become loss; and like the figure of night in *Visite de la nuit*, he is described as 'l'errant en soi-même'. Would you say that Supervielle's view of man and creation is far more pessimistic at this point in his career than at the time of writing *Montévidéo*? Study the following points of style: the appropriateness of the unrestrictive free verse form; the use of repetitive structure, antithesis and occasional run-on effects; the value of the shorter lines for special emphasis; the balance between abstract statement and illustrative imagery; the way in which elementary traditional images are renovated in this context.

Is Supervielle as successful in this more rhetorical vein as in the pictorial and narrative one? Does his view of God appear to be more serious and meaningful here than in *Prophétie*? Compare this poem with Hugo's *Booz endormi* as a picture of the mysterious pact between man and the divine: has Hugo's poem a greater dignity? Which has the deeper spirit of humanity?

SUBJECTS FOR DISCUSSION

1. Supervielle once said, 'Je suis peut-être encore davantage que le poète de la nuit, le poète des commencements, des naissances'. Does this selection of his poems lead you to agree?
2. 'Faire en sorte que l'ineffable nous devient familier tout en gardant ses racines fabuleuses': how well does Supervielle fulfil this stated intention?
3. 'Poète des métamorphoses, des échanges, des passages clandestins' (G. ANEX): does this seem a good description of Supervielle?
4. Is it apparent that vision is more important in Supervielle's poetry than ideas?

5. Henri Michaux wrote of Supervielle: 'il se plaisait à être gracieux et courtois avec les mots, les états, les créatures, dans un immense désir de rassurer, de calmer, de pacifier et, par le charme des mots rendant le réel inoffensif, de faire que les choses soient simples et non plus redoutables'. Would you agree that his poems work this kind of charm?

6. 'More naïve than mystic, more primitive than metaphysical, he seems to have the spontaneous, imaginative speculations of childhood, whose innocence and inexperience sees no barrier between the real and the unreal, the material and the fantastic' (D. BLAIR). Discuss and illustrate.

Paul Eluard

L'Amoureuse

For a guided commentary on this poem, see *The Appreciation of Modern French Poetry*, pp. 143–5.

La courbe de tes yeux...

A joyously lyrical poem, *La courbe de tes yeux...* expresses the double richness of the poet's love which is at once protective and yet provocative of ever-new experience. For the poet, who has a love-spell spun round him by a magical figure similar to the fay who presses on his eye-lids in *L'Amoureuse*, time and life are re-defined exclusively in terms of the present relationship (lines 1–5). From this contact issues a cluster of images which describe the woman's eyes and their effect: unifying all the elements (light, water, wind; air, sea and vegetation) and orchestrating the various sensations (lines 6–10). The poem closes where it began, with the idea of the circle (the dancing-ring, the halo or the globe of the world), with the image of the cradle or nest (a dark or nocturnal hollow from which light emanates), and with a statement of the poet's and the world's absolute dependence on his beloved's gaze (lines 11–15). How does this circular development support the central theme?

Note how many images of roundness and encirclement come together in the first three lines. (The image 'Auréole du temps' deserves a special comment: this halo is, as it were, the superior spiritual expression of time, surrounding the eyes and surrounding the heart, which explains the poet's subsequent acknowledgement that it is only since her eyes have encircled him that time has come alive and that he has been living life instead of mere existence.) After this particularly dense succession of images, the almost monosyllabic simplicity of lines 4–5 stands out in contrast to convey the poet's childlike wonderment. Study how suggestively the image of dawn is developed in slight touches throughout the poem (compare 'Ailes couvrant le monde de lumière' with 'l'Aube exaltée ainsi qu'un peuple de colombes' in Rimbaud's *Le Bateau ivre*; think of 'Bateaux chargés de ciel' as a treasure of luminosity transported over the high seas towards its ultimate harbour; note how the brood of dawns hatches out, new-born, from the nest of the night sky, surrounded by the morning perfumes). In the second stanza especially the influence of light seems to extend everywhere: caught on the leaves, seen as twinkling dew on the moss (or as a light foam of dew), in the form of smiling expressions, colours, wings catching glints and spreading a canopy of light over the whole world – a host of impressions all building up finally to the subject 'Le monde entier'. And this in turn depends totally upon the eyes, suggestions of which are never lost: examine how the poet indirectly evokes their delicate shape, their feminine fragrance, their moistness and brilliance in the images of the second stanza. How do the first two lines of the final stanza draw together threads of various images and weave them into a rich whole? (Study particularly the key-word 'éclos' and the dual suggestion of security and space, intimacy and infinity, enclosure and expansive aspirations.) The final lines are more than a restatement of the poet's dependence; they are an intensification. The poet's whole being is now involved, not just his heart; the image of encirclement becomes one of total fusion. The woman's eyes have given birth to an intense feeling of being alive, of being a part of the same innocent, natural world which she seems to represent.

Analyse the metrical structure which, even though the poem is irregular according to the traditional rules of French versification, suggests a reassuring regularity. Another feature which helps stylistic unity is the number of major sound schemes which run through the poem, including the attenuated rhyming of several lines (note especially the use of a final [r] sound).

Tu te lèves l'eau se déplie...

Here is a love poem which, in a sort of liturgical incantation, celebrates the power of a mysterious feminine 'toi'. The woman (or perhaps one should say Woman) is seen as an almost divine principle of creation capable of producing a continual genesis in the poet's vision.

The simple cause-and-effect structure of the first two lines makes the woman a majestic, natural figure who controls the normally capricious water-element, here unfolding in an expansive gesture of delight. In the first two stanzas, notice the use of antithesis (to what effect?), the growing authority of the 'tu' figure and, on a phonetic level, the assonance which links the final word of each line. In the barren chaos of the world (paradoxically the 'désert' here is full of noise), the woman creates moments of buoyant, perfect peace (the phrase 'bulles de silence' carries with it associations of formal perfection and ethereal mobility, suggestions of that self-contained roundness and wholeness implicit in the images of 'Courbe...rond...auréole' in *La courbe de tes yeux...*, as well as the idea of serene contemplative silence). What is the purpose of the apparent contradictions between water ('bulles') and land ('désert'), between silence and song, between darkness ('nocturnes') and colour ('arc-en-ciel')? The woman, now a universal spirit, destroys both space (line 8) and time (line 9) but only in order to recreate in a constant Phoenix-like process; so that she is perpetual change and perennial likeness. For the poet, the world is continually being renewed in the likeness of the woman, such is her power (cf. her lifegiving force in *La courbe de tes yeux...*).

Study the effects which can be gained from the variation in sentence- and line-lengths and from the typographical divisions.

Compare this poem with Baudelaire's vision of woman in *Avec ses vêtements ondoyants et nacrés...*

Sans âge

For a guided commentary on this poem, see *The Appreciation of Modern French Poetry*, pp. 146–9.

Je ne suis pas seul

This poem is the first of *Médieuses*, a collection of poems which were meant to establish, in Eluard's own words, 'une espèce de mythologie féminine'. Certainly one can feel the presence of some delightful 'goddess' of Nature in these lines; even though she remains discreetly unnamed and separated from the adjectives which represent her, she is very much the poet's companion, never leaving him (look at the title) and blending so indistinguishably with the natural world that under her influence '*le* jardin' becomes feminine and in his dreaming, induced by love, she becomes the poet's Eden.

The description of the woman/garden is unfolded in gentle, adulatory phrases, all cast in similar moulds of syntax and versification, harmonized by the use of internal and terminal rhyme, assonance and alliteration, and all arousing by their pure enthusiasm the reader's expectation of an imminent main subject. What is the effect of breaking this pattern with the isolated 'Fidèle' and of surprising that expectation? One can also sense from the recurrent verse-pattern something which, although taking on a great variety of expressions, remains true to itself (cf. 'Tu es la ressemblance' in the previous poem); something which shuttles fluently and gracefully between state of emotion and state of nature, between subjective and objective worlds. In what tone are the last three lines spoken and how do they give the poem a change of direction?

With its picture of a woman figure at one with the familiar and the tiny as well as the cosmic, with its equation of love, dream and a surreal world of harmony, this poem contains themes essential to Eluard's poetic vision. Compare the description of the woman here with that found in *Tu te lèves l'eau se déplie...*

Critique de la poésie

When Eluard tried to publish this poem in the occupied France of 1943, the German censors refused permission to print; it was however published in Switzerland a year later, a few months before the Liberation. A glance back at an earlier work helps to explain the title; in 1931 Eluard had given the same title to a poem which was violently revolutionary and ended with the lines: 'Je crache à la face de l'homme plus petit que nature/Qui à tous mes poèmes ne préfère pas cette *Critique de la poésie*'. Why do you think he chose to give this poem the same title?

The opening stanza begins with a dramatization of fire, a symbol of awakening (an important image in Eluard, as seen in *L'Amoureuse* and *Sans âge*) and of things consumed in an ardent and luminous unity. But might one also see this awakening by fire as a more ominous and urgent one: that of the German destruction? Be that as it may, the images in this first stanza speak of a poetic ideal of unity (man's heart and hands merged with the earth and the richness of the vegetal realm), solidarity (man merged as friend with man) and all-embracing happiness (an experience which is an intermingling of sweetness, lightness, the sustenance of fresh springs and a homely sun).

The second tableau keeps the idea of unity (after 'Le bonheur en un seul bouquet', 'Maison d'une seule parole' and the picture of joined lips), of people brought together in a common place and a common spirit, of a light joined with a liquid quality to bring man promise and fulfilment. What does the phrase 'paupières transparentes' evoke in this context? But the images here are perhaps slightly more ambiguous: could one draw from them the suggestion of an impoverishment, a deprivation and a mutism, as well as a certain pathos? And one notices that the description of the lavishness of nature (so often a symbol of fertility in Eluard: cf. *Je ne suis pas seul*) tends to fade away.

The third tableau takes the change of scene even further. Study the development from a natural to an urban setting, from the warmth ('bon soleil') and suppleness ('léger fondant') of the first stanza to the rigid monotony ('glacée d'angles semblables') of the townscape, from the close-knit comradeship of 'toute une forêt d'amis' to the solitude of the inward-looking poet, in exile and out of harmony with his surroundings. It is in this part, too, that the vision of 'fruits en fleurs', freedom and innocence is acknowledged as a dream (cf. the end of *Je ne suis pas seul*), thus accentuating the gulf between poetic imaginings and the harsh stuff of reality.

A crucial feature of the poem is, of course, the chilling refrain, the bare journalistic statements reporting the murders of two poets (Lorca was shot by General Franco's troops in 1936; Saint-Pol-Roux, then 80, died a few days after German soldiers had attacked his home) and one of Eluard's colleagues in the French Resistance. Examine the effects of these interpolations in relation to each of the imaginative stanzas, and in general the challenge they seem to offer to the poetic, versified language.

Bonne justice

Bonne justice was written in 1949 at a time when Eluard was reaffirming his faith in a universal fraternity of mankind; it states his ideal with a convincing authority which springs from the simple directness of the language, the persuasive use of repetition and example, and the tidy syllabic structure of the poem. One notices the deliberate balance between man at peace and man in danger, between creation and destruction, fruitfulness and deprivation, between man joined in a perfect interchange with nature and a rounded cyclic unity (cf. the many images in Eluard to this effect) and man cut off from the world as a means of personal salvation. In style, there is a matching balance between the confident, assertive rhythm of the first stanza and the unsettled, anxious rhythm of the second. The third human 'law' takes one from everyday realities (whether homely or harsh, concerned with fertility or self-preservation) to the realm of the ideal; and clearly it is the most important to humanity and its well-being, deserving a climactic two-stanza development. Eluard promotes to a law of mankind the ambition for a better world which has haunted idealists from the beginning of time; he sees this law not as a changeless absolute but as a continually evolving ideal, constantly perfecting itself, which embraces everyone. Notice again that we have light and water, dream and reality, past, present and future, innocence and knowledge, instinct and intellect, brought together in reconciliation. How effective do you find the conclusion?

Compare this poem, both in its form and content, with *Sans âge*.

Semaine

Being well aware that the number seven is traditionally a number with occult significance, Eluard often used seven stanzas or seven divisions to make up his poems, as if to confer on the contents a surreal power. Here he links the number with the idea of the week, so that the poem, which is like an inspired diary of the poet's love, is given a satisfying form as well as a magical aura.

The poem opens with the by now familiar association of love with the dynamic and expansive life of the natural world, with the fusion of the universal and the personal (looks and words, the human forms of expression, being scattered liberally among leaves and wings, rivers and sky). After the flux of poetic enumeration, the second 'day' with its two short sentences stands out in contrast, conveying the ingenuous, sentimental pleasure of the poet in love: how do these words surprise? In the third stanza, note the use of paradox and opposition to suggest that love can be both unique and universal, solitary and altruistic. The fourth section is more enigmatic: why should the poet cast blame on his heart and body? The poem, which was published three years after the death of Eluard's second wife, Nusch, appeared (under a slightly different form) in *Le Phénix*, a collection of poems celebrating the feeling of love rekindled in the poet's heart by Dominique Lemor, whom he later married. This couplet refers perhaps to the poet's emotional pain at Nusch's death, which in spite of his new-found love still lingers on.

The two decasyllabic quatrains which form the fifth section reintroduce specifically the theme of time suggested in the title. The poet recalls a day of radiant love which illuminated the whole world (cf. images of vision and visibility elsewhere in Eluard's work). Study the notions of time and light; the intermingling of abstract and concrete; and, on the phonetic level, the links between the terminal words in these eight lines. The sixth part, carrying on the idea of light, creates a highly complex image by the deliberate juxtaposition of parallel sentences; the blending of light and dark in the penumbra of dawn mists (cf. *Sans âge*: 'Montez les marches de la brume') preludes the sexual union where the splendour of the feminine body is offered to the poet's deep-felt desires. Eluard closes the poem with enthusiastic emphasis on the qualities of the woman: her mixture of change and stability ('saisons fidèles'), of revelation and mystery ('te couvres...t'éclaires'), the constructive power of her love, both artificial and natural, her sheltering, restful presence ('maison', 'lit') and her promise of generation ('mûrit', 'lit', 'fruit'). She provokes in the poet the feeling of surging, inexhaustible life with which the poem began and also a feeling of security and reliability; she is like the week which is constituted of ever-passing particles of time and yet is also a compact unit, a stable measure laid along the track of time.

Finally, analyse the appropriateness of the different verse-forms to the thematic presentation as a whole, and the variations in the rhythmical structure which create an effect of modulation in a basically parisyllabic metre.

SUBJECTS FOR DISCUSSION

1. 'Le vers d'Eluard (...) c'est l'aile éblouissante d'aube d'un papillon triomphant, c'est la jeunesse universelle' (L. SCHELER). Discuss.
2. Study Eluard's preference for imagery which relates feeling to the four elements (earth, air, fire and water). Does any consistent pattern of association emerge?
3. To what extent has Eluard succeeded in making his poetry accessible to everybody?
4. Though abandoning many of the traditional techniques of prosody, what variety of means does Eluard use to ensure a formal unity in some of his poems?
5. 'The presence of woman and the poetic images released in Eluard's sensibility by contact with her (...) are of supreme importance. They promise man success in his battle with the oppressive forces which would confine his gaze to the material universe' (J. H. MATTHEWS). Investigate the links between Eluard's social vision and his love-inspired vision.
6. Consider Eluard's description of the poet as a 'rêveur éveillé'.

Henri Michaux

Emportez-moi

This is one of Michaux's early poems, published in 1929, in which one can see a Baude-lairean inspiration (as in the poem *Mœsta et errabunda*: 'Emporte-moi, wagon! enlève-moi, frégate!/Loin! loin!') and even a reminiscence of Mallarmé's *Brise marine* ('Fuir! là-bas fuir! Je sens que des oiseaux sont ivres/D'être parmi l'écume inconnue et les cieux!'). Its theme is the journey beyond, the desire to be *ailleurs* (*Ailleurs* and *Lointain intérieur* are the titles of two of Michaux's works). But the familiar details of the first stanza are deceptively so and in form the poem is highly original. Michaux is not content to be carried on a single vague lyrical wish. He explores the depth and subtlety of this wish by allowing it to generate, in an uninhibited play of creative association, a cluster of widely different but complementary images (a technique somewhat similar to that used in *Icebergs*). There is the desire to be elsewhere in time, space and form; to be drawn into the train of some surging motive force ('l'étrave' is the bows of a ship) or dispersed in its wake; to be absorbed into smoothly textured surfaces with no asperities; to be taken out of his singularity and made part of a nebulous collective identity; to become bodiless and airy, and yet to be carried within the vital rhythms, lines of communication and sensual points of contact of the body; to be exterior and interior mobility, an easy traveller in outer and inner space; to be simultaneously dynamic and passive, eliminated yet precariously preserved; to be projected afar in a horizontal plane and yet, perhaps more essentially, thrust downwards in the vertical (a surprising last adjustment and an ambiguous one since it could represent a kind of self-burial or an integration into the secretive life of *la profondeur*). Note how the regular decasyllabic lines of the beginning make way for a less predictable rhythm as the theme acquires more unusual facets; how the poem gains its cohesion, not from rhyme, but from a technique of repetition and the gradual accumulation of image.

La jeune fille de Budapest

This poem depicts the kind of unreal and magical feminine figure which haunts a good deal of Surrealist poetry. One thinks of Eluard's 'Elle est debout sur mes paupières' and 'Tu te lèves l'eau se déplie', or of Desnos's 'J'ai tant rêvé de toi que tu perds ta réalité'. In all these cases, the woman acts as a mysterious intercessor between the poet and a 'surreal' state of experience, waving a wand over the laws of time, space and substance, and dissolving the boundaries between fact and fantasy, reality and imagination. As with *Emportez-moi*, a main theme here is that of stepping outside the bounds of one's own person and personality, of effecting a kind of transmigration or transubstantiation. (In fact, this poem might easily have grown from the detail of 'Dans l'haleine de quelques chiens réunis' and 'Dans les poitrines qui se soulèvent et respirent' of the previous piece.) Study the way in which the ideas of weightlessness and ubiquity are developed; the extent to which this is a paradoxical experience, a coming together of contradictions. Does it surprise you that Michaux should define the girl so specifically as 'de Budapest'? What are her predominant characteristics? Notice the use of the tenses; the slight reversal of rôles which takes place in this *rencontre* (with first the poet immersing his almost non-existent person in her, who is seen as an enveloping mist or water, then the woman, now absent, pressing her diminutive presence upon him); and the force of the final words '. . .que tu n'es plus'. What effects does Michaux draw from his phrasing: from the fact that each poetic line is kept as a separate punctuated compartment; from the dual structure of so many of the lines; from the omission of 'de' and the repetition in 'Longues belles herbes. . .', describing their miniature Eden; from the double stress of 'tu t'appuies maintenant'?

Dans la nuit

It is interesting to quote here a few of Michaux's comments from *Un Barbare en Asie*, his account of travels in the Orient: 'L'Hindou est *religieux*, il se sent relié à tout'; 'Toute pensée indienne est magique (. . .) Une grande partie de ce qui passe pour des pensées philosophiques ou religieuses n'est autre chose que des *Mantras* ou prières magiques, ayant une vertu comme "Sésame, ouvre-toi"'; 'Alors il dit AUM. Sérénité dans la puissance. Magie au centre de toute magie'. But, apart from Eastern outlooks and practices, it is in the oldest traditions to see a link between the poetic word and magical efficacy. Mallarmé writes of one of his sonnets, 'En se laissant aller à le murmurer plusieurs fois on éprouve une sensation assez cabalistique'. These words apply equally well to Michaux's text. It is a contemplative chant, inducing a kind of union between himself and the body of the night (cf. Rimbaud's 'j'ai senti un peu son immense corps' in *Aube*, his coming together with a great force of nature). A trance-like effect and a sensation of being invaded or enveloped by a vast uniformity is produced by the un-relieved repetitions of word, sound and rhythm (note particularly all the little switch rhymes and approximate echoes: 'nuit...uni', 'Et fumes...Et mugis', 'tout autour... haut...partout'). And yet there are subtle variations within the monotony: the two isolated end-stopped lines ('Mienne, belle, mienne.' and 'Nuit qui gît, Nuit implacable.') which stand out against the fluency of the rest, marking points of transition in the poem and drawing attention to the question of possession or non-possession (cf. Rimbaud's *Ma Bohème*, '*Mes* étoiles au ciel avaient un doux frou-frou'); the change to a second person address in the central section after the word 'mienne', which gives a greater intimacy and leads to suggestions of fertility and fullness; the passage from night described in the feminine form as 'Mienne' to night as masculine power ('roi... lui'), and from the poet as initiating agent to Night as absolute overlord (note the modification of syntax, sound and presentation accompanying this new emphasis); and, despite the harping recurrence of the one word 'nuit', the variety of properties of night which are touched upon in this highly imaginative description (sea-swell and shore, liquid invasion and draining suction, smokiness and sound, the infinite and the infinitesimal). One critic has said that this cannot be called a poem, any more than one would call the chants of a religious sect repeating 'Seigneur! Seigneur! Le Seigneur va venir!' a poem. Would you agree?

Compare this poem with Supervielle's *Visite de la nuit*.

Icebergs

For a guided commentary on this poem, see *The Appreciation of Modern French Poetry*, pp. 146–9.

Clown

For a guided commentary on this poem, see *The Appreciation of Modern French Poetry*, pp. 153–5.

Portrait des Meidosems (extracts)

Portrait des Meidosems, the larger work from which these various extracts are taken, describes in detail the nature of a race of imaginary creatures. But behind the veil of foreignness and fantasy it is not difficult to see a study of human duality, perhaps one of the most refined in French poetry since Baudelaire. The name 'Meidosems' suggests 'demi-semi', creatures living in a half and half world, tormented by the con-tradictory properties and impulses of their own irremediably pliable nature: 'âme à regrets et projets, âme pour tout dire'; 'Tout éruption, si on l'écoutait, mais c'est un nœud indivisible'; 'D'une brume à une chair, infinis les passages en pays meidosem'; 'L'élasticité extrême des Meidosems, c'est là la source de leur jouissance. De leurs malheurs, aussi' – such are the descriptions of them to be found elsewhere. Michaux heightens the idea of a dual nature by having masculine and feminine forms ('Meido-semme') of these beings.

From the thematic point of view, notice the loss of their own form, substance and identity; the absorption into a great current of nature and unity with the elements, whether water, fire or air; the fluidity and spontaneity of movement of these transmigrations; the image of being carried in an upward surge; the escape from physical wound and spiritual frustration and tedium; the idea of a purification and of a superhuman euphoria or *extase*; the desire to transcend solitude and become a parcel of an immeasurable unity, knowing mysterious spiritual communications; and then the reverse side of all this, the wounds, the fatigue, the relapses, the waiting dissatisfaction of their regular life ('fatiguées à mort', 'Au moins, ce ne sont pas des plaies', 'Sans doute elle a une fin', etc.).

One might compare aspects of Michaux's text and inspiration here with details of Baudelaire's *La Chevelure* ('l'arbre et l'homme, pleins de seve'; 'glissant dans l'or et dans la moire'), where the imagination is transported on a rich play of sensations and finally takes flight in a world of shimmering light; Rimbaud's *Le Bateau ivre* ('Je sais les cieux... et les trombes/Et les ressacs et les courants'), where access is given to vast tides and rhythms, 'la circulation des sèves inouïes' and strange Sargassos of vegetal life; or *Aube* ('les ailes se levèrent sans bruit'). Each of these poets depicts in his own way the 'misère et grandeur de l'homme', with emphasis on the privileged moments of release.

Note the fine shading and variety in Michaux's descriptions and imagery, with the 'Meidosemmes' slipping with equal ease from 'rameaux' to 'pédoncules', the mere flower-stalks; with their movements changing in tempo and sensation according to whether they are rising in the sap of short grass, aspens or flowers; with the feeling of joy provoking simultaneous images of fear and warm security; with the transmutation being felt as waterfall or fire or sudden airy openings in the earth, etc.

Dans le cercle brisant de la jeune magicienne

The title touches on themes encountered already in Michaux: magic, the young woman, the attraction of some other sphere of influence in which one's own personality is broken down or at least not left intact. But the main theme, not emerging explicitly until the dramatic final line, is that of the disruptive power of a strange force of love (cf. 'Emportez-moi sans me briser, dans les baisers' in an earlier poem), love like a thunderbolt, coming and departing in a flash (cf. 'maintenant que tu n'es plus' at the end of *La jeune fille de Budapest*). It is obviously not a love-poem in the style of Verlaine's 'O triste, triste était mon âme/A cause, à cause d'une femme', but more reminiscent of Rimbaud's *Le Bateau ivre*: 'Fermentent les rousseurs amères de l'amour' and 'L'âcre amour m'a gonflé de torpeurs enivrantes'. Michaux's poem has a similar excited and energetic lyricism, a kaleidoscope of startling images, and the feeling of being overwhelmed by a multiplicity of impressions which words can hardly hold. It is as if a creative vein had been suddenly struck and burst open: it is notable that in the heat of experience the devastating force is a cascade of images and sensations; only as it disappears is it recognized and named as 'amour' (love or loved one). Study the controlled structure of this piece: the repetitive syntax (recurring in a circular pattern and acting as a rhythmical life-line in the heart of multiplicity and potential confusion); the way in which each of the three sections expands in intensity, and ends with a reference to the poet himself; the structural progression from 'tu parais et tu pars' to 'tu pars...et tu disparais'. Note the ideas of projection through space and time; of apparition and illumination; of the order of the world, matter and reason being overthrown; of being burned ('brûlante'), exploded ('fusées'), torn ('déchirés'), traversed ('vrilles' are gimlets), lashed ('cinglement'), submerged ('dévala', 'déboulent'), invaded (the mysterious oriental-sounding figure 'Phou' launching his troops). Note also the variety of the senses through which the experience makes its impact. One cannot determine whether this violent upheaval is divine ('ostensoir', 'prières', 'cathédrales'), satanical (the wildness of witches' 'sabbats'), scientific ('magnésienne' means containing magnesium and therefore burning in the air, 'aluminiée', coated with a luminous protective surface of aluminium, 'draguée', mechanically dredged or scooped from a quarry), bestial ('dragonne', 'retours à la caverne', 'meutes'), childlike (the comparison with children shouting their excitement and joy as they play inside a barrel) or insane ('démente', 'folle', 'égarement'), and yet paradoxically it is named without hesitation as 'amour'.

Ainsi, ce jour-là fut . . .

This text comes from *Misérable Miracle* (1956), an account of Michaux's explorations with certain drugs. One should not misjudge the poet's position with regard to drugs, however, nor the quality of this passage as a piece of writing'. In order to discover and chart more and more of his mental, imaginative and poetic territory, Michaux has taken measured doses of hallucinogenic substances in scientific situations (one thinks again of Rimbaud: 'La première étude de l'homme qui veut être poète est sa propre connaissance, entière; il cherche son âme, il l'inspecte, il la tente, l'apprend'). But there is no love of false paradises, no cult of trance-like euphoria and little sign of addiction. As for the passage itself, it is a remarkably orchestrated exercise in style, far removed from the occasionally brilliant but unselective juxtapositions of image thrown up by much Surrealist 'automatic writing'. It is a piece of poetic prose, but it has more to offer in terms of imaginative vision, linguistic originality, rhythmical patterning and internal cohesion of sound and detail than many which have paraded under the name of 'prose-poem'. It is interesting to add here that Michaux's life-long compulsion to cross boundaries and break open the walls of narrow compartments extends equally to the traditional distinction between prose and poetry.

The passage is particularly revealing as a condensation (and possibly a more rational exposition) of so many themes, words and images found elsewhere in his poetic work. How many such links can you see? (Some of the vocabulary calls for clarification: 'images de pacotille' means shoddy or second-rate mental images; 'ambulacraires' refers to the little tube-feet with a suction mechanism by which echinoderms such as the sea-urchin move; 'astérie' is just such an echinoderm, the star-fish; 'ravinements virevoltants' are spinning or swirling landslides or collapsing hollows in the ground.) One could fruitfully compare this passage with Rimbaud's *Le Bateau ivre*.

SUBJECTS FOR DISCUSSION

1. The title of one of Michaux's major works is *Ailleurs*. Study the variety of forms that this 'elsewhere' assumes in his imagination, and the features they have in common.
2. 'Michaux, poet of turbulence': discuss.
3. A. Rousseaux has said of Michaux's poetry, 'Dans ces livres qui vont si loin vers l'extrême de l'homme, c'est l'humain que j'admire le plus'. What evidence do you see of these two sides: a tendency to go beyond the limits of the human, and yet a deep and moving human quality?
4. Baudelaire once wrote, 'De la centralisation et de la vaporisation du *Moi*. Tout est là'. How appropriate to Michaux's poems might this quotation be, with its idea of a tormented personality, caught between the contradictory needs of self-possession and self-dispersion?
5. Analyse in detail Michaux's ability as a *rhythmical* artist.

6. 'Une sensibilité de mage ou de fée constamment surexcitée et survoltée' (G. Bounoure): is this a good description of Michaux's most common poetic mood?

Robert Desnos

J'ai tant rêvé de toi

This poem concerns the fine balance of the poet's affections, poised at a critical point in time, wavering uncertainly between reality and dream, possible and impossible contact. In his dreams, the loved woman is losing her reality, and although her physical being seems close ('*ce* corps vivant' '*cette* bouche'), it is out of reach (cf. 'atteindre ce corps vivant' with 'l'étreinte à laquelle j'aspire' of *Comme une main à l'instant de la mort*). One even wonders whether he has ever seen this woman, since he has dreamed of her 'depuis des jours et des années' without, it seems, confronting her 'apparence réelle'. How does Desnos give the impression that a critical moment in his relationship has arrived? The repetition of 'J'ai tant rêvé de toi' creates a rhythmical pattern; what is the more specific value of the parallel positioning of 'peut-être' and 'sans doute'? The couple are destined not to meet: she becomes unreal while he is real ('mes bras habitués...poitrine'); and, yet, faced with her reality, he himself would become 'une ombre'. They switch from side to side of the 'balances sentimentales' in which dream is weighed against reality. The image of the scales is structurally the fulcrum of the whole poem; by what means does Desnos reinforce the balance between the first and the second halves of the poem?

The stress now moves on to the idea of the poet as sleep-walker, half in and half out of reality. Still the woman is unattainable ('je pourrais moins toucher ton front et tes lèvres...'). But in what way does the conclusion appear optimistic? And at what point exactly does the tipping of the scales towards optimism occur? Notice that, whereas earlier in the poem the word 'ombre' is felt almost to be a synonym of 'fantôme', it develops its associations with sunlight ('ombre' becoming more 'shadow' and less 'ghost'). As shadows imply sunlight, so the deepening unreality which the poet feels ('plus ombre cent fois...') implies a greater intensity in the woman's radiant presence. His dream-realm is neither vague nor diffuse but sharply defined, with shadow and sun seeming more acute, more real than in ordinary reality (cf. the visual recording of this experience in the paintings of Chirico, Tanguy and Dali, all Surrealists). Desnos has moved from the unreal to the surreal. Draw out the richness of the sundial image ('le cadran solaire de ta vie') which combines the ideas of radiance, shadow and time.

The concern with dream, sleep, reality and unreality, shadow and sun, is typical of the Surrealists. Compare their importance in this poem with their rôle in Eluard's poetry (in *L'Amoureuse*, for example). Could one call this poem a love poem in the customary sense?

Non, l'amour n'est pas mort

For a guided commentary on this poem, see *The Appreciation of Modern French Poetry*, pp. 157–60.

Comme une main à l'instant de la mort

For a guided commentary on this poem, see *The Appreciation of Modern French Poetry*, pp. 160–3.

A la faveur de la nuit

The furtive *voyeur* creeping under cover of night, the lover obsessed by his 'mystérieuse', the poet confronting in all lucidity the barrier between illusion and reality: Desnos fits all these rôles in this uncomplicated little poem. The 'meeting' between poet and woman (who is unaware of his presence) can scarcely be called such, so many are the separating factors: the cloak of night, the window, the curtains (and we must remember that it is her shadow he sees, not her reality). Yet it is a situation he wishes to maintain ('N'ouvre pas cette fenêtre...'); why? Why does he want her to close her eyes? After the wishful gesture of kissing his beloved's eyes, brutal reality impinges on his dreams ('Mais...'). Study the contrast in tone between lines 7–8 and lines 9–10; the different effects of the wind (at once unstable and protective); the sudden introduction of images. The bathos of the revelation ('ce n'est pas toi') is heightened by the self-persuasive insistence earlier ('c'est toi, ce n'est pas une autre, c'est toi') and partly redeemed by the concluding admission of lucidity in self-deception. Why the recurrent stress on opening and closing? Does it underline any deeper oppositions? In this poem at least, Desnos prefers the safe cocoon of his imaginings to exposure to the real world. Mary Ann Caws sees this poem as a good example of what she calls 'Desnos's self-involvement' and what André Breton called his narcissism; would you agree? How does his rôle compare with that of Apollinaire in *Rosemonde*?

From the stylistic point of view, study the full effects of the opening infinitives, the rhythmic repetitions, the variations in sentence-length and the important play of assonance and alliteration.

La Voix de Robert Desnos

This midnight incantation which opens *Les Ténèbres*, a collection published in 1927, vibrates with the Surrealists' vision of a universe dominated and renovated by the poetic voice (an idea expressed beautifully in Eluard's *Sans âge*). But, in the end, the poem draws its power not so much from the magnetic 'voix de Robert Desnos' as from the pathos of his unreciprocated love.

Apparently irrational in their fitful movements from particular to abstract, private to universal, the opening images do have an imaginative cohesion derived from common suggestions of the fragile and the ephemeral. How can these images be said to resemble the idea of 'le minuit passé'? Midnight, the witching hour, rather than the time of recumbent sleep is the time of upright action: the clockhands are pointed skywards like steeples and poplars, the naked god-like figure rises and the ritual begins. What elements of contrast strike you in the first invocation ('j'appelle à moi')? Study the way in which the poet's voice, in this calling up of forces, draws into its wake the abject and the massively powerful, the immense and the diminutive, natural phenomena and human activities (some concerned with death and destruction, some with life and construction): a host of disparate ingredients culminating in the very specific and obsessive 'celle que j'aime'. Why is there the sinister repetition of 'les assassins' (cf. the partnership of love and death in *Comme une main à l'instant de la mort*)?

In the description of the response to Desnos's voice, trace the recurrent motifs of renaissance, revolt, submissive love and universal obedience. Study the mood of creative dynamism, the stress on passionate irrational forces, the excited interpenetration of world and poet, the idea of an exchange of rôles. The poet's confident pleasure as the surreal potentate reveals itself in the vigorous sound-play: 'les *peupl*iers *pl*ient', '*mar*ée...*mour*ir', '*tremblem*ents...*m'ébranl*ent' and '*our*agans *roug*issent' (instead of 'rugissent') etc. What is the effect of the repeated interpolation 's'il est possible' on your view of the efficacy of his verbal operation? Is the emphasis on visual appearances ('rougissent. . .mes lèvres', 'me vêt' etc.) of any significance? Why is the reference to 'la chair' such an appropriate conclusion to the pageant of metamorphoses and a perfect stepping-stone into the finale? The spiritless end to the parallels of invocation and response transforms the poem into one of melancholy. Love is the ultimate experience ('rien n'est perpétuel sur terre/Sauf l'amour,') and without it, the divine powers of the poet are meaningless.

What do you make of the title (cf. Desnos's use of his own name in *Non, l'amour n'est pas mort*)? Does the structure of the poem seem suited to the theme? Do you find it too obvious? What does the poet gain (if anything) from abandoning punctuation?

Compare this poem with Rimbaud's *Après le déluge* as the vision of an attempted transformation of the world.

Ombres des arbres dans l'eau. . .

This apparently artless poem lacks the emotional resonance of the previous five (it was written at a much later date) but incites a response by its inner contradictions, its play of opposites and the poet's own ambiguous attitude (one of wonder or distaste, joy or pain, uplift or depression, at the duality of life?). The writer is struck by the clarity of reflection in the murkiness of the water (although this first appears as 'si nette si claire si propre'); it is a fascination of opposites and a contemplation of the border between two worlds which thrills the Surrealists (look in some of Eluard's poetry, for instance). Though it is known that the reflective quality of a mirror depends on its black or opaque underside, does the contradictory 'si sale' seem disconcerting here? What is the stylistic effect of lengthening the third line especially after the neatly cadenced rhythm of the first two lines? Is there any progression in the series of words following 'lourd de. . .'? The brilliant colours of the kingfisher, the flowers and the passing boats are all reflected in precise detail. Does the use of 'ne. . .que' express continued astonishment or disappointment (at a surface illusion which barely disguises a polluted reality)? What connections can be made between these rather simple observations at a river-side and the larger, more complex problems of perception found earlier in Desnos poems where the poet's vision explores the real and the unreal, the actual and the virtual, the seen and the dreamt, *l'envers et l'endroit*?

SUBJECTS FOR DISCUSSION

1. 'Monologues haletants, obsédés, à la fois familiers et oratoires, et comme dictés les yeux fermés un soir d'exceptionnelle exaltation' (R. BERTELE). Discuss this description of the poems of *A la Mystérieuse* and *Les Ténèbres*.
2. Commenting on the litanic structure of some of Desnos's poems, Mary Ann Caws sees its function as 'assuring uninterrupted communication between apparently contradictory concepts and images'. Illustrate this observation on form and content.
3. 'There is no real love in *A la Mystérieuse*, only a sentimental narcissism which thrives on the emotions of dreams.' Would you accept or reject this comment?
4. Show the importance that Desnos gives to the play of opposites in his poetry.
5. 'Desnos's poems are, for the reader, like glimpsed moments of a private, passionate drama, moments of balance or crucial moments of intensity which can foreshadow anticlimax.' Discuss.
6. Rosa Buchole has said of one of Desnos's works, 'Tout chavire dans une légère folie étonnée et dansante'. Is this a good description of the poems here?

Index of First Lines

The first figure refers to the text of the poem; the figure in bold type refers to the notes on the poem.